ARISTOTLE ON ARTIFACTS

SUNY series in Ancient Greek Philosophy
Anthony Preus, editor

ARISTOTLE
ON ARTIFACTS

A Metaphysical Puzzle

Errol G. Katayama

STATE UNIVERSITY OF NEW YORK PRESS

Published by
State University of New York Press, Albany

For information, address State University of New York Press,
State University Plaza, Albany, N.Y., 12246

Production by Cathleen Collins
Marketing by Fran Keneston

Library of Congress Cataloging in Publication Data

Katayama, Errol G., 1962–
    Aristotle on artifacts : a metaphysical puzzle / Errol G.
Katayama.
        p.   cm. — (SUNY series in ancient Greek philosophy)
    Includes bibliographical references and index.
    ISBN 0-7914-4317-5 (alk. paper). — ISBN 0-7914-4318-3 (pbk. :
alk. paper)
    1. Aristotle—Contributions in metaphysics.   2. Metaphysics.
3. Aristotle—Contributions in concept of substance.   4. Substance
(Philosophy)   I. Title.   II. Series.
B491.M4K38   1999
110′.92—dc21   98-51014
                                                             CIP

10   9   8   7   6   5   4   3   2   1

To My Wife, Olga

Contents

Notes on Translations and Abbreviations

All translations are my own. They are based on translations by Apostle (The Peripatetic Press) and Peck (Loeb Classical Library). I have also consulted other translations (see Bibliography under "Primary Sources"), but have focused especially W. D. Ross's translation of the *Metaphysics*.

The following abbreviations are used:

Categories   Cat
De Interpretatione   *De Int*
Posterior Analytics   *An Po*
De Generatione et Corruptione   *De Gen et Corr*
Physics   *Phys*
De Caelo   *DC*
De Anima   *De An*
De Somno   *De Som*
History of Animals   *HA*
Parts of Animals   *PA*
De Motu Animalium   *De Motu*
Generation of Animals   *GA*
Metaphysics   *Meta*
Nicomachean Ethics   *EN*

Acknowledgments

This book is based on a Ph.D. thesis submitted to the University of Toronto in 1996. In the course of writing the thesis and revising it for the State University of New York Press, I have incurred a considerable debt to a number of people. I would like to thank especially my Ph.D. supervisor, Lloyd Gerson, and my advisors, John Rist and Brad Inwood, for their guidance. I am grateful to Alan Code, Sheldon Cohen, Michael Ferejohn, Martha Husain, Sean Kelsey, and Tony Preus for their comments. I owe thanks also to Pat Weldon, Jane Finnan, and Greg Klotz for their editorial suggestions. Finally, a personal thanks to my parents and to my wife, Olga (to whom I dedicate this book), for their support.

Introduction

1. Synopsis

Artifacts (man-made physical objects, such as houses and beds) are not substances in Aristotle's *Metaphysics* because substances are metaphysical principles that exist as eternal actualities. There are only three kinds of substances: God, heavenly spheres, and animals and plants (that are capable of reproducing). God is an eternal thinking activity. Heavenly spheres that eternally revolve around heaven exist as actualities (that is, they are indestructible and are in motion continuously). Animals and plants partake of the eternal and the divine by means of reproduction; since species are eternal, their forms have been passed on from one generation to another and have always existed as actualities.

The *existence* of metaphysical principles does not depend on other principles, otherwise, they fail to be principles. This, however, does not mean that they all have the same status; on the contrary, there is hierarchy among them. God, the ultimate independent being, is the substance *par excellence*; Its existence and activity do not depend on any other being. Next comes heavenly spheres, which need God to guarantee their continuous motions; thus, their activities depend on another being, although not their existence as such; that is, God does not cause the existence of heavenly spheres but only their motions. At the bottom of the ladder are animals and plants (that are capable of reproducing). They need heavenly spheres to produce the climate necessary for their existence, but heavenly spheres (and for that matter God) do not cause the existence of these organisms (except the spontaneously generated ones); thus, God and heavenly spheres are only necessary, but not sufficient, conditions for the self-reproducing animals and plants to exist eternally. These animals and plants are substances because they have their own principles to cause and to perpetuate the existence of their own species.

1

Suppose none of these three kinds of substances were to exist; then an Aristotelian universe would be such that only elements exist as heaps in concentric spheres—earth in the center of the universe, surrounded by water, then air, and fire, in that order. It is unclear whether *aether*, the fifth element, could exist independently from living heavenly spheres as a heap; analogously, it is also unclear in the case of *pneuma* in relation to living things. However, whatever the status of *aether* and *pneuma* may be, all phenomena in the universe could ultimately be explained by three kinds of substances and elements (plus *aether* and *pneuma*). For example, spontaneously generated organisms, mules, and artifacts are not substances because their existence depends on heavenly spheres, horses, and artisans, respectively. There will be no artifacts without artisans, no mules without horses, and no spontaneously generated organisms without heavenly spheres.

In contrast to these nonsubstantial beings, substances are prior in *logos* (formula or definition), in knowledge, and in time. For example, on the one hand, the *logos* of mule includes the *logos* of horse; for it is the form of the horse that causes the coming-to-be of mules. The knowledge of what it is to be mule presupposes the knowledge of what it is to be horse. And mules must be temporary posterior to horses, since the existence of mules presupposes the prior existence of horses. On the other hand, the *logos* of horse does not include the *logos* of any other being (except to the extent that the necessary condition of their existence depends on God and heavenly spheres); the knowledge of what it is to be horse does not depend on the knowledge of what is it to be any other thing; and since its species is eternal, it is prior in time. Analogously, the same relationship, that which obtains between horses and mules, also holds between artisans and artifacts, as well as heavenly spheres and spontaneously generated organisms, respectively.

In the sublunary world, composites, and not their forms, exist on their own. Yet, the indestructible forms, not the destructible composites, are substances—for metaphysical principles are indestructible. The form of a composite exists as an eternal actuality in the form of a *dynamis*. The form, as a *dynamis*, of a composite maintains the life of an organism, and it is the very same *dynamis* that generates its offsprings; thus the same *dynamis*, which is the cause of both an organism's existence and its offsprings, is passed on from one generation to another. It is in this way that the form of a composite is separate: the *dynamis* is separated from a father to produce another separate being with the same *dynamis*. It is this *dynamis* that exists as an eternal actuality.

Aristotle criticizes that Plato has not really explained how his Forms can be causes, as stated in the *Phaedo*. To posit Forms as paradigms and sensible beings as the things that participate in them is to use empty words and poetic metaphors. In contrast, Aristotle's forms exist in the sensible beings as actualities and are the causes of both the existence of sensible beings as well as coming-to-be of their offsprings. Their forms are transmitted from one generation to another in the form of *dynamis*. Males, who have the complete form (that is, who have the *dynamis*), are substances most of all; whereas females and children, who have incomplete forms (hence, lack the *dynamis* in some sense), are substances in a qualified sense. In reproduction, although both males and females are the principles of generation, it is the males who supply the motion that have the *dynamis* to pass on their forms, while the females who serve as matter lack this *dynamis*. Male children, who cannot reproduce, will however eventually attain this *dynamis* of adult males, if nothing prevents them from growing into adulthood.

The understanding that the form is a *dynamis* holds the key to resolving the most notorious Aristotelian dilemma: whether the form, understood as the substance of a composite, is individual or universal. The form of a composite exists as *dynamis* from one generation to another. Hence, it is not an individual, since the same *dynamis* is shared by more than one being, nor is it universal in the sense that it is predicated of many, since the *dynamis* of an offspring does not necessarily share the same *dynamis* of another offspring; yet they can all be predicated by the same universal. For example, Pelus and Achilles share the same *dynamis* but not with that of Nicomachus and Aristotle (unless all four happen to share the same ancestor); but that notwithstanding, they are all human beings. Therefore, substance is neither individual nor universal, but it is somehow both individual *and* universal (both in a different sense). On the one hand, it is not an individual in the sense that it is a composite of form and matter. The form is an individual when it attains its completeness (that is, realizes its full actuality) as an individual adult composite. If the form is prevented from reaching its completeness for whatever reason, as in the case of monstrosity, Aristotle calls it the universal most of all. The mark of the complete form is its *dynamis* to reproduce its offspring. On the other hand, it is not a universal in the sense that it is predicated of many, but it is universal in the sense that the same *dynamis* is shared by one's ancestors. The *dynamis* contains both the individual and the universal components. It is because of these two components that exists in the semen in the form of *dynamis* (which acts on the menstrual fluid) that make it possible to pass on the *dynamis* of the father to his offspring *via* semen.

2. Project

As we can surmise from the synopsis of this book, it deals with many different, but related, metaphysical issues. However, I would like to emphasize that the project of this book is to determine the substantial status of artifacts in Aristotle's *Metaphysics*. It is only to this extent that other metaphysical problems (such as Aristotle's account of substance, separability, and eternity) are dealt with. Hence, the title of my book: *Aristotle on Artifacts: A Metaphysical Puzzle*.

It is curious to note that despite ever-growing scholarship on Aristotle's *Metaphysics*, one of the conspicuous lacunae is a comprehensive treatment of artifacts. The obvious need for such an exposition can easily be seen: unless we can explain the substantial status of artifacts clearly, we cannot be said to have understood Aristotle's concept of substance. Such an explanation provides a valuable litmus test for our grasp of what it is to be a substance. Yet, what we find in the literature is a cursory examination, or at best a token discussion, of the ontological status of artifacts. For the most part, artifacts are mentioned just in passing. Very few scholars have recognized what turns out to be a very cryptic argument.[1] My task is to elucidate the argument against the substantial status of artifacts found in the *Metaphysics* (as we shall see, the task of this book ultimately comes down to explaining this one argument); in so doing, I hope to fill an important gap in Aristotelian literature on the topic of substance.

3. Method

A most profitable and unexpected exegetical dividend to be gained from examining those passages where Aristotle questions the status of artifacts is that they provide us with a rather firm framework in which to understand Aristotle's theory of substance in the *Metaphysics*. To illustrate my method, allow me to begin with the following allegory.

Suppose two thousand years ago someone discovered a box containing a jigsaw puzzle, which had been buried in a damp cellar for about one hundred and fifty years. The box and some pieces had been severely damaged by moisture and vermin so that neither the title nor the cover-picture on the box could be discerned. Let us say there are about ten thousand pieces. Let us also suppose that for the last two millennia, countless numbers of people have made heroic attempts to solve it, but without success. Many frustrated people have speculated as to why no one has yet convincingly put all the pieces together. Some have suggested that crucial pieces have been lost or damaged and, consequently, it is a hopeless task to try restoring the original picture. Others claim that the box contains several different puzzles that they try to solve by assembling different sets of what they believe to be related pieces. A third group contends that in the course of centuries, because of some preconceived idea of how the puzzle should fit together, some people have contaminated the content by introducing a number of "foreign" pieces. The members of the third group then try to eliminate these pieces, but more often than not they do so on the basis of their own preconceived idea of what the puzzle should look like.

Nonetheless, heroic and dauntless attempts to solve the puzzle continue, made by those who are quixotic by nature but find themselves in a discouraging predicament. Through their tireless efforts, most people have more or less come to accept that the puzzle is a picture of a Greek statue. A torso, shoulders, hands, and legs have been quite adequately pieced together. But the problem is that no one has convincingly identified the subject of the statue; for the face is missing. Of course, many people have attempted to reconstruct it, but instead of the expected face of a Greek god or hero, it always ends up looking like a disfigured lump such as we might see in modern sculptures. Some are not perturbed by this and happily accept such an anachronistic solution.

Now suppose someone notices that there is a handful of pieces that contain purple specks. He is not the first one to notice them, but no one else has looked at them seriously. They were always treated in a cursory manner, fitted to the whole puzzle after the other pieces had been assembled.

Our investigator steps back and asks the following question: on the assumption that this is a picture of a statue, what could these purple specks be? He remembers that Greeks had a tendency to paint purple (ὄστρεον) what they conceived to be the most important part of the statue—the eyes.[2] Given this insight, he collects all the pieces with purple specks and fits them together. He finds that they are indeed eyes. But there is a windfall, for these eyes come together, not in isolation, but with the surrounding features. While he is piecing the eyes together, he sees that he is also constructing the eyebrows, the forehead, the bridge of the nose, and so on. Using this method, he is able to reconstruct the face, thereby identifying the subject of the statue, and from there he successfully pieces together the rest of the puzzle.

Let me now compare the above jigsaw puzzle with Aristotle's *Metaphysics*. Just as the one who solved the puzzle assumed that it is a picture of a Greek statue, I shall assume that, regardless of one's conception of Aristotle's science of being, one of the central theories of the *Metaphysics* is that of substance. The scattered passages where Aristotle argues against the substantial status of artifacts are my pieces of purple specks. They are purple—that is, the most important passages—because they are key to the crucial task of elucidating the previous argument, which turns out to be very obscure. If we cannot adequately explain why artifacts are not substances, or, if they are substances, why Aristotle raises serious doubts about their substantiality, then we cannot say we have grasped Aristotle's concept of substance; that is, we have not understood one of the central theories of the *Metaphysics*.

When we collect all four passages where Aristotle questions the substantial status of artifacts, we shall see that Aristotle gives only one argument against the substantiality of artifacts in the entire corpus of the *Metaphysics* and that he always uses it in the same context. Note that the argument comes with the context, just as the purple specks came with the surrounding picture. And we may identify the "face" of the *Metaphysics*— what it is to be a substance—by examining the relationship between the argument and its context in the four passages. With such a method I shall reveal the criteria of substantiality. By means of these criteria we can then establish a framework from which to understand the rest of the *Metaphysics*.

Typically we find scholars first develop Aristotle's doctrine of substance and then, in passing, offer reasons why artifacts are not substances. My method is the reverse. I shall *begin* by examining why Aristotle doubts that artifacts are substances. And as a result of that examination, I shall disclose the criteria of substantiality, which will enable us to identify substances. Consequently, we shall be in a position to discover the ontological status of artifacts.

Now how do we know that we have discovered the right criteria? We have reason for believing that we have correctly identified the criteria of substantiality to the extent that we are able to do the following: we can present a consistent view of Aristotle's *Metaphysics*, shed new light on a long-standing controversy, and suggest solutions to cryptic passages that until now have not been adequately explained. And, as a consequence, we have established a reliable framework for understanding Aristotle's *Metaphysics*.

My immediate goal, however, is rather modest: to elucidate the argument against the substantial status of artifacts found in the *Metaphysics*. I shall develop the context only to the extent that it will help me solve this problem. Whether I can illuminate the entire philosophy of Aristotle by appealing to such a context remains to be seen. But there will be a *prima facie* reason for believing that this context will lead to a fruitful exegesis if the metaphysical puzzle about artifacts is resolved.

4. Context

There is only one argument in the *Metaphysics* against the substantial status of artifacts, and this argument always occurs in the same context. My approach is to extract these passages from the surrounding context and to discover the criteria of substantiality by examining the connection between the argument and its context. I should, however, like to avoid making unwarranted inferences or reaching false conclusions on the basis of passages taken out of context. But this turns out to be rather tricky; for in order to limit the discussion, I am bound to take some passages out of context. A sentence is found in a paragraph, a paragraph in a chapter, a chapter in a book, a book in a treatise. The pertinent passages must be taken from the context appropriately. But the question is this: how do I know when I have succeeded in doing so?

The first step is to identify the criterion of relevance, and this is determined by the purpose of my investigation, which is to elucidate Aristotle's argument against the substantial status of artifacts. So, whether the context is relevant to my discussion will be determined by whether it provides us with information that is required to solve the puzzle.

The second step is to make sure that the relevant *information* itself is not taken out of context. The interpretation of a passage is inaccurate when the context adds new information that undermines it. On the other hand, if the interpretation is not affected at all by placing the passage back into the context, then it is likely that such a passage, on which the interpretation is based, has been properly selected.

In order to ensure this, as far as possible, it is necessary to do two things: (1) establish the essential connection between the particular passage and its context; and (2) show why there is no more significant connection between the particular passage and another text. The first condition is relatively easy to meet; or, at least in order to defend an interpretation of a passage adequately, it is the responsibility of an exegete to establish such a connection. The second condition is more problematic. But wherever appropriate, I argue why in principle a given context will not affect our interpretation. By appropriate I mean this: task (2) is taken up only when there is a plausible reason for believing that the passage in question may be directly relevant to our discussion; that is, I do not exhaustively discuss every unrelated passage and argue why it is irrelevant. It is unreasonable to strive for a level of accuracy inappropriate to a particular exegetical endeavor. I exercise discretion and good judgment, trying to live up to the wise counsel of Aristotle himself: the mark of a wise person is to seek the accuracy that is appropriate for a given task.[3]

5. Developmental Issues

After the publication of Jaeger's *Aristoteles* in 1923[4]—regardless of the accuracy of his account of Aristotle's intellectual development—scholars could no longer take for granted a unitary notion of Aristotelian thought either among his treatises or within the *Metaphysics* itself. Therefore, I must comment on the issue regarding the development of Aristotle's thought and the relative chronology of his writings with respect to the present topic.

I emphasize that my topic is not the development of Aristotle's concept of the ontological status of artifacts, but his argument against their status as substances, found only in the *Metaphysics*. Since there is only one argument on this subject throughout the *Metaphysics*, there is no development in his view regarding it.[5]

The crucial point is that the passages in question are B4, K2, H3 and ∧3. Aristotle gives the same argument in the so- called theological book ∧, and in one of the central books of the *Metaphysics*, as well as in his book of *aporiai* (and its doublet). Furthermore, in the course of our discussion, A9 and M5 (the introductory book and its doublet) and Z7–9 (another passage from the central books) are analyzed. I show that there is a consistency in what some scholars consider to be conflicting works; that is, I relax the tension supposed to exist among different books of Aristotle's *Metaphysics*, especially between what some call the theological book ∧ and the onto-logical material in the central books Z–Θ.

My task is to present, as an alternative to developmental interpretations, the consistent view of Aristotle's concept of artifacts in the *Metaphysics* and, as a consequence, that of substances. I do so by using the four passages (B4, K2, H3 and ∧3) as the framework, and by offering suggestions to counter popular developmental interpretations. Thus, this unitary exposition (within the context of our discussion), if it is successful, would make the developmental thesis of the *Metaphysics* otiose.

As far as other works of Aristotle are concerned, since I rely on passages from the *De Anima* and especially the *Generation of Animals* to solve problems in the *Metaphysics*, the chronological assumption I need to make is that these two treatises are late works of Aristotle, an assumption that is not controversial.[6]

However, a further assumption that I shall make, which may not be readily granted by all, is that the *GA* is a *later* work than the *Metaphysics*.[7] If this assumption is granted, I can elucidate the argument against the sub-stantial status of artifacts in the *Metaphysics*. Of course, the crucial question is: why should anyone concede this point?

In the course of our discussion, I indicate why this assumption is a reasonable, or at least not an unreasonable, one to make. The main reasons are as follows:

1. There is no passage in the *Metaphysics* itself that helps us completely elucidate the argument; that is, not all the relevant information is available in the *Metaphysics*.
2. The relevant context is the topic of coming-to-be; hence, if some living things are substances most of all because of the manner in which they are generated, then the distinction between the generation of animals and the production of artifacts holds the key to our solution.

3. In the *Metaphysics*, Aristotle is ambivalent about the status of artifacts. Nowhere does he unequivocally claim that artifacts are not substances. I suggest that the explanation lies in his theory of embryology.
4. There is a development in Aristotle's embryology from *Meta* Θ to the *GA*.

Thus, my analyses will indicate that, if indeed there is a solution to this problem, we can reasonably expect to find it in the *GA*.[8]

My method, however, is different from that of some scholars[9] who appeal to Aristotle's biological doctrine as the framework in which to interpret the *Metaphysics*. My exegesis of the *Metaphysics* is based on nothing but its text; that is, the text of the *Metaphysics* itself leads us to the biological work of the *GA*. The importance of this methodology is that I can justify my appeal to the *GA*.

In this regard, Gerson[10] raises an interesting issue. Is it possible to solve metaphysical problems by means of subontological principles (that is, the principles that pertain to special science, such as biology, and not to metaphysics)? Or, can only metaphysical principles solve them?

I agree with Gerson that the study of a special science *per se* is irrelevant to the study of being *qua* being. My textual analysis of the pertinent passages of the *Metaphysics* reveals the following: Aristotle's *Metaphysics*, as it stands, is deficient in solving our problem, and there is every indication that the solution to the metaphysical problem is found in the *GA*. In the *GA* Aristotle can no longer appeal to his old principles to account for the development of an embryo. He needs to introduce a new principle (or at least modify an old one) to save the phenomenon. Although the new principle is found and employed within his physical treatise, this introduction has a great impact on his metaphysics because it is the very principle that determines the *substantial* status of both living things and artifacts. It solves a metaphysical problem raised in the *Metaphysics*, hence, it can be construed also as a *metaphysical* principle.

The theory of substance is one of the central problems of Aristotle's *Metaphysics*. Therefore, once a new metaphysical principle is introduced (which is the key to determining the substantial status of artifacts), the introduction of such a principle has serious ramifications for other metaphysical problems (for example, whether a substance is individual or universal).

I do not assume that there is a new *metaphysical* principle in the *GA*, nor do I begin with any preconceived idea of what Aristotle's *Metaphysics* is about. To avoid reading my prejudices and biases into the text, the context itself dictates as much as possible the direction in which I proceed. If I am successful, I have established the reasonableness of appealing to the *GA* to look for a new principle to solve the metaphysical problem of the *Metaphysics*. We should bear in mind, however, that because I am operating on the assumption that the *GA* is a later work than the *Metaphysics* when I am applying the new principle found in the *GA* to solve the substantial status of artifacts in the *Metaphysics* (which is incomplete as it stands), I am going *back* in time. That is, I present what would be the view of Aristotle had he the chance to reconsider the status of artifacts by appealing to the new principle that he introduces in the *GA*, where he gives an account of his embryology—the generation of substances.

6. Summary

In chapter 1, I argue that there is no evidence in the *Metaphysics* to warrant the inference that all living things are substances most of all or substances in some qualified sense. Mules and spontaneously generated organisms are suspects (and women and children are somewhat ontologically deficient). That being so, we cannot *a priori* look for the differences (such as internal-change, psychic activity, and intrinsic unity) that we find between living things and artifacts as criteria for substantiality. Consequently, we need to establish another criterion (or criteria) for it.

In chapter 2, I begin my account of Aristotle's theory by identifying the four passages (B4, K2, H3, and Λ3) where Aristotle argues that artifacts are not substances. From these passages, I establish that in the *Metaphysics*, Aristotle offers only one argument against the substantial status of artifacts, which is: the form of an artifact does not exist apart from the composite; hence, it is possible that an artifact is not a substance. Furthermore, I note that this argument always occurs in the same context (that is, in a context where Aristotle defends the view that the form is ungenerable and indestructible). Then, I analyze the connection between the argument and the context and discover that eternity is a criterion of substantiality.

Since we shall find that the immediate context common to all four passages provides us with insufficient information, I expand the context to Aristotle's discussion of coming-to-be (which occurs in B4, H3, and Λ3). In chapter 3, by examining an *aporia* found in B4 (and its doublet in K2) along with the passages where Aristotle criticizes Plato's theory of Forms, we discover that actuality is another criterion of substantiality. Thus, I conclude that a substance is somehow an eternal actuality.

In chapter 4, I turn to Z7–9 where Aristotle discusses the principles of coming-to-be. I expose the crux of the problem that we need to solve: whether the form, understood as the substance of a composite, is individual or universal. We shall see that in these passages, Aristotle does not provide the crucial difference between the generation of natural substances and the production of artifacts.

Having identified the crucial passages as B4, K2, H3, and ∧3 in chapter 2, and having examined B4 and K2 as well as A9 and M5 in chapter 3, and Z7–9 in chapter 4 (and since H3 does not provide us with any further information), in chapter 5 I turn to ∧3 (and *GA* 2.1) where the important distinction between art and nature is drawn: art is a principle in another and nature is a principle in itself. By analyzing Aristotle's concept of a principle, we shall discover why a substance must be an eternal actuality, separable from the destructible composite. A principle in principle must be separate from that of which it is a principle; a primary principle of coming-to-be must be eternal, and as a cause it must exist in actuality. And we shall learn that although art is a principle that exists potentially in the mind of an artisan and nature is a principle that exists actually in the form of a male parent, the simple distinction between actuality and potentiality is inadequate to capture the crucial difference between art and nature. For, although the form of a house exists potentially in the mind of an artisan and the form of the son also exists potentially in his father, art is understood as in another while nature is understood as in itself.

In chapter 6, by examining other relevant passages from the *Generation of Animals* (and with the help from the passages of the *De Anima*) we shall discover that, in contrast to potency (the *dynamis* of the complete form), Aristotle introduces power (the *dynamis* of the incomplete form), which is somehow both an actuality and a potentiality at the same time. The mark of the power is that it can realize its own potentiality without further assistance from any external cause. I call this process self-realization. And it is the form, understood as an active *dynamis* (which is neither individual nor universal, but somehow both individual and universal in a different sense), that exists in the male parent (as potency) in the motion of semen and in the principle of growth (as power) that makes it possible for the form of destructible substances to exist as an eternal actuality.

In light of our discussion, in the final chapter I present Aristotle's overall metaphysical view (that is, the πρὸς ἕν relationship that exists among different kinds of substances as well as with other nonsubstantial beings). By appealing to Aristotle's doctrine of *connate pneuma*, I speculate the most likely view of Aristotle on the ontological status of (among other living things) women, children, mules, and spontaneously generated organisms. And within this overall metaphysical framework, I determine the substantial status of artifacts. Since the principle of art is a potentiality, and not an active *dynamis*, the products of art, such as artifacts, are not substances at all. Artifacts belong to a group of nonsubstantial *pragmata*, such as heaps. Therefore, I conclude that artifacts are simply *things*.

7. Notes on Appendix D

Different sections of passage B4, 999a24–999b20, are referred to throughout the book. To facilitate an integrated analysis and avoid repetitions, this section is analyzed in Appendix D, rather than discussed in fragments throughout the book.

In Appendix D, I am especially interested in showing the connection among different sections of the B4 passage, that is, in exposing Aristotle's train of thought or in showing how one idea leads to the next. But the content is also important. Although the B4 passage is dialectical, it is safe to assume that Aristotle is committed to its arguments, because he advances the same views in other passages of the *Metaphysics*. For example, he offers the same argument against the substantial status of artifacts in the same context elsewhere.

When I appeal to the just mentioned passage in the main text, I take for granted that the arguments represent Aristotle's view. To sceptics I suggest this approach: consider the aporetic passage B4, 999a24–999b20, as representing Aristotle's view until I have presented a consistent and coherent picture of his position. For example, I show from the previous *aporia* that the criteria of substantiality are eternity and actuality, and I also confirm this from other passages.

There is evidence to suggest that the *aporiai* of B themselves may not be merely dialectical, for in M2, the text begins as follows:

> It has been stated in our discussion of difficulties (ἐν τοῖς διαπορήμασιν) that it is impossible for [the mathematical objects] to exist in the sensible things, . . . (1076a38–b1).

Here, Aristotle refers to the discussion of difficulties (that is, the *aporiai* in B2, 998a7–19) as though it represents his view—his argument against the existence of mathematical objects in sensible things.[11] Although the passage does not in itself establish that every single aporetic discussion in B is not dialectical, it gives us some reason for believing that at least some can be taken as representing Aristotle's own view.

However, as far as my topic is concerned, I assume that *only* the passage B4, 999a24–999b20, represents Aristotle's view.[12] I appeal to the information obtained by this analysis, where appropriate, to defend my position.

For ease of reference, I have divided the passage of B4 into five main sections.

Chapter One

Substances Most of All

In the *Categories*, artifacts fall under the category of substance; however, in the *Metaphysics*, Aristotle introduces degrees of substantiality by identifying a certain group of beings as "substances most of all." A widely held view is that all living things are such substances. Accordingly, many scholars have argued that artifacts are not substances (with or without qualification) by appealing to the differences that we find between living things and artifacts, such as internal-change, psychic activity, and intrinsic unity. I shall, however, show that there is no clear evidence for such a position; nowhere in the *Metaphysics* does Aristotle identify mules and spontaneously generated organisms as either substances most of all or substances as such. To understand why artifacts are not substances in the *Metaphysics*, we need to establish criteria beyond those uniformly applicable to all living things.

1.1. *Categories*

If we examine the categorical schema of *Categories* (i.e., substance, quality, quantity, and so on), artifacts fall under the category of substance. In *Cat* 2, Aristotle introduces the technical terms "said of a subject" and "present in a subject."[1] By means of these terms, he establishes the following classification: (1) those that are said of a subject but are not present in a subject (e.g., man is said of an individual man but is not in any subject); (2) those that are present in a subject but are not said of any subject (a particular whiteness is present in a body but is not said of any subject);[2] (3) those that are both said of a subject and present in a subject (knowledge is present in a soul but is also said of a subject, such as, grammatical knowledge); and (4) the primary substances—those that are neither present in a subject nor said of a subject (an individual man or an individual horse). Everything can be classified as either a primary substance or a thing whose existence depends on the existence of a primary substance; hence, it is impossible for any other things to exist if primary substances did not exist (2a34–b6).

Primary substance is also described in a number of other ways: for example, it indicates a 'this'[3] because it is something individual[4] and numerically one. In contrast, man or animal indicates a sort of quality; that is, it indicates a secondary substance. Furthermore, primary substance has no contrary (for there is nothing contrary to an individual man) nor admits of a more and a less (for one man is not more or less of a man than another), and the most distinctive characteristic is that, while remaining numerically one and the same, a primary substance admits of contraries by changing (for a man becomes pale or dark) (3b10–4a21).

Note, however, that these criteria are applicable to an individual artifact, such as an individual jackknife as much as to an individual horse or an individual man. For an individual jackknife is not said of a subject nor is it in a subject. On the contrary, other things are said of or present in it; for example, knife (which indicates a kind of thing—that is, a secondary substance) is said of an individual jackknife or a particular sharpness is present in it. It is also a 'this,' an individual, and numerically one. Furthermore, there is nothing contrary to an individual jackknife, but rather it admits of contraries—the most proper mark of a substance. For, just as an individual man, "being one and the same, becomes at one time light and at another time dark, warm and cold, and vicious and virtuous" (4a18–21), similarly an individual jackknife, being numerically one and the same, can undergo similar qualitative changes: it can become tarnished, hence change its color; it can become hot or cold, depending on the temperature; and, if its edge is dulled, it could even lose its "virtue." Artifacts, then, must be primary substances.[5]

1.2. Z7

The *Metaphysics* introduces features of substantiality that are absent from the *Categories*, including an enriched notion of the degrees of substantiality. Of course, even in the *Categories*, Aristotle allows for degrees of substantiality, but in a weaker sense. For example, he says, "the species is more of a substance than the genus" (2b7–8) because, among other reasons, the species is a subject for the genus (2b19–20). Similarly, because primary substances are subjects for all other secondary substances (such as, species and genus), the former are identified as substances most of all (μάλιστα) (2b15–17). But, since no species is a subject for any other species, "as many of the species themselves that are not genera, none of them is more of a substance than another" (2b22–24). This is also the case with the primary substances themselves, for "an individual man is not more of a substance than an individual ox" (2b27–28). So, degrees of substantiality exist because of the different levels of subjects. But within the same hierarchical level, one is no more a substance than another.

But that is no longer the case in the *Metaphysics*. For example at Z7, 1032a19, Aristotle identifies a certain group of beings (men and plants) as substances most of all, suggesting that in contrast to them, there is another group of beings that are substances with qualification,[6] that is, Aristotle is employing the familiar phrase from the *Categories*, substances most of all,[7] in a different sense.[8] In Z7, 1032a19, Aristotle mentions "a man or a plant or some other of these things" as substances most of all. Most scholars[9] assume that Aristotle is here referring to all living things. But this is far from clear. Just previously he classifies three kinds of coming-to-be: things that come to be by nature, art, and chance. It is in this context[10] that Aristotle identifies substances most of all:

> Natural comings-to-be are those whose coming to be is from nature; and that from which they come to be is what we call matter; and that by which [they come to be] is something which exists by nature; and "what" [comes to be] is a man or a plant or some other of these things, which indeed we call substances most of all. (1032a15–19)

So, Aristotle is explaining how the things that come to be by nature come into existence. And it is in this context that he refers to "a man or a plant or some other of these things" as "substances most of all;" that is, he refers to the sort of things that come to be by nature but not by art or by chance. He continues:

> Universally, then, that from which they come to be is nature and that according to which they come to be is nature (for what comes to be has nature, for example, a plant and an animal) and that by which [they come to be] is the nature, which is called according to the form, and it has the same form [as that which comes to be] (but the form exists in another; for man generates man). (1032a22–25)

In other words, Aristotle identifies only the living things that come to be by nature as substances most of all. It is only after having done so that he then turns to the other modes of coming-to-be:

> So in this way come to be the things that come to be through nature, but other comings-to-be are called "makings." And all makings are either from art[11] or from potentiality or from thought. And of these, some occur both spontaneously and from chance just as among things that come to be from nature, for these too, in some cases,

the same things come to be both out of seeds and without seeds. But concerning these things we must examine later. (1032a25–32)

Here Aristotle introduces spontaneously generated organisms as a subset of "the things that come to be *from* nature" (1032a30). But their examination is *postponed*,[12] indicating that they (that is, "the things that come to be from chance") were not included in his discussion of "the things that come to be by nature," even though they come to be *from* nature. Thus, Aristotle has not included living things that come to be from chance, such as spontaneously generated organisms, in the class of things called substances most of all.[13]

But the superlative μάλιστα (most of all) suggests that there are things that are substances, but not most of all. Are spontaneously generated organisms, then, substances in some qualified sense? Before we turn to this question, let me analyze the term "nature," for, since Aristotle identifies substances most of all among[14] "the things that come to be by nature," the standard in which to measure the degree of substantiality may be discovered if this term is clarified first.

Unfortunately, the actual formulations of Greek phrases are of no help because Aristotle expresses himself in many different ways. In Z7, to denote natural comings-to-be, he employs the following phrases: "the things that come to be *by* nature" (1032a12); "things that come to be *through* nature" (1032a26); and "in the things that come to be *from* nature" (1032a30).[15]

The problem with attempting to identify the things that can be construed as natural substances is that the term "nature" is used in many senses.[16] For example, in *Phys* 2.1, in contrast to the things that exist by art, Aristotle lists animals, their parts, plants, and elements as natural substances.[17] But in Z16 he denies that the parts of animals and elements are substances because they are mere potentialities (1040b5–10). In *Phys* 2.6, Aristotle identifies the things that come to be from chance as the things that come to be contrary to nature (197b34). That means spontaneously generated organisms are the things that are generated contrary to nature.

A similar problem also arises with regard to the status of mules. In *GA* 2.7–8, Aristotle identifies "the race of mules"[18] (747a24–25) among animals as the only one that is infertile, and one[19] reason for its sterility is that it is generated contrary to nature.[20] In *HA* 6.23, Aristotle describes the trick that the breeders employ to generate mules such that under normal circumstances mules would not be generated.[21] The fact that mules are generated contrary to nature is also emphasized in Z8, 1033b29–33.

This, however, does not mean that things that are contrary to nature are not in some sense according to nature. For example, in his biological works, Aristotle says, "even that which is 'contrary to nature' is in a way 'according to nature'" (*GA* 4.4, 770b16).[22] Furthermore, in the case of spontaneous generation (that is, of things that are generated contrary to nature), the process involves nature. For example, the heat of the sun generates organisms by acting upon natural residue[23]—such as mud and putrefying matter[24]—that is, in a way spontaneously generated organisms are also generated according to nature.

Given the complexity of the use of the term "nature," we cannot simply appeal to phrases such as according to nature and contrary to nature as if they were univocal. It seems that the only recourse we have in determining the sense in which Aristotle applies the word "nature" (or any other phrase that contains the word "nature") is to surmise the sense from its immediate context.

From the context of Z7, it is clear that Aristotle excludes "the things that come to be by chance" from the class of "the things that come to be by nature." Now, although in Z7 he includes "the things that come to be by chance" among the things that come to be from nature, and in Z9 he refers to them as "the things which are *formed* by nature" (1034a33), it is not clear whether the former are to be considered as natural substances at all. Consequently, spontaneously generated organisms are not substances most of all, and there is no clear evidence that they are even substances in a qualified sense (in this passage).

But, then, we find ourselves in a quandary: what possible things are there that would qualify as substances, but not most of all, if we cannot assume that either "the things that come to be by art" or "the things that come to be by chance" are such substances? Because of the lack of better alternatives, one could argue that in contrast to substances most of all, spontaneously generated organisms and mules must be natural substances in some sense of the word.

But there are other alternatives. First note that the topic of the previous discussion is coming-to-be.[25] And it is in that context that Aristotle appeals to the celebrated formula, "man generates man"[26] (1032a25), sometimes reformulated as "man from man" (1034b2), to refer to a natural coming-to-be. If these formulae express the norm of natural coming-to-be or generation, whatever deviates from that norm may lose some degree of substantiality.[27] An instance that worries Aristotle is mentioned in Z9:

> One must not expect with respect to every thing that it is like "a man [comes] from a man"; for also "a woman [comes] from a male man."[28] (1034b1–3)

In the *GA*, a female is described as "a deformed male" (737a28), because the menstrual discharge, which is impure semen, cannot supply the principle of soul. That is why in some animals, females can only produce wind-eggs

(730a27–34). Now although they are deformed males, Aristotle specifies that they are *naturally* deformed (775a15–16) and they are necessary by nature (767b9). Females also have a vital role in reproduction, because both male and female are the principles of generation: the former is the principle in the sense of *form*, which supplies the principle of motion, while the latter is the principle in the sense in which it serves as *matter* (732a1–11). Note that in Z7, immediately after Aristotle identifies some things as substances most of all, he describes the role of matter in generation as potentiality (1032a20–22) as if to indicate its subordinate role. So if male and female are to be understood in terms of form and matter,[29] respectively, then the former is more of a substance than the latter, because form is more of a substance than matter (Z3, 1029a5–7, 27–30). We can thus understand why in I9, Aristotle raises the question, puzzling to us, of whether or not a female differs from a male in form or species (1058a29–b25).

Another interesting case is a child. An adult male is said to be prior to a child with respect to substance (Θ8, 1050a4–7). Throughout the *GA*, Aristotle emphasizes that a boy resembles a woman.[30] That is evidence to suggest that females[31] and children, who are generated by nature, may not be considered by Aristotle as substances most of all because they lack the important principle of generation—complete form.[32]

Thus, in Z7, there is no warrant for the view that all living things are substances most of all, and there is no clear evidence to suggest that some living things, such as spontaneously generated organisms, are substances even in a qualified sense (although they might be).[33]

This conclusion has an important bearing on the discussions that we find in the literature on artifacts. Most (if not all) scholars, who argue that artifacts are not substances, assume that all living things are substances most of all, or at least substances in a qualified sense.

1.3. *Status Quaestionis*

There are at least three views that other scholars have entertained:[34]

1. Artifacts are not substances because they do not have the principle of internal-change that is exhibited by living things.[35]
2. Artifacts are not substances because they possess no psychic activity.[36]
3. Artifacts are not substances because the intrinsic unity of nature, as opposed to the accidental unity of art, is the criterion of substantiality.[37]

A fundamental problem with all of these three views is that they either explicitly or implicitly assume that all living things are either substances most of all or at least substances with qualification. But this assumption is dubious, for there is no clear evidence in the *Metaphysics* to warrant such an assumption.

There are five[38] passages in the *Metaphysics* that seem to support the view that all living things are substances most of all or at least substances with qualification: Z7, 1032a18–19; Z8, 1034a3–4; Z17, 1041b28–31; H3, 1043b22–23; and Λ3, 1070a17–19. I have just discussed the Z7 passage in chapter 1.2, so I begin with the Z8 passage.

1.3.1. Z8, 1034a3–4

By referring to the common genus of a horse and an ass, Aristotle has just explained how one can account for the generation of mules—which he has identified as contrary to nature:

> Consequently, it is clear that it is not at all necessary to establish a form as a paradigm (for most of all we should have looked for [such forms] in these things [natural things]; for these things most of all are substances; but it is sufficient that what generates produces and is the cause of the form in the matter. (Z8, 1034a2–5)

Exactly what Aristotle is saying here in this passage is not clear. Is he saying that we could dispense with the Platonic Forms of all living things altogether because we can account for their generation by appealing to the natural substances, such as a horse and an ass, which are substances most of all? In saying so, does he consider mules[39] (which are generated contrary to nature [1033b33]) and spontaneously generated organisms (not discussed until the next chapter, Z9) as such substances?

The crucial Greek text is this: "μάλιστα γὰρ ἂν ἐν τούτοις ἐπεζητοῦντο· οὐσίαι γὰρ αἱ μάλιστα αὗται" (1034a3–4). But what does ἐν τούτοις refer to? Apostle (1966) translates it as "physical substances,"[40] and the reason for this translation is found in the previous passage "ἐν τοῖς φυσικοῖς" (1033b32). Aristotle was emphasizing the similarity between the production of artificial things and the generation of natural things in the previous paragraph (1033b 19–26). Does ἐν τούτοις refer to artifacts? Given the context, probably not.

Since in Z7 Aristotle has identified substances most of all as being only among the things that come to be by nature, this is the most conservative and safest reading. If indeed the phrase refers to ἐν τοῖς φυσικοῖς (the most likely candidate in this context), then the phrase ἐν τούτοις does not include all living things; that is, it excludes mules and spontaneously generated organisms. Furthermore, there is no positive evidence that things not included as substances most of all can even be considered as substances with qualification.

1.3.2. Z17, 1041b28–31

In Z17, Aristotle identifies the form as the cause and the substance of the thing. And having explained how this is so in the cases of a syllable (such as "*ba*") and of flesh, he says:

> Since some things are not substances, but as many things that are substances are formed according to nature, the substance would appear to be this nature, which is not an element but a principle. (1041b28–31)

Aside from the fact that he seems to have excluded syllables and flesh, there is no clue as to what he means by "things that are formed (συνεστήκασι)[41] by nature." The context is simply uncertain.

Thus, again, the text does tell us what things are natural substances (either with or without qualification).

1.3.3. H3, 1043b22–23

Here, Aristotle suggests that one might posit only nature as a substance among the destructible things. In the immediate context (1043b18–23), artifacts are contrasted with things that are formed (συνέστηκεν) by nature. In the previous chapter, H2, Aristotle discusses things that are only "analogous" (1043a5) to substance. According to Lewis (1994), in H2 Aristotle admits that "such items as honeywater, bundles or books or boxes, thresholds and lintels, or breakfast and supper, or broadening the range of cases winds, or even ice . . . are not substances at all." Lewis also includes eclipses and sleep as well as hands and feet in the list of what he calls "pseudo-substances"(265). Hence, one could argue: given that Aristotle has rejected the examples selected from the following genera (artifacts, elements, natural phenomena, and parts of animals), what are left (living things, including mules and spontaneously generated organisms) are the things that are formed by nature.

This argument can be strengthen by noting the phrase "things that are *formed* (συνέστηκεν) by nature" in contrast to "things that *come to be* or *are generated* (γίγνεται) by nature;" the first phrase is a broader term than the second. In Z9, spontaneously generated organisms are called "the things that are formed by nature" (1034a33); although the expression "things that *come to be* or *are generated* by nature" excludes spontaneously generated organisms, the phrase "things that are formed by nature" includes them. So, even if spontaneously generated organisms are not substances most of all, they can be considered as substances in some sense of the word.

Unfortunately, even if the phrase "things that are *formed* by nature" is broader than "things that *come to be* or *are generated* by nature" and hence includes the spontaneously generated organisms, we cannot assume that the expression is equivalent to "all living things," for it has a much wider connotation. It includes things such as animals, their parts, plants, and elements.[42] Secondly, even if we take into account the context in which Aristotle employs the expression "things that are formed by nature," that is, the context in which, according to Lewis, he has rejected such things as substances, there is no way of knowing from the context whether Aristotle has selected examples from *some* or *all* of the genera to which he denies substantiality. Furthermore, there is a problem deciding whether or not mules can be considered as "things that are formed by nature" in this context.

1.3.4. Λ3, 1070a17–19

Here, Aristotle endorses Plato for positing as many Forms as those that come to be by nature. This passage should be examined in the context of Λ3 discussion. Ten lines earlier the text reads:

> After these things (μετὰ ταῦτα ὅτι), each *substance* comes to be from a synonymous [thing] (for those that [come to be] by nature are substances and the rest (τὰ γὰρ φύσει οὐσίαι καὶ τὰ ἄλλα)); for [a thing] comes to be either by art or by nature or by luck or by chance. (1070a4–9)

First, we need to clarify the translation of the following sentence: τὰ γὰρ φύσει οὐσίαι καὶ τὰ ἄλλα. According to Elders (1972), grammatically, " τὰ γὰρ φύσει and τὰ ἄλλα are the subject of the sentence, οὐσίαι the predicate" (100). Thus, he concludes that "products of art, chance, and spontaneity are substances" (100).[43] This seems right, for Aristotle seems to be saying that the reason each *substance* comes to be from the synonymous thing is that both "things that come to be by nature" and the rest are substances.

But this interpretation throws doubt on the very meaning of the word "substances." For now unlikely things, such as things that come to be by luck and chance and health (1070a16), become substances. So if we adhere strictly to the grammar of the sentence, we will have to accept that a number of things that are not considered to be substances *are* substances, unless Aristotle is using the word substance to cover all things that come to be (which includes forms in other categories as well). But such an extensive meaning will be of no use in determining what is a substance.

I suggest an alternative reading. In his commentary on line 1069b35, which begins with the phrase μετὰ ταῦτα ὅτι, Ross[44] says this phrase is "one of the clearest indications of the fact, apparent throughout chs. 1–5, that Aristotle is jotting down notes for a treatise (or lecture), not writing a treatise in its finished form." He also refers to Alexander's remark[45] that the book is confused and disordered.

If the passage is to be taken as a note, Aristotle is simply reminding himself (or his "hearers") that not only natural substances but also other *things*, including things that come to be by art, chance, or spontaneity, all come to be by something that has the same name (ἐκ συνωνύμου);[46] that is, the point at issue is not that τὰ ἄλλα are substances, but rather that they come to be in the very same way as natural substances. The advantage of this interpretation is that it is consistent with what we find in Z7–9 (as we shall see in chapter 4.1).

So either we strictly adhere to the grammar, in which case the word "substances" is used equivocally, or we accept a possible interpretation that is consistent with other writings of Aristotle (on the assumption that it is a note to serve as a reminder and not a carefully formulated statement). If we accept the former interpretation, the sentence does not establish that there are substances other than things that come to be by nature because the word "substances" would include other categories. But if we accept the latter interpretation, then only things that come to be by nature are substances. Either way, we can only conclude that things that come to be by nature are substances.

There is another possibility: only those things that come under the category of substance are substances. For example, in the case of the things that come to be by art, things like houses are substances but not things like health. There is evidence for this interpretation; the immediate context is this:

> In some cases a "this" does not exist apart from the composite *substance*, like the form of a house, unless it is art (but there is no generation and destruction of these things, but in another way the house without matter and health and all others according to art exist and do not exist), but if indeed [a "this" exists apart from the composite], it is in cases of things that [come to be] by nature. And indeed that is why Plato did not speak wrongly when he said that there are as many Forms as those that [come to be] by nature (if indeed there are Forms), but there are no [Forms] of things, such as fire, flesh, and a head; for all these are matters, and the last one is [the matter] of a substance most of all. (1070a13–20)

Note that Aristotle identifies a house as a *substance*. And yet when he endorses Plato for positing Forms, he excludes all art (including artifacts). What is most revealing is that Aristotle excludes elements (like fire) and parts of animals (like flesh and a head) from the rest of natural substances, as if to suggest that until now he has been including them among the things that come to be by nature, which in turn suggests that Aristotle has been using the word substance rather loosely, as we indicated earlier.

Whatever may be the case, it is clear that when Aristotle identifies things that come to be by nature as substances most of all, he means things that are *generated* by nature (as in the case of plants and animals): (i) elements and parts of animals are excluded; (ii) he says that the head is the matter of a substance most of all (among the things that come to be by nature only animals and plants have heads);[47] and (iii) in ∧1 he identifies animals and plants as destructible substances (1069a31–32).

Now the question is this: do things that are generated by nature include spontaneously generated organisms? The answer to this depends on whether Aristotle classifies them as things that come to be by chance or by nature. The text is not clear. But, as we saw in chapters 1.2 and 1.3.1, in Z7–9, they were excluded from things that come to be by nature. So there also is a *prima facie* reason to exclude them from things that come to be by nature in our present passage.

Are they substances with qualification? Aristotle calls artifacts substances, as if to imply that if they are not substances most of all like things that are generated by nature, then they are substances in some sense of the word. But it is unclear in what sense Aristotle is using the word "substance" to denote artifacts. There is an indication that Aristotle even includes nonsubstantial beings, such as elements and parts of animals, as those that come to be by nature when he identifies them as substances in line 1070a5–6. Again, the text is not clear. Similarly, we cannot determine the substantial status of things that are generated by chance. Hence, we cannot conclude from ∧3 that spontaneously generated organisms are substances, with or without qualification.

1.4. The Summary

Our findings on the five passages herein are summarized in Appendix B. From this summary we can see that passage (1) unequivocally excludes spontaneously generated organisms as things that are generated by nature (i.e., as substances most of all), nor is there any indication that they are substances with qualification. The contexts of passages (2)–(5) do not license us to infer that all living things are natural substances, with or without qualification. Thus I conclude that there is no evidence in the *Metaphysics* to warrant the inference that Aristotle believes that all living things are natural substances, with or without qualification.

Chapter Two

Separate

We cannot simply employ living things *per se* as paradigms to argue why artifacts are not substances. Instead of starting with a preconceived idea of what substances are, I shall begin by analyzing the argument against the substantial status of artifacts in the *Metaphysics*, for Aristotle gives only one such argument and it occurs always in the same context. By examining the argument in its context, I shall argue that, since the key to understanding the argument lies in Aristotle's conception of separation, eternity is a criterion of substantiality.

2.1. The Argument in Its Context

There are four passages in the *Metaphysics* where Aristotle argues that artifacts are not substances: B4, 999b17–20; K2, 1060b16–28; H3, 1043b18–23; and Λ3, 1070a13–20. In each passage, Aristotle's argument against the substantial status of artifacts occurs in the immediate context in which he is discussing *the topic of coming-to-be*, which specifically includes the identification of form as ungenerable[1] (or indestructible in K2). Since there is a close connection between ungenerable and indestructible,[2] we can see that the argument occurs always in the same context. The pertinent passages with the common immediate context are as follows:[3] B4, 999b4–20 (and its doublet K2, 1060b23–28); H3, 1043b14–23; and Λ3, the whole chapter.

In each passage, Aristotle gives the same argument against the substantial status of artifacts, which is: the form of an artifact does not exist apart from the composite; hence, it is possible that an artifact is not a substance. Let me take each of them in turn.

2.1.1. B4, 999b4–20 (and its doublet K2, 1060b23–28)

The argument that is found in B4[4] is this: the form of an artifact does not exist apart from the artifact; hence, it is possible that the artifact is not a substance.

Its doublet, K2, 1060b23–28, reads:

> Furthermore, is there anything apart from the composite or not (and by [the composite] I mean matter and what [comes] with it)? For if there is not anything, then all things in matter [would be] destructible; but if there is anything, then this would be the form or the shape. But it is difficult to determine that this is so in some cases and not so in others, for in some cases it is obvious that the form is not separate, for example, [the form of] a house.

Given that the composite is form and matter, the best candidate for what exists separate from the composite is the form. But this is not always the case; an obvious exception is the form of an artifact, such as that of a house.

It is not clear how we should take the term *separate*. If it is meant as a criterion of substantiality,[5] then the argument is this: the form of an artifact does not exist separate from the composite; hence, it is possible that an artifact is not a substance.

2.1.2. H3, 1043b14–23

In the passage 1043b14–18, having identified the form as the ungenerable and indestructible element, which is the substance, Aristotle continues:

> But it is not yet clear if the substances of destructible things are separate; except it is obvious that it is not possible for some cases— those things that are not able to exist apart from individual things, for example a house or utensil. But perhaps neither these things themselves nor any of the others that are not formed by nature are substances, for one might posit only nature as a substance in destructible things.

So he questions whether it is possible for a substance, understood as the form and not the composite, to be separate. What is certain is that there is an obvious exception, which is again the form of an artifact, such as that of a house. So perhaps these things themselves, referring to the composites, are not substances.

Thus, the argument is this: the form of an artifact does not exist apart from the artifact; therefore, an artifact is perhaps not a substance.

2.1.3. ∧3, the Whole Chapter

Aristotle begins ∧3 by noting that neither the matter nor the form is generated. He next draws a distinction between nature and art by means of the principle of coming-to-be. He reminds us that there are three sorts of substances: matter, nature, which is a "this," and the composite of the two. Having established the above points, he says this:

> In some cases a "this" does not exist apart from the composite substance, like the form of a house, unless it is art (but there is no generation and destruction of these things, but in another way the house without matter and health and all others according to art exist and do not exist), but if indeed [a "this" exists apart from the composite], it is in cases of things that [come to be] by nature. And indeed that is why Plato did not speak wrongly when he said that there are as many Forms as those that [come to be] by nature (if indeed there are Forms), but there are no [Forms] of things, such as fire, flesh, and a head; for all these are matters, and the last one is [the matter] of a substance most of all. (1070a13–20)

Aristotle denies that a substance (understood as a "this," that is, the form) of an artifact exists apart from the composite, except with qualification. But if there is a "this," which exists apart from the composite, it is found in nature. And since Aristotle endorses Plato's claim that there are Forms of the things that exist by nature, this also suggests that the natural composite things, rather than the artifacts, are substances.

Thus, the argument is this: the form of an artifact does not exist apart from the composite except with qualification (that is, in the sense in which art is said to be separate); hence, it is possible that an artifact is not a substance.

2.1.4. The Oddities

Let me now examine the oddities that are found in the previous argument.

(A) Since, in every passage, Aristotle identifies the substance with the form, and it is the separation of the form itself that is the issue, we expect that the argument would be this: the form of an artifact does not exist apart from the artifact; hence, it is possible that the *form* of an artifact is not a substance. And yet in H3, Aristotle argues that the form of an artifact does not exist apart from the artifact; hence, it is possible that the *artifact* is not a substance. In other words, while he identifies the form of a composite as the substance in H3, what he doubts or affirms is not the substantiality of the form but rather that of the composite itself. Also in ∧3, he says that the head is the matter of a substance most of all, but the head cannot be the matter of the form but only of the composite; that is, Aristotle affirms the substantiality of the composite and not the form.

There is no apparent reason for this shift of emphasis of the term substance from the form to the composite. Except in H3, where he presents the previous argument, Aristotle points out that a name (τὸ ὄνομα) can signify both the form and the composite. But he says that this distinction makes no difference to the investigation of sensible substances. The difference seems to occur in the context of the discussion of essence (1043a38–1043b4). Since the argument occurs always in the same context (that is, Aristotle is engaging in the same kind of investigation of sensible substances), there is good reason for believing that, in passages B4 and K2, it is also the substantiality of the composite itself that is questioned. On this assumption, I have analyzed B4 and K2.

(B) Aristotle is *clear* about the fact that the form of an artifact does not exist apart from the artifact, for he says "it is clear (φανερόν)" (B4, 999b19) and "it is obvious (δῆλον)" (K2, 1060b28 and H3, 1043b20). In Λ3, he states unequivocally that the form of a house exists apart only with qualification. Yet in H3 and Λ3, Aristotle hesitates to conclude, from that fact, that an artifact is not a substance, for he says "perhaps (ἴσως)" (1043b21) and "if indeed (εἴπερ)" (1070a17) respectively, when he affirms that only the things that (are formed/come-to-be/are generated) by nature are substances. But why?

Furthermore, although in Λ3, Aristotle calls a house "a composite *substance*" (1070a14), in H3 he refers to artifacts as "those that are among destructible things (τῶν φθαρτῶν)" (1043b18) or "individual things (τὰ τινά)" (1043b20), avoiding (or not using) the word "substances" when he is referring to artifacts. And of course, as we saw in chapter 1.3.4, there is a further problem of ambiguity in Aristotle's use of the word "substance" in Λ3.

Thus, it appears that in the *Metaphysics*, Aristotle is ambivalent about the status of artifacts; nowhere does he unequivocally declare that artifacts are not substances. But it is clear to Aristotle that what undermines their substantiality (with or without qualification), if indeed they are substances in some sense of the word, is the fact that their forms are not separate. I have analyzed B4 and K2, taking into account Aristotle's ambivalence.

So my exposition of the ontological status of artifacts must answer the following: (1) Why is it clear to Aristotle that the form of an artifact is not separate (except with qualification in Λ3)? and (2) Why does he hesitate to conclude from (1) that an artifact is not a substance (with or without qualification)?

I answer (1) in chapter 5.2.3 and (2) in chapter 6.1.1. But for now, from the prior analyses of the four passages and taking into consideration the oddities of (A) and (B), I can reasonably conclude that Aristotle gives only one argument: the form of an artifact does not exist apart from the composite; hence, it is possible that an artifact is not a substance.

Since Aristotle gives only one argument against the substantial status of artifacts, I need to elucidate this argument, in order to understand why Aristotle questions their substantiality.

2.1.5. An Objection

My analyses of these four passages notwithstanding, one could argue that although I have shown how material from the passages could be used to formulate an argument for the conclusion that it is possible that artifacts are not substances, I have fallen short of establishing that such an argument can actually be found in them. Another consistent reading of these passages is that Aristotle simply raises the question as to whether a substantial form can exist apart from the composite and states that, at least in the case of some things, this is clearly impossible (artifacts are such things). Aristotle, in these passages, does not commit to the view that, if the form of some destructible thing cannot exist apart from the individual, then that destructible thing is not a substance; rather, he believes that no substantial forms of destructible things are separate.

I do not have any argument that would exclude the possibility of this (or any other) alternative reading. What I shall do instead is present a consistent interpretation of Aristotle's *Metaphysics* based on my analyses of these four passages (in conjunction with other textual evidence that would support my reading)[6] and let the reader decide to what extent I have been successful.[7]

2.2. Separation

The crux of the argument is Aristotle's conception of separation: apart or separate[8] from the composite. But what does it mean?

I shall now review some of the existing literature on the topic of separation. Unfortunately, none of the scholars have discovered the sense of separation that can clarify the just mentioned argument and shed meaning on the phrase apart or separate from the composite.

In his Berlin thesis, Chen (1940) understands the main sense of separation as that which is self-sufficient (175). He identifies two[9] main types (173–174): (1) "χωριστὸν ἁπλῶς" and (2) "χωριστὸν τῷ λόγῳ." (1) is the central term that is applicable to a composite, while (2) is applicable to the substance of a composite rather than other categories.

Chen describes the previous distinction in his *Sophia*[10] as follows. In both cases, *chōrismos* is understood as "separability from secondary categories" (225). In the case of a composite, it means "the permanence of the individual thing amid the change of its accidental attributes" and in the case of the form of a composite, it means "the essence of a concrete thing does not contain anything belonging to a secondary category" (226). The essence corresponds with definition, for what "is true of one is *eo ipso* true of the other" (226). Spellman[11] also introduces a similar kind of separation.

She calls it "independent being," which is "the ontological correlate of separation in definition."

The problem with this distinction is that it is very difficult to see how it can help us elucidate the present argument. In H3 and Λ3, while Aristotle questions the status of artifacts as substances, he declares that natural things are substances. The key is to explain how it is possible for the form to exist apart from the composite in the latter, while this is not so in the former. We are therefore looking for the separation that exists between the form and its composite, and not that between the composite and its accident. Hence, (1) is not applicable. But neither is (2), for the "ontic χωριστή" of Chen or the "independent being" of Spellman alone cannot distinguish artifacts from substances, because both artifacts and substances have the same internal composite structure in such a way that the essence and other categories can be ontically (Chen) or ontologically (Spellman) separated in the same way.[12]

According to Fine,[13] substantiality can imply two kinds of separation (38–39): definitional and ontological (capacity for independent existence (IE)). "A is definitionally separate from B just in case A can be defined without mention of (the definition of) B" (35); and "A is separate from B just in case A can exist without, independently of, B" (35), respectively.

The problem with definitional separation is that it is hard to see how one can distinguish the form of artifacts from that of substances without appealing to the factor of intrinsic unity (which presupposes an unwarranted assumption that all living things are substances).[14] The problem with IE is that it applies only to the separation between the composite and the accidents (see 36, especially where Fine appeals to H1, 1042a28–32 and M2, 1077a30–b11), and not to the separation between the form and the composite.

When Fine introduces IE, she eliminates the important connection between separation and the temporal priority (which is crucial for my thesis). First, Fine appeals to the passage from Z1[15] where, according to her, Aristotle argues that substance is prior in three ways: in nature, definition, and knowledge (35). She interprets the text so that the natural priority is understood in terms of the separation that exists between substance and the other categories. She admits that in Z1 Aristotle does not explain what he means by separate. So in order to elucidate the text, she turns to Δ11, 1019a1–4, where Aristotle explains natural priority. She understands this passage to say that "A is naturally prior to B just in case A can exist without B but not conversely" (35). On the assumption that natural priority has the same sense in Z1 and Δ11, she integrates the above two passages to derive IE.

But there are a number of problems with Fine's argument. First of all, her view is based upon an unargued textual emendation (which she claims to be unnecessary for her argument) at 1028a32–33, where she adds φύσει and deletes χρόνῳ from Jaeger's text.[16] But if this emendation is unnecessary for her argument, I am at a loss as to how she can justify her conception of IE. The text reads, καὶ λόγῳ καὶ γνώσει καὶ χρόνῳ; that is, in his conception of separation, Aristotle argues for the temporal priority of substance. Then, Fine cannot appeal to the explanation of natural priority found in Δ11, but only to the temporal priority. Her conception of ontological separation cannot be derived from Aristotle's explanation of temporal priority.

Now suppose that somehow she could justify her emendation; that is, in Z1, φύσει is a plausible gloss on χρόνῳ. Such a gloss no longer seems plausible when one considers other passages of the *Metaphysics*.

In Z1, Aristotle says the first (τὸ πρῶτον), and not the prior (τὸ πρότερον), is said in many senses (1028a31–32). Aristotle distinguishes different senses of the first when he defines the different senses of principle in Δ1:

> It is common to all principles to be first from which [a thing] either exists or comes to be or is known (1013a17–19).

So if Aristotle had in mind the previous three senses of the first in Z1, given the close connection between time and coming-to-be,[17] it is difficult to see how χρόνῳ can be replaced by or understood as φύσει in Z1.

If we accept that τὸ πρῶτον and τὸ πρότερον are interchangeable,[18] the problem is compounded, for in Z13, we find the following passage:

> For neither in formula nor in time nor in generation[19] are affections able to be prior to the substance, for otherwise they will be separate (1038b27–29).

Note the connection that Aristotle makes between the temporal priority (along with other priorities) and separation. In Z13 as in Z1, Aristotle argues for the priority of substance over other categories. Fine must therefore explain how Z13 can be made consistent with her interpretation (and/or emendation) of Z1.

Furthermore, in *Phys* 8.9, 265a22–23, Aristotle draws a distinction between priority in nature and in time,[20] as if to suggest that they differ with respect to priority.[21]

In light of the previous passages and considering the absence of Fine's justification for her emendation, it seems more reasonable to read Z1 with the temporal sense intact.

But Irwin[22] argues that he prefers the text of Asclepius 377, 7–8, with the deletion of καὶ χρόνῳ (which is equivalent to Fine's emendation) because of the following reasons:

1. Asclepius gives only three explanations and the first one is derived from the line 1028a23–24, where χωριστόν is associated with nature;

2. separability and natural priority are usually connected (he refers to the above passage of Δ11); and

3. we expect the list of priorities and their respective explanations to be either the same (ABC/ABC) or chiastic in order (CBA/ABC); although Irwin's emendation follows the same order, the order we find in the manuscript is neither the same nor chiastic and, therefore, the text "is open to suspicion" (554).

The problem with Irwin's argument is that he does not take into account the passage of Z13 where Aristotle seems to argue for temporal priority. And as far as the order of the list and that of its explanation is concerned, in Θ8 (where Aristotle argues that actuality is prior to potentiality) we find the following order (ABC/ACB); that is, the order is neither the same nor chiastic. Thus, since Aristotle does not always follow Irwin's expectation of the order, Irwin's claim that the text is open to suspicion loses its force.

However, we find Frede and Patzig[23] defending a similar interpretation. Their solution depends not on emending the text, but on dispensing with the most obvious assumption that, in this passage, Aristotle provides us with the argument for all three kinds of priority; that is, the argument for temporal priority is missing. By referring to the Δ11 passage as Fine and Irwin did, Frede and Patzig argue that separation should be understood in terms of either natural or substantial priority. Consequently, they believe that the temporal priority plays no role in the discussion of Z.

In contrast to the theses of Fine, Irwin, and Frede/Patzig, the advantage of my interpretation is that I need not dispense with the most natural assumption, or emend the text, or rely on an *ad hoc* hypothesis (that by separation Aristotle had in mind the sense of natural priority found in Δ11) to explain this obscure passage of Z, which has troubled most scholars.[24] I suggest a possible solution consistent with the sense of separation that I shall be defending, for the pertinent sense of separation is closely connected with the *temporal* factor. Instead of eliminating the importance of temporal priority (with Frede and Patzig), I shall establish its importance with respect to the criteria of substantiality.[25]

Now, Fine defends two senses of separation: one that is applicable to the composite in the sense that the composite exists as a separate independent being, and another that is applicable to the form in the sense that the form exists separate in thought. This is a standard interpretation of Aristotle's view on separation,[26] but a number of scholars have found this dichotomy to be inadequate. For example, Morrison[27] (who also holds a similar dichotomy) complains that Aristotle equivocates on the word "separation" and that Aristotle's solution is only verbal:

"Separation" has become ambiguous, and form has been shown to be "separate" in a sense quite different from the original sense in which substance was held to be separate.

So it seems that scholars have not yet discovered the sense of separation that will help us elucidate the argument. However, let me now go back to Chen's thesis, for he makes a very interesting distinction that will help us find the appropriate sense of separation.

Chen[28] suggests this promising distinction when he attempts to explain Λ3, 1070a13–18. According to Chen, "apart from" in this passage should not be understood as an instance of separation, but as the continual existence of the form. This is accomplished through reproduction. No such continuity exists in the case of artifacts, for what persists is not the form of an artifact but the craft. However, he points out that the distinction between the continual existence of the form of living things and that of craft contradicts Aristotelian epistemology, because not only the craft but also the forms of artifacts in the mind of an artisan continue to exist from one generation to another.

The advantage of Chen's interpretation is that it takes into account the actual context in which the argument is found, namely, the discussion of coming-to-be. The interesting point he makes is that the form of both an animal and an artifact can be passed on or transmitted in one way or another from one generation to another. The former is accomplished by means of reproduction, and the latter by means of teaching[29] the art. For example, a builder who has the form of a house in his mind can teach another how to build a house. In the process of teaching the art, the form of a house is also transmitted; the form is passed on, not only from the mind to the actual house when the house is being built, but also from one person to another.

This comparison is very important to my thesis because it is the transmission of forms by means of reproduction that is the key to solving our problem. The solution lies in determining the very special way in which the form of an animal can be passed on from one generation to another (in contrast to the way art is passed on, whether to an actual artifact or to another person). To determine this, I first need to clarify in what way the form of an animal differs from that of an artifact with respect to separation.

The major problem with Chen's interpretation is that he denies that the term "apart from" used in the just mentioned context indicates separation. This is a very unfortunate denial, for separation is a criterion of substantiality. We need to distinguish whether or not a thing is a substance by appealing to the way in which the form is "apart from" the composite. The term "apart from" must be understood as a criterion of substantiality.

2.3. The Connection

In chapter 2.1, I establish that Aristotle has one argument against the substantial status of artifacts, and that this argument always occurs in the same
context. So there is *prima facie* reason to believe that there is an important
connection between the argument and its context; in Aristotle's mind, the
two topics are always connected.[30] In each of the four passages (B4, 999b4–20
and its doublet K2, 1060b23–28; H3, 1043b14–23; and ∧3, the whole chapter),
there is a connection between the ungenerablility (or the indestructibility)
of the form and its separability. Thus, the sense of separation that I am
seeking is closely connected with Aristotle's concept of ungenerable and
indestructible. I now show that, for Aristotle, this concept of ungenerable
and indestructible means eternal.

My procedure first identify (without analysis) the connections between
the argument and its context that Aristotle makes in all four passages, then
I step back and examine their significance. Let me take each in turn.

2.3.1. B4, 999b4–20 and Its Doublet K2, 1060b23–28

The connection we find in B4 is this: if the form is ungenerable, then it must
exist apart from the composite.[31]

Its doublet K2, 1060b23–28,[32] states that a composite is made up of
matter and what exists with it. If there is nothing apart from the composite,
all things in matter will be destructible. If there is something that is
indestructible, then it exists apart from the composite. The best candidate to
be something indestructible is the form. So, the connection is this: if the
form is indestructible, then it must exist apart from the composite.

2.3.2. H3, 1043b14–23

Having pointed out that no one makes or generates a form (b17), Aristotle
identifies the form as ungenerable. Then, he questions whether it is possible
for it to exist apart. There is an obvious exception, which is the form of an
artifact such as a house. Thus, the connection that Aristotle is questioning is
this: is it always the case that if the form is ungenerable, then it exists apart
from the composite?[33]

2.3.3. ∧3, the Whole Chapter

Aristotle begins by noting that neither the matter nor the form is generated.
And it is in this context that Aristotle denies that the form exists apart from
the composite, except with a qualification in the case of artifacts, but he
affirms such separation in the case of natural things. Thus, the connection is

this: given that the form is ungenerable, it exists apart from the composite, either with or without qualification.[34]

2.3.4. The Analysis

The analysis of the argument in the context of the passages shows the connection between the ungenerability (or the indestructibility) of the form and its separability. The sense of separation is closely connected with Aristotle's concept of ungenerable and indestructible. But the question is this: what do ungenerable and indestructible mean? Let me return to the same passages for clues.

In H3 (chapter 2.3.2), Aristotle makes the following distinction:

> It is necessary that it [a substance] is either eternal or destructible without being destroyed and has come to be without coming-to-being. (1043b14–16)

Here Aristotle introduces two kinds of ungenerable and indestructible: (1) eternal (ἀΐδιον); and (2) destructible without being destroyed and having come to be without coming-to-being (φθαρτὴν ἄνευ τοῦ φθείρεσθαι καὶ γεγονέναι ἄνευ τοῦ γίγνεσθαι).[35] I call (1) the eternal and (2) the noneternal sense of ungenerable and indestructible.[36]

What could Aristotle mean when he says that a substance is eternal? Is he referring to God or to a heavenly sphere? Let me examine the context. In H1, Aristotle delimits the scope of his discussion:

> But let us now discuss those that have been agreed upon as being substances. And they are sensible substances which all have matter. (1042a24–26)

Aristotle limits his discussion to sensible substances, and there is no indication in H3 or anywhere in H that Aristotle has changed his topic; therefore, God is eliminated from the discussion. In H4, this is what Aristotle says:

> But as regards natural eternal substances, it is another account. (1044b6)

This suggests that the discussion is limited to sensible destructible substances. Thus, Aristotle is not referring to heavenly spheres.

As a matter of fact, immediately after Aristotle introduces the two senses of ungenerable and indestructible, he says:

> It has been shown and also it has been made clear from other [discussion] that no one makes or generates the form, but a "this" is made, and the composite comes to be. (1043b16–18)

Note the immediate context. Aristotle is discussing the fact that the form of a composite is ungenerable. Since God and heavenly spheres are eliminated and given the immediate context, it is reasonable to conclude that by a substance he is referring to the form of a destructible composite. So, Aristotle identifies two ways in which the form of a composite can be ungenerable: the eternal and the noneternal sense of ungenerable.

Now there is a connection between ungenerability and separability. The question, however, is this: to which sense of ungenerable is Aristotle referring when he denies that the form of an artifact is not separate? He denies either that (1) The form, understood as eternal, exists apart from the composite; and (2) The form, understood as ungenerable and indestructible in the noneternal sense, exists apart from the composite.

The alternative (2) seems impossible, for *all* forms (both substances and accidental forms) are ungenerable and indestructible in this sense. Accidents,[37] points, whiteness, formulae,[38] and forms in general (especially, the forms of artifacts)[39] are all said to be ungenerable and indestructible in the noneternal sense.[40] Thus, the form understood in the noneternal sense of ungenerable cannot suggest substantiality, for this sense of ungenerable includes nonsubstantial forms.

In other words, Aristotle cannot be referring to (2) when he questions the substantiality of artifacts. This finding accords with $\wedge$3, 1070a13–18 (chapter 2.3.3). In this passage, the form of an artifact is said to be ungenerable and indestructible in the noneternal sense. Furthermore, Aristotle denies separation in one sense, but affirms separation with qualification. So, separation with qualification is connected with the noneternal sense of ungenerable, and it is in this context that Aristotle questions the substantiality of artifacts. Accordingly, the noneternal sense of ungenerable cannot suggest substantiality.

Thus, in H3 Aristotle could only be referring to (1), the eternal sense of ungenerable, when he doubts the substantial status of artifacts. Consequently, eternity is a criterion of substantiality.

Based on the results of the current analyses, the following three issues emerge:

1. the two senses of ungenerable and indestructible;
2. the two ways in which the form of a composite is said to be separate—with and without qualification; and
3. eternity as a criterion of substantiality.

Let me take each in turn.

2.3.5. The Two Senses of Ungenerable and Indestructible

They can also be found in *De Caelo* 1.11.[41] Thus, the two senses of ungenerable and indestructible that have been discovered in these passages of the *Metaphysics* cannot simply be something that I have invented or read into the text, for Aristotle himself makes the same distinction in another treatise. What is significant about the *DC* is the context in which Aristotle identifies the different senses of ungenerable—the context in which he is arguing for the *eternity* of the universe. Hence, it is not surprising that he also makes this distinction in H3 where he identifies a substance as eternal.

Based on the two senses of ungenerable, I now go back to Λ3 for an interpretation of a rather cryptic passage. Ross[42] and Elders[43] both appeal to the explanation given by ps.-Alexander[44] in the passage where Aristotle refers to the noneternal sense of ungenerable and indestructible (1070a15–17). While Ross is uncommitted, Elders endorses ps.-Alexander. Their argument is as follows. The sense of ungenerable and indestructible, which is discussed in Z8, is relevant both to the forms of artifacts and to other forms such as those of living things (Ross simply refers to forms while Elders speaks of substantial forms). But Aristotle is clearly referring to the forms of artifacts alone; therefore, he must be referring to the way in which the forms of artifacts can be ungenerable and indestructible, that is, the way they exist in the mind of a craftsman and "come into being or pass away, according to whether the craftsman begins to think them or ceases to do so."[45]

This argument is based on a false assumption and therefore is compelled to rely on an *ad hoc* hypothesis. Let me take Elders's version first. It is a mistake to assume that the noneternal sense of ungenerable and indestructible is applicable *only* to substantial forms. This can be seen clearly not only in the passages that we have examined earlier (in chapter 2.3.4) but also in Z9 itself (a chapter closely connected to Z8), for the text reads:

> But it is not only concerning substance that the account shows that the form does not come to be, but the common account holds similarly in the case of all primary [categories], for example, quantity, quality, and the other categories. (1034b7–10)

My criticism of Ross's version is this. Although in Z8 Aristotle indicates the noneternal sense of ungenerable and indestructible, we cannot conclude that in Z7–9 he is arguing that forms are ungenerable and indestructible in the noneternal sense *only*.[46]

My contrasting version is this. There is no need to introduce another sense of ungenerable and indestructible (for which there is no evidence) to clarify Λ3. Here, Aristotle refers to the way the form can be ungenerable and indestructible without any suggestion of substantiality. In other words, Aristotle is pointing out that even if the form of an artifact is not separate in the way in which the form of a natural thing is separate, the form can be understood as ungenerable and indestructible in another way (1070a15–16), which does not suggest eternity. And this is an important point to stress, because he has just argued that *all forms* are ungenerable (1069b35–36).

2.3.6. The Separation of the Form of a Composite—
With and Without Qualification

Let me pose two questions. (1) Why do most scholars accept that the separation applicable to the form of a composite is separation in thought only?[47] (2) Is there other evidence for the just mentioned distinction?

(1) The text that has most hindered the detection of the pertinent sense of separation is *Phys* 2.1. It reads as follows:

> Consequently, in another way the nature of the things that have the principle of motion in themselves would be the shape or the form, which is not separate except according to formula (193b3–5).

On the strength of this passage, many scholars[48] have accepted only one sense in which the form of a composite can be separate—separate in formula or thought. But if we examine the passage more closely, the text reads as follows: "of things which have in themselves a principle of motion" (193b3–4). We can only infer that the form considered *in this sense* is separate only according to formula. This is indeed reasonable, for how could a principle of *internal*-change be separate except in notion or thought? It is because this principle is "not in other things or outside" (192b29) of that of which it is a principle, but exists in a thing "according to itself and not accidentally," that it is the principle of *internal*-change. That is why, unlike a doctor who also happens to be a patient, the principle is not at one time *separate* (192b26–27) from that of which it is a principle.

By internal-change Aristotle means locomotion, quantitative change, and qualitative change.[49] The principle of generation is not included, for nothing generates itself. In *Phys* 2.1 Aristotle has not excluded the possibility that the form, understood as the principle of *generation*, is separate in some other way than according to formula or thought. As a matter of fact, I shall show that the principle of generation is indeed in a way "in another" (ἐν ἄλλῳ).[50] But for now it is sufficient to note that the prior text leaves open the possibility that the principle of generation can be separate in another way.

(2) Is there other evidence for the two ways in which the form of a composite is said to be separate? In the *Metaphysics*, there is a passage that distinguishes the two kinds of separation that are applicable to the form of a composite. In H1, Aristotle draws the following distinctions:

> An underlying subject is a substance; in one sense it is the matter (and by matter I mean that which is not a "this" in actuality but is a "this" potentially); in another sense it is the formula and the shape, which being a "this" is separate in formula; the third is a composite of them, of which alone there is coming-to-be and destruction, and it is separate without qualification, for some of the substances according to formula are separate while others are not. (1042a25–31)

Note that some substances according to formula (that is, the forms) are said to be separate! Several scholars believe that in the previous passage Aristotle is referring to either God or heavenly spheres or man's active intellect.[51]

But their belief is not reasonable if we examine the context. I have already shown that in H, God and heavenly spheres are eliminated from the discussion. As far as the active intellect[52] is concerned, there is no evidence in the whole of H that Aristotle had this in mind. Thus, in the earlier passage of H1 Aristotle is not referring to God, heavenly spheres, or man's active intellect.

On the contrary, it is within the context of the discussion of sensible, destructible substances that in H3, as we have seen, Aristotle questions the substantiality of artifacts and affirms the substantiality of natural things. He does so with reference to whether the form exists apart from the composite. This suggests the possibility that, in contrast to the form of an artifact, the form of a natural being is also separate in another sense than merely separate in formula.

In Λ3 Aristotle admits that the form of an artifact is separate with qualification (in contrast to that of natural beings). In light of the recent discussion of H, we can see that this means that the form is separate in thought, for art exists in the mind of an artisan.[53]

It is one of my tasks to explain how the form of a natural being can be separate in another way. But for now it is sufficient to note that *Phys* 2.1 does not undermine my finding that forms of composites can be separate in two ways. Rather, H1 confirms it.

2.3.7. Eternity as a Criterion of Substantiality

In chapters 4.2 and 5.1.1, I confirm that eternity is a criterion of substantiality by examining other passages. But I am now in a position to emphasize the connection between the two crucial factors that I have raised in this chapter: separation and temporality. If in the case of substances, the form of a destructible composite is eternal, we can see why it has to be separate from its composite; for if it is eternal, it existed *prior* (temporally, that is) to the generation of the composite.

But how is this possible? My aim is to determine in what sense the form of a composite can be eternal. But before I turn to this task, I must first identify another criterion of substantiality. Eternity is only a necessary, and not a sufficient, condition for substantiality; otherwise, Platonic Forms might turn out to be substances,[54] and Aristotle denies that. Let me now turn to this second criterion of substantiality.

Chapter Three

Eternal and Actual

By examining the two crucial passages[1] from the *aporiai* and Aristotle's criticism of Plato's theory of Forms (where in both passages Aristotle discusses the ontological status of artifacts), I show that: Aristotle is seeking an indestructible (that is, eternal) principle within the destructible things to account for coming-to-be; and he points out that a Platonic Form cannot be such a principle of coming-to-be. At stake in these discussions is the second criterion of substantiality—actuality. Thus, I shall conclude that the form of a substance is an eternal actuality.[2]

3.1. *Aporiai*

I turn to the following three *aporiai*: B4, 999b4–20; its doublet K2, 1060b23–28; and K2, 1060a3–36 (which might be construed as relevant to my discussion).[3]

3.1.1. B4, 999b4–20

The immediate context is this: Aristotle identifies the form as an element in the destructible things, and it is described as ungenerable and indestructible.

In B4, 999b4–12, Aristotle argues for the necessity of something eternal to account for the coming-to-be of destructible things, because there cannot be an infinite regress of what comes to be and because nothing can come to be out of what is not. Aristotle is not here referring to the ultimate principle of coming to be, that is, the Unmoved Mover, but the principle that exists within the destructible things. First of all, there is no evidence in the B4 passage that Aristotle is referring to the ultimate principle. Second, I have shown that we have good reason for believing that the form, understood as ungenerable in the eternal sense, is the criterion of substantiality. Accordingly, I understand the text of B4[4] thus: Aristotle argues that the form is the eternal element in a destructible thing, accounting for the coming-to-be of

41

the latter; that is, the form is a principle of coming-to-be.[5] So, the connection between the wider and the immediate context is this: given that the principle of coming-to-be is eternal, the form, which is such a principle, is eternal; thus, it must exist apart from the destructible composite.[6]

Hence, there are two kinds of eternal principles: one for the eternal substances, such as the Unmoved Mover, and the other for the destructible substances. The possibility of two kinds of eternal principles is the subject of the tenth *aporia* (B4, 1000a5–1001a3). Here, Aristotle questions whether the principles[7] (1000a7) of destructible things and indestructible things are the same. If they are same, why are some things destructible while others are not? The same question is posed in this way:

> Why is it that things which are [composed] of the same [principles] are some of them eternal with respect to their nature but others destructible? (1000a21–22)

By indestructible things, Aristotle means those that are *eternal*. If the principles of destructible and indestructible things differ, are the principles of destructible things destructible or indestructible? If they are destructible, then there must be another principle to account for their existence, since all things that are destructible will be destroyed into their own composition. Since an infinite regress of destructible things is not possible, the principles are indestructible. But how can we account for the difference between destructible and indestructible things, if the principles for both of them are indestructible? This is either impossible or requires a lengthy discussion.[8] Aristotle complains that the problem has not been dealt with at all by his predecessors (1000b32–1001a3).

The solution to this *aporia* is the key to understanding how the form can be apart from the composite. If the form of the composite is eternal while the composite itself is destructible, then the form existed before the composite is generated, and after it is destroyed the form will continue to exist. The problem is to *distinguish* how this eternal principle of destructible things differs from that of eternal entities.[9]

3.1.2. K2, 1060b23–28

In this passage, the wider context is missing. In its place, there is a problem about science or knowledge (ἐπιστήμη). The *aporia* is this: if knowledge is of universals but a substance is not a universal, how could there be a substance, if knowledge is concerned with principles?

In B4, there is also a problem of knowledge. The *aporia* is this: we cannot have knowledge of individual things since they are infinite in number; hence, in order to have knowledge of them, we do so insofar as there is a universal. And if that is so, we need to posit the genera. But how is it possible for such things as genera to exist apart from individual things?

If we compare the context of these two passages,[10] there is *prima facie* reason for believing that the problem of knowledge is the wider context in which Aristotle questions the substantial status of artifacts and, hence, that it is relevant to our present discussion. But is this true?

First of all, generically speaking, these two passages are found within the context of epistemological problems. Specifically, the *aporiai* are not the same: K2, 1060b19–23 is not the doublet of B4, 999a24–b4, but of B6, 1003a5–12. So the connection between them may not be as close as a cursory inspection might suggest.

The important point is that epistemological issues are irrelevant to my discussion,[11] because they cannot *in principle* distinguish between artifacts and substances. This can be seen first by examining Aristotle's objection to the *method* of Platonic enquiries.[12] According to Aristotle, the reason Plato and the present-day thinkers (i.e., people in the Academy) went astray is that they propose metaphysical entities based only on logical or mathematical enquiries (which are only prior in formula (τῷ λόγῳ))[13]—that is, they rely only on epistemological enquiries.[14] One of the consequences of that method is that substances and other things, notably artifacts, can no longer be distinguished.

In A9, 990b12 Aristotle alludes to the arguments from the sciences (τοὺς λόγους τοὺς ἐκ τῶν ἐπιστημῶν). This is one of his epistemological objections to Plato's theory of Forms. Details have been preserved, among the fragments of the *Peri Ideōn* (On Ideas), by Alexander in his commentary on the *Metaphysics*.[15]

The gist[16] of Aristotle's arguments is this: according to Alexander, Aristotle presents the following three arguments offered by the Platonists. (1) If every science deals with something that is not a sensible individual thing, then this would have to be some other thing (apart from the sensible things), which is eternal. And this sort of thing is called an Idea. (2) Since individual things are infinite and indeterminate, but the objects of science are determinate, there is something apart from individual things called an Idea. (3) If medicine is the science not of this health but of health without qualification, and similarly if geometry is the science not of this equal or this commensurate but of these without qualification, then health itself, the equal itself, and the commensurate itself exist. These are Ideas.

One of Aristotle's objections is that the arguments do not prove that there are Ideas but only that there must be something that is common that is apart from sensible individuals. Another objection is that, since art also deals with some one thing apart from individual things (e.g., the art of building is not of this individual bench or bed but of bench without qualification or bed without qualification), then just as in the case of science, there must be Ideas of these artifacts. Platonists want to deny the existence of such Ideas.

In other words, from an epistemological standpoint, the Platonists argue for the necessity of the existence of Forms. Holding that knowledge or science deals with one and the same thing apart from the sensibles, they argue that there must be objects that are eternal and determinate. Then we would need to posit Forms of artifacts, because the object of art is not indeterminate individual artifacts, but what is common (eternal and determinate) and is apart from them. In Aristotelian language, just as in the case of science, art[17] is also of universals.[18] Aristotle's criticisms suggest that we cannot distinguish between Forms of artifacts and those of substances by appealing to epistemological considerations alone.

Let me now turn to Aristotle's own position. In Z4, where Aristotle discusses the topic of essence (Z4–6), he begins by announcing that he is first going to make logical remark (λογικῶς) (1029b13). In Z10–12, he deals with the problem of definition and formula (λόγος), and generally speaking in Z13–16, he focuses on the topic of universals—the objects of knowledge. Although such discussions are ontological in nature, they are closely related to epistemological issues. Ross[19] notes: ". . . ZH are occupied mainly with *logical* analysis of sensible substances into form and matter" (emphasis added).

We can see why, relying only on the schema of categories (which is the focus of Z), we cannot distinguish between artifacts and substances. I began the first chapter with Aristotle's doctrine of substance in the *Categories* and found we could not distinguish artifacts from substances. In the discussion of separation,[20] we found something similar with separation by formula or thought. What is more, even at the ontological level where a number of scholars have made an ontological separation,[21] we still could not distinguish between artifacts and substances. The reason is that the structure of composite beings, insofar as they are composite, does not differ, and the relation that exists between substance and other categories, or between form and matter, is the same.[22]

This is an important point to stress. Throughout the *Metaphysics*, (e.g., at Z3, 1029a5),[23] Aristotle uses artifacts as examples to illustrate what he means by substances and employs them in his logical or ontological investigations of the nature of substances. From the perspective of a hylomorphic structure of a composite, there is no difference between artifacts and natural substances; therefore, in such contexts, Aristotle can appeal to artifacts as if there are substances. He does so most likely for the methodological[24] reason: for it is easier to grasp the nature of artifacts.

Even in the context of his discussion of coming-to-be (which I turn to in the next chapter), Aristotle assumes the close analogy between the coming-to-be of artifacts and that of other beings, including, the generation of animals. However, what should be noted is that it is only when he is discussing the topic of coming-to-be that Aristotle questions the substantial status of artifacts. In the first chapter, I examined five passages[25] where he affirms that natural beings are substances (with or without qualification). What is interesting to note is that in all these passages, Aristotle is discussing the topic of coming-to-be.[26] This overwhelming evidence suggests that Aristotle's distinction between substances and artifacts lies in the doctrine of coming-to-be.

Thus, there is good reason for believing that neither an epistemological nor an ontological consideration (which relies only on the structure of composites) will undermine my interpretation, which will be based solely on the topic of coming-to-be, for we cannot *in principle* distinguish artifacts and substances by means of such considerations. In other words, the principle that will distinguish artifacts and substances is *not static* but *dynamic*.

The advantage of this delineation is that it now gives us at least one clear criterion for what is and what is not relevant to our discussion; that is, I have shown why there is no further connection between epistemological issues and our discussion.[27] Since I need not concern myself with epistemological questions and since K2, 1060b23–28 lacks the wider context, it cannot provide us with any further relevant information.

3.1.3. K2, 1060a3–36

There are certain passages in K2, however, that might be construed as relevant. But, there, Aristotle is discussing a totally different problem. This discussion is very important to my topic, because the kind of separation (as well as the kind of principle) that I am seeking depends on clearly distinguishing the different kinds of separation (and of principle). The passage in question is K2, 1060a3–36. I split it into two sections:

1. K2, 1060a3–27 (which purports to be the doublet[28] of the eighth *aporia*, where Aristotle questions the substantiality of artifacts in B4); and
2. K2, 1060a27–36 (which purports to be the doublet[29] of the tenth *aporia*).

Let me examine them each in turn.

3.1.4. K2, 1060a3–27 and B4, 999a24–b20

Despite the superficial resemblance between the K2[30] and B4[31] passages, Aristotle is talking about totally different problems. In K2, he is questioning the *object* of the science that is being sought (ἡ ζητουμένη ἐπιστήμη), and he denies that it is an individual, genus, or species. In B4, he is questioning the possibility of knowledge (πῶς ἐνδέχεται λαβεῖν ἐπιστήμην) of individuals, given that the object of knowledge is universal. Thus, in the two passages the term ἡ ἐπιστήμη (knowledge or science) is used in two different ways.

Furthermore, in K2,[32] Aristotle uses the term παρά or χωριστόν (separate) in the way that a thing exists on its own totally separate from the sensible substances. But in B4,[33] by παρά (apart from), he means the separation that may be possible between that which is predicated of matter, namely form, and the composite. Thus, the term παρά is used in two different ways in B4 and K2.

Finally, in K2,[34] Aristotle is employing the terms παρά and χωριστόν with reference to the way a thing exists according to itself (καθ' αὐτήν). The first half of this passage of K2 reminds us of Aristotle's objection to Platonic Forms in A9. He complains that to account for the causes of things, those who posit Forms introduced things equal in number to them "just as if someone, wishing to count but believing that he cannot do so with fewer things, counts by creating more things" (990b2–4). In the latter half of K2, Aristotle denies that this kind of separation—separate and according to itself (χωριστὴ καὶ καθ' αὐτήν)—is applicable to the form of sensibles because it is destructible.[35] Furthermore, to account for the existence of an order (τάξις), we need an eternal, separate, and permanent principle.

Let me now contrast the context of K2 and B4.[36] K2: παρά or χωριστόν indicates separate and according to itself and does not exist in any of sensible things (χωριστὸν καθ' αὐτὸ καὶ μηδενὶ τῶν αἰσθητῶν ὑπάρχον), and Aristotle is discussing the principle of order (τάξις). B4: παρά indicates separation that exists between the form and its composite, and Aristotle is discussing the principle of coming-to-be.

Furthermore, it is in B4, 999a24–b20 that Aristotle questions the substantial status of artifacts, not in K2, 1060a3–27. In K2, he raises the same question about artifacts in a different context in 1060b23–28.

3.1.5. K2, 1060a27–36 and B4, 1000b20–31

The difference in context between K2 and B4 can also be seen if we compare the tenth *aporia* discussed earlier with what is supposed to be its doublet— the passage that immediately follows K2 (in chapter 3.1.4). Note the prepositional phrases in these passages. In K2[37] it is ὑπό plus accusative, and in B4[38] it is ἐκ plus genitive. The former concerns the relation that exists between a principle and what comes *under* it; the latter concerns the relation that exists between a principle and what comes *from* it or is made *out of* it. Thus, Aristotle is using two different senses of the relationship that exists between a principle and that of which it is the principle.

3.1.6. The Summary of B4 and K2

Let me now summarize the results of chapters 3.1.4 and 3.1.5. In K2 we see that the object of science (ἡ ἐπιστήμη) that is sought is neither individual, genus, nor species but something separate according to itself, which does not exist in any sensible thing (χωριστὸν καθ' αὑτὸ καὶ μηδενὶ τῶν αἰσθητῶν ὑπάρχον); παρά or χωριστόν indicates separate and according to itself (χωριστὸν καὶ καθ' αὑτόν); Aristotle is discussing the principle of order (τάξις); and a principle is that which stands in relation to what is *under* it. In B4 we see that Aristotle questions the possibility of knowledge (ἡ ἐπιστήμη) of individuals, given that the object of knowledge is universal; παρά indicates the separation that exists between the form and its composite; Aristotle is discussing the principle of coming-to-be; and a principle is that which stands in relation to what comes *from* it or is made *out of* it.

To summarize, in K2 Aristotle raises the question of the relationship that exists between the Unmoved Mover and the sensible world,[39] but in B4 he questions the relationship that exists between the form and its composite. If the passages are conflated, then we obliterate the different significance of separation and principle as well as of ἡ ἐπιστήμη. In elucidating the argument against the substantial status of artifacts, it is especially important to differentiate the different ways of separation (as well as the different uses of principle). We have seen how the interpretation of separation I am seeking has eluded most scholars.[40] The preceding conflation is another reason for this.[41]

3.2. Aristotle's Criticism of Plato's Theory of Forms (A9, 991b1–9 and Its Doublet M5, 1079b35–1080a8)

In A9, Aristotle mentions or discusses his objections to the doctrine of Plato and other Platonists. It is very difficult to tell in some cases how one objection is related to the next. Here I simply take the passages that come together as a section common to A9 and M5. The common passages are A9, 991a8–b9 and M5, 1079b12–1080a8.

I do not take up M5, because aside from minor changes in expression, the content is exactly the same. So let me focus on A9. Aristotle begins with the following question:

> What indeed do the Forms contribute to the eternal things among the sensibles or to those which come to be and are destroyed? For they are the causes neither of motions nor of any changes in these things.

Aristotle is concerned with the problem of accounting for motions and changes in both eternal and destructible things. This is the problem we have already encountered in B4. Aristotle's response to the Platonists is that the description of Forms as patterns and of the others as what participate in them is a mere use of empty words and poetic metaphors; that is, it has no explanatory force. It is in this context that we find the pertinent passage. The text reads:

> Furthermore, it would seem impossible that the substance and that of which it is the substance are separate (χωρίς); how, then, could ideas, which are substances of things, be separate (χωρίς) [from them]? But in the Phaedo it is said in this way, that the Forms are the causes of being and coming-to-be; however, even when the Forms exist those that partake [of them] do not come to be unless there is that which will set them in motion (τὸ κινῆσον); and many other things come to be, for example, a house or a ring, of which we deny that Forms exist. Consequently, it is clear that it is possible even for the rest to be and to come-to-be by means of these sorts of causes that [produce] those things that have been mentioned now.

Before I analyze this passage, I will first mention a number of controversies that have arisen from it but that are outside the scope of my present discussion:

1. The historical accuracy of Aristotle's objection to the theory of Forms with regard to separation.[42]
2. The accuracy of Aristotle's interpretation of the *Phaedo* and of his objection to Plato for not positing "that which will set a thing in motion" (τὸ κινῆσον).[43]
3. The accuracy of Aristotle's report of the denial of the Forms of artifacts.[44]

The aforementioned controversies are irrelevant to my discussion because they do not help us elucidate the argument in question. Let me now return to A9.

Aristotle's criticism seems to be this. First, he questions the intelligibility of supposing that the Forms (which are the substances of things) exist apart (χωρίς) from those things. In the *Phaedo*,[45] Forms are supposed to be the cause of both the existence and the coming-to-be of sensible things. The implication is that Plato does not explain how Forms (which exist apart from the sensible things) can be the causes of their existence and especially of their coming-to-be. For even if Forms exist, what is needed to generate things is "that which will set a thing in motion" (τὸ κινῆσον), since Forms are not movers. Furthermore, there are other things that are produced, such as artifacts, of which no Forms exist; that is, they come to be without Forms.

This being so, all other things might come to be in the same way. In general, Forms are useless in accounting for the coming-to-be of sensible things.

Let me identify the context. Assuming that no Forms of artifacts exist, Aristotle appeals to the production of artifacts as an example of things manufactured without any assistance from Forms. So Aristotle denies Forms of artifacts when he criticizes the view that Forms can be principles of coming-to-be. Thus, Aristotle refers to the ontological status of artifacts in the context in which he is discussing the principle of coming-to-be. This is the wider context that we have also identified in B4.

From this context, I would like to focus on the following points: separation, that which will set a thing in motion (τὸ κινῆσον), and the production of artifacts. Let me take each in turn.

3.2.1. Separation

In chapter 2.2, we saw that separation is a criterion of substantiality. Yet in the present passage, we find Aristotle criticizing Plato for separating Forms from sensibles. We need to understand why in one context Aristotle endorses separation while in another he seems to reject it. In Z16, we find the answer. Aristotle says:

> Furthermore, what is one would not be in many ways at the same time, but what is common exists in many ways at the same time; consequently, it is clear that none of universals exists apart from the individual things separately (οὐδὲν τῶν καθόλου ὑπάρχει παρὰ τὰ καθ' ἕκαστα χωρίς). But those who say that the Forms [exist] are right in one respect by separating them (χωρίζοντες αὐτά), if indeed they are substances, but are not right in another respect, because they say that what is one over many is a Form. (1040b25–30)

Here, Aristotle does not deny but, rather, endorses the idea that separation is a criterion of substantiality. The problem he sees with the Platonic Forms is that they are universals;[46] and, by being universals, the Platonic Forms cannot be separate.[47] But in what way can they not be separate?

Note that when Aristotle says that no universal exists apart (παρά) from the individual, he adds the term χωρίς; he seems to be indicating that there are different senses of apart from. We have so far encountered, among others, the following three different senses of separation:

1. separate by itself and not existing in any of the sensible things (χωριστὸν καθ' αὐτὸ καὶ μηδενὶ τῶν αἰσθητῶν ὑπάρχον) (e.g., the Unmoved Mover);
2. apart from the composite, in the way in which the eternal form is separate from its composite; and

3. a qualified apart from, in the way in which the form exists in the mind of a person (i.e., separate in formula).

(1) and (2) indicate the way in which substances are separate, while (3) does not.

Although Aristotle does not tell us what he means by "παρὰ τὰ καθ' ἕκαστα χωρίς", the expression is most likely equivalent to (1), given that in K2 we saw that he refers to this kind of separation when he criticizes Platonic Forms. However, my concern is whether or not universals can be separate in the sense of (2).

It is clear that regardless of what "παρὰ τὰ καθ' ἕκαστα χωρίς" means, universals cannot be separate *in the way in which substances are separate*,[48] for Aristotle says that those who posited the Forms are right "in separating them (χωρίζοντες αὐτά), if these are indeed substances." So even if substances can be separate in two different ways (in the sense of (1) and (2)), universals cannot be separate in both ways.

3.2.2. That Which Will Set a Thing in Motion (τὸ κινῆσον)

Aristotle denies that a Form can function as τὸ κινῆσον. But what does τὸ κινῆσον mean? Is it used in the sense of an efficient cause or a final cause? If τὸ κινῆσον refers to an efficient cause,[49] then Mabbott's interpretation[50] seems to be correct; for he says, "The forms cannot cause motion in objects if separate from them." And this seems to accord with Aristotle's view in *Phys* 3.2, 202a6–9[51] that the mover must be in contact with the moved.

But is Mabbott's view correct? In *Phys* 7.2, 243a3–6[52] Aristotle argues that there is no intermediate between the proximate mover, which is an efficient cause, and the moved. In this passage, by motion he only means locomotion, qualitative change, and quantitative change (243a6–8); missing from the list is generation.[53] But why? Perhaps, separation *per se* is not the problem. I will come back to this problem, after I consider final causes.

Suppose τὸ κινῆσον refers to a final cause. In the *Phaedo*, equal things are said to *desire* or *strive* to be like the equal (75a2). This suggests that the Forms are final causes. If so, separation has nothing to do with it; for Aristotle's Unmoved Mover is said to be separate.[54] Why cannot the Forms be movers in the same way as the Unmoved Mover? The answer can be found in Λ6, 1071b12–17.[55] The Forms cannot cause motion or change, even if they are to be understood as final causes, because they are not in actuality; according to Aristotle they are potentialities.[56] As a matter of fact even if the Forms, understood as final causes, are not separate, they cannot cause motion because it is always that which is in actuality that sets a thing in motion.[57]

Thus, regardless of whether τὸ κινῆσον is to be understood as an efficient or a final cause, the Platonic Forms cannot be movers,[58] for they are potentialities. However we understand Aristotle's omission of generation in *Phys* 7.2, separation *per se* is not the issue. It is because Platonic Forms are potentialities that they cannot be movers. The important point is that what is τὸ κινῆσον must be in *actuality*.

Let me now step back and analyze the importance of this. In chapter 3.1, I argued that the form, understood as a principle of coming-to-be, is eternal; and in 2.3, we saw that this sense of ungenerable and indestructible suggests a separation of the form from the composite. I concluded that this is a criterion of substantiality. But if a principle of coming-to-be is τὸ κινῆσον, then it must also be in actuality. That means that substance, understood as a principle of coming-to-be, is *both* eternal and actual;[59] that is, both eternity and actuality are essential for substantiality.[60]

Let me now turn to the view of Ross who came very close to identifying the two criteria, but failed to appreciate the importance of his identification. The most instructive importance of Ross's failure is the *reason* why he failed.

In his commentary on Z8,[61] Ross[62] says that among the composites "[w]here what is produced is a new substance, its form must have pre-existed in another individual", but as far as other forms (such as quality, quantity, and so on) are concerned "they need not have pre-existed actually", but "may have existed only potentially." And he continues:

> ἄνθρωπος ἄνθρωπον γεννᾷ,[63] but there is no corresponding principle λευκὸν λευκὸν γεννᾷ. I.e. in the former case the form is eternal; in the latter it comes into being instantaneously; it supervenes in a moment on a change which has taken time.

Ross emphasizes actuality and eternity! In his Introduction, Ross explains that the eternity of the form is attained "by virtue of the never-failing succession of its embodiments" (cxxiii), and this must be so because "the form must pre-exist actually (i.e., as embodied in the male parent)" (cxxii). This is not necessary in the case of artifacts:

> The form of house exists actually before the building of a particular house, for it is already embodied in other houses; but Aristotle would probably say that when the first house was being built the form existed only potentially (cxxii–cxxiii).

The crucial distinction that Ross draws between the embodiment of the form in actuality in the case of a male parent, as opposed to that of a house, is that in the male parent it is necessarily so, while in the house it is contingently so. But he does not quite explain *why* this must be the case. His failure to do so seems to stem from his understanding of the term "eternity,"

which is "the never-failing succession of the embodiment of the form;"
Ross emphasizes only that as long as there are things that embody the form
in actuality, the form is eternal. On this point, he is vulnerable to criticism.

Shields[64] criticizes Ross's view. Shields identifies the forms that are
ingenerable[65] as "substantial universals"[66] (370), such as the species man
and the genus animal. These substantial universals are ingenerable because
they are "always *instantiated*" (370; emphasis added). Then Shields argues
that there are other nonsubstantial properties that are also what he calls
sempiternal. They are expressed in terms of propositional statements, such
as "all men are capable of learning grammar" or "all humans have skin"
(370) and so on. But if that is so, then there are other forms that are ingenerable. But if sempiternal is the basis for ingenerability, then it is not the case
that only substantial forms are ingenerable. So, since Aristotle identifies the
particular forms of individuals as substances, and since they are destructible, "substantiality as such does not determine whether a form is generable
or not" (371).

The ambiguous words are "embodiment" (Ross) and "instantiation"
(Shields), which are equivalents of the Platonic expression "participation."
They are, for Aristotle, empty words and poetic metaphors, because they
do not account for the coming-to-be of things. That is, an account that
appeals merely to such expressions leaves out the crucial explanation of
how a thing comes to embody, instantiate, or participate in a given form, be
it a substance or any other category. In other words, the account leaves out
the *actual* cause.

Because Ross did not understand why for Aristotle substance must be
both eternal and in actuality, he identifies living things, "held together by
nature," and "unified by an inherent power of initiating movement" (cxiv),
as substances. I shall argue that not all living things are substances,[67] for not
all forms of living things preexist as an actuality, for example, spontaneously
generated organisms or mules. The forms of these exist potentially, in the
heat generated by the sun or in horses, respectively, and it is the sun and
horses that exist in actuality that produce them.[68] Thus, a substance is an
eternal actuality, because it must be a principle[69] of coming-to-be, and this
principle is *always active*.[70] My task is to explain how this is possible.[71]

3.2.3. The Production of Artifacts

What is interesting is that Aristotle gives a hint of how he will replace
Plato's theory of Forms. He says that "it is clear that it is possible even for
the rest (τἄλλα) to be and to come to be by means of these sorts or causes
that [produce] these things that have now been mentioned [a house and a
ring]."[72] Note that the rest (τἄλλα), including substances, come to be in the

very same way as the artificial products. That means that it is the production of artifacts that holds the key to understanding how substances and the rest come to be.[73] We shall see the importance of this in Z7–9, which I discuss in the next chapter.

Before I do so, let me summarize A9:

The context is this: Aristotle is discussing the principle of coming-to-be. In this context we learn the following: the form, which exists apart from the composite, must not be a universal; the form, which is a principle of coming-to-be, must be in actuality; and the production of artifacts holds the key to understanding how substances and the rest (τἆλλα) come to be.

In light of the above analyses of B4 and A9, we understand the argument in this way: the form of an artifact is not both eternal and in actuality; hence, it cannot exist apart from the composite in the way in which substances (which are both eternal and in actuality) do; hence, it is possible that an artifact is not a substance.

How is it possible for the form of a substance to be an eternal actuality? I deal with this perplexing issue in the next three chapters.

Chapter Four

Individual or Universal

A clear understanding of the principle of coming-to-be holds the key to elucidating the argument against the substantial status of artifacts. One of Aristotle's criticisms against Plato's theory of Forms revolves around it; that is, because of the very nature of Platonic Forms, they cannot account for the coming-to-be of things. Even if they were to exist, they would be useless. For example, artifacts are produced even though there are no Forms of them. Aristotle, thus, argues that other things, including substances themselves, can come to be in the very same way. I now turn to Z7–9.[1] It is in these passages that, by appealing to the production of artifacts as a paradigm, Aristotle analogically explains every type of coming-to-be and that we can confirm the two criteria of substantiality—eternity and actuality. However, they invite the most notorious Aristotelian dilemma:[2] whether the form, understood as the substance of a composite, is individual or universal.

4.1. The Scope

In Z9, 1034b7–19, Aristotle concludes his discussion of Z7–9 by making the general claim applicable to all forms: that they do not come-to-be and that the form (as well as matter) must preexist. Aristotle's discussion is not limited to what scholars call substantial forms, but includes other forms[3] that come under the schema of categories.[4] Thus, we cannot take the passages from this context (i.e., Z7–9) and simply assume that any statement about the forms that is found in them establishes Aristotle's theory of substance.[5] Nor can we assume from this context that these forms are ungenerable in one sense only, the noneternal as opposed to the eternal sense.[6] This is so even though Aristotle argues that one does not make sphericity, except accidentally in Z8, 1033a29–30 (which seems to be the noneternal sense of ungenerable). In chapter 2.3.4, we saw that throughout the *Metaphysics*, this sense of ungenerable is applicable to forms and formulae in general, including such things as accidents, points, and whiteness. What we should note instead is that Aristotle here appeals to the noneternal sense of ungenerable, when he is discussing the forms of artifacts, just as we saw in Z15 and Λ3.[7] Furthermore, the context does not make it clear whether the noneternal sense of ungenerable is also applicable to the forms of natural substances,[8] as opposed to the forms of artifacts; or even if it is applicable to the former, since Aristotle does say forms in general (H5, 1044b22), it does not follow that the form of a natural substance cannot also be ungenerable in the eternal sense.[9] But rather I shall confirm the view that the eternal sense of ungenerable is only applicable to natural substances.

Aristotle only distinguishes between substance and nonsubstance in the concluding chapter of Z9 by means of actuality and potentiality. A substance must preexist as an actuality. We meet again a passage where Aristotle identifies the principle of coming-to-be with the form as a substance that is an actuality. An interesting question is this: does the form of artifacts preexist actually or potentially? And if actually, does it preexist in actuality *in the very same way* as the form of a natural substance?[10] I come back to this problem in the next two chapters.

Let me now emphasize the scope of Z7–9. In the opening passage of Z7, 1032a12–15, we can see that, first of all he is analyzing the coming-to-be of forms according to each of the categories: a "this," quantity, quality, and place[11] (they correspond to substantial, quantitative, and qualitative changes, and locomotion, respectively).[12] Thus, Aristotle is referring to all changes (including locomotion) and not only to substantial change when he speaks of the things that come to be. Secondly, he analyzes forms that can be classified by the heading of nature, art, or chance; that is, his discussion includes the coming-to-be of all forms, and he identifies the *common* factors that explain them. This is a very ambitious enterprise.

Because of the magnitude of his task, Aristotle focuses only on the relevant similarities rather than on the important differences among the different kinds of coming-to-be. From our standpoint, this is very disappointing, for if the principle of coming-to-be holds the key to solving the problem, then what we need to discover is the essential difference between the principle of the production of artifacts and the principle of the generation of natural things, the difference that makes only natural things substances. Nevertheless, the following examination of Z7–9 turns out to be very fruitful; it exposes the crux of our problem.

In Z7, Aristotle identifies the three common factors—ὑπό τινος, ἔκ τινος, and τί—as the principles of coming-to-be operative in the production of artifacts and natural things as well as in other cases. In the opening passage of Z8, he is more explicit:

Since what comes-to-be comes to be by something (ὑπό τινος) (by this [by something] I mean that from which the beginning of motion originates), and out of something (ἔκ τινος) (let this be not the privation but the matter; we have already determined in what sense we mean by this), and it comes to be "what" (τί) (and this is either a sphere or a circle or whatever else it may happen to be) (1033a24–28).

So, having eliminated privation from his discussion, he identifies ὑπό τινος, ἔκ τινος, and τί as efficient cause, matter, and form, respectively. I shall focus on efficient cause, for this is where the essential difference lies.[13]

In the case of natural generation, Aristotle identifies ὑπό τινος vaguely as "a thing which exists by nature" (1032a18)—which suggests that a thing that exists by nature is a composite individual. However, he immediately moves to a more general level, for he gives an account of natural generation *universally* (1032a22):

And that by which the nature, which is said according to the form, [comes to be] is the same in form but it is in another;[14] for man generates man. (1032a24–25)

After commenting that things that come to be by chance or luck also come to be in a similar fashion, he turns his attention to artificial production. In a nutshell, he identifies the efficient cause of things that come-to-be by art as the form in the soul (1032b21–23). By "form," he means the "what it is to be of each thing and the first substance" (1032b1–2), "the formula in the soul" (1032b4), "knowledge" (1032b5–6), and "substance without matter" (1032b14), and he argues that "in a way health comes to be *from* health and a house *from* a house" (1032b11–12).

Aristotle does not say health generates health or that a house generates a house,[15] as in the case of man; he only says that health comes to be *from* health and a house *from* a house. Although he also employs the expression "a man *from* a man" (1034b2), in the case of artificial production, Aristotle formulates their coming-to-be carefully[16] in this passage. Since he makes a qualification "in a way," he is very aware of the important distinction between the production of artifacts and the generation of natural substances, even though in Z7–9 he never explains it.

Why does Aristotle want to establish such a close analogy between natural generation and artificial production, even at the cost of obscuring the important difference between them? Perhaps the answer lies in the passage that I examined in chapter 3.2.3. In criticizing Plato's theory of Forms, we saw Aristotle indicating how he can account for the coming-to-be of all things without appealing to the existence of Forms:

And many other things come to be, for example, a house or a ring, of which we deny that Forms exist. Consequently, it is clear that it is possible even for the rest to be and to come-to-be by means of these sorts of causes that [produce] those things that have been mentioned now. (991b6–9)

In Z7, Aristotle identifies substances most of all only from the things generated by nature; he excludes other things, including artifacts.[17] But if he is going to appeal to the production of artifacts as a paradigm of the way in which everything else comes to be, especially the generation of substances most of all, then he needs to show why it is an appropriate paradigm. He can do so if he has established the similarity that exists between the generation of natural substances and the production of artifacts.

In Z8, Aristotle argues that Platonic Forms are useless, because we can account for the generation of natural substances, like Callias and Socrates, in the same way we explain the production of artificial objects, such as bronze spheres. In Z9, he also explains the coming-to-be of spontaneous things similarly.[18]

For my purposes, however, the problem is focusing on the difference, rather than the similarity, between the production of artifacts and the generation of natural substances; although man comes *from* man and *in a way* a house *from* a house, what I need to distinguish is the qualification that Aristotle makes; although a house comes *from* a house, unlike man, a house does not generate a house.[19] Let me, therefore, analyze the analogy that Aristotle establishes between the production of artifacts and the generation of animals and see what exactly is left unexplained.

In the case of artifacts, the form in the mind of an artisan is the principle of coming-to-be. What an artisan makes is the shape in the matter, for example, a sphere in a particular piece of bronze. Aristotle argues that we can account for the generation of animals in the same way (1034a4–7). That is why we do not need to set up Forms as paradigms, because they can be sought in the animals themselves just as the forms of artifacts are found in the mind of artisans.

Aristotle maintains that the form always preexists in any coming-to-be. He can therefore summarize it by a formula, such as man from man, health from health, or a house from a house; as a result, we do not need to posit Platonic Forms. But in Z7–9, Aristotle does not give us any hint as to how the production of artifacts and the generation of animals differ. My task is to explain this crucial difference—the difference between the way in which the form of an artifact exists in the mind of an artisan and the way in which the form of an animal exists,[20] such that we can distinguish their *manner* of coming-to-be.

4.2. Eternity and Actuality

Let me go back to Z7–9 and see if we can discover the essential factors that distinguish the generation of natural[21] substances from other comings-to-be by focusing our attention on Aristotle's celebrated formula—man generates man (ἄνθρωπος ἄνθρωπον γεννᾷ). In chapters 1.2 and 1.3.1, I argued that in Z7 and Z8, Aristotle identifies substances most of all only among the things that are generated by nature; among other things (such as health) he does not include mules, spontaneously generated organisms, and artifacts as substances most of all. I concluded that the previous passages do not support the view that all living things are substances either with or without qualification. I have also shown how this is so in the case of all the other passages in the *Metaphysics*. However, I have only made a negative conclusion. Let us see what positive conclusion I can derive from the analysis of the five passages (see Appendix B for its summary).

In passages (1) and (5), Aristotle identifies the manner in which the natural things are generated by the formula ἄνθρωπος ἄνθρωπον γεννᾷ.[22] As a matter of fact, I can argue consistently in each of these five passages that, regardless of whether they are said to be generated (γίγνεται) or formed (συνέστηκεν) by nature, the generation of natural substances can be understood in terms of this formula. But why would Aristotle identify only the things that are generated by nature as substances? What is the main difference between them and the rest of the things? The clue is provided in other treatises of Aristotle.

Such a clue is found in the *Generation of Animals*. Although Aristotle says that generation is a function common to all living things (731a31) in *GA* 1.23, he makes the following qualification in *GA* 2.1:

> This [the nutritive part][23] is what is generative of another like itself, for this is a function of all things (both animal and plant) which are complete in nature. (735a17–19)

But what does the qualification, complete in nature, mean? What living things are not considered to be complete? Aristotle is much more explicit in *De An* 2.4:

> For the most natural function in living things, as many of those that are complete and not defective or are generated by chance, is to produce another like itself, on the one hand an animal [produces] an animal, and on the other hand a plant [produces] a plant, in order that they may partake of the eternal and the divine insofar as possible; for all [things] desire this, and it is for the sake of this that all act as many of those that act according to nature. (415a26–b2)

So the two kinds of living things that are not complete are those that are defective, like mules,[24] and things that are generated by chance. Aristotle's key point is that the goal of these complete natural things is to partake of the eternal and the divine by means of reproduction (expressed by the formula ἄνθρωπος ἄνθρωπον γεννᾷ),[25] which neither mules nor spontaneously generated organisms[26] (nor, of course, artifacts) are able to do *per se*. I say *per se* because, as we noted, Aristotle does make a qualification in Z7–9 to explain all comings-to-be by appealing to the earlier principle of synonymy.[27]

On the assumption that Aristotle employs the words αἴδιον and ἀεί interchangeably,[28] I have confirmed the discovery in chapter 2.3.4 that eternity plays a role in one of the criteria of substantiality. However, in order to distinguish clearly between substances and other things, that is, between the primary and the secondary application of the ἄνθρωπος ἄνθρωπον γεννᾷ formula, we need to appeal to another criterion. This we can see by returning to the last sentence of Z9:

> But the peculiarity of a substance, to grasp from these things, is that it is necessary for a substance other than the one which it produces to pre-exist in actuality, for example, an animal if an animal comes to be; but it is not necessary for a quality or a quantity [to pre-exist] except potentially only. (1034b16–19)

Note that a substance must preexist in actuality. Thus, I have confirmed the findings of chapters 2 and 3 that a substance is somehow an eternal actuality. But we should again emphasize the context—Aristotle is discussing the principle of coming-to-be. Substance as a principle of coming-to-be (or more specifically of generation) is somehow an eternal actuality.

We have now reached the crux of the problem. How is it possible for a destructible substance to be an eternal actuality?

4.3. The Dilemma

Let me introduce the problem by noting that there is an apparent discrepancy between Z8, 1033b19–26 and Λ5, 1071a27–29. In Z8 Aristotle claims that the forms are "suches" and, thereby, implies that they are universals and, as a consequence, says that the forms of Callias and Socrates are the same; on the other hand, in Λ3 he identifies the form as a "this"[29] and, as a consequence, recognizes the difference between your form and mine.

Many scholars have tried to resolve these apparent inconsistencies by a developmental explanation.[30] Let me offer a possible way of avoiding this by pointing out the context in which Aristotle makes his two claims.

I argued that in Z7–9 Aristotle is discussing the coming-to-be of things at a certain level of generality because his project is to explain the coming-to-be of all things analogically by appealing to the production of artifacts as a paradigm. Consequently, he is speaking at a universal level. This is exactly what Aristotle himself states in Λ4:

> The causes and the principles differ for different [things] in one sense, but in another sense, if one were to speak *universally* and according to *analogy*, they are the same for all. (1070a31–33)

And he says in Λ5:

> Indeed, the primary 'this' in actuality and the other which is in potentiality are the primary principles of all. But then with respect to them universals do not exist, for an individual is a principle of an individual; for a man is a principle of a man universally (but no one is [a universal man]), but Peleus is a principle of Achilles, your father of you, and this B of this BA, but in general B is of BA without qualification. (1071a17–23)

It is in this context that Aristotle mentions the individual form in Λ5, 1071a27–29. Therefore, it is only when we are speaking universally that we have the same form (a "such"), but otherwise the form is a "this," for the primary principle exists actually. Thus, the apparent inconsistency can be resolved.[31]

But why does Aristotle emphasize the individual forms in Λ? Let me examine the context. In Λ, Aristotle's main concern is with the Unmoved Mover—which is both one in formula and one in number (1074a36–37). That being so, the contrast between the Unmoved Mover and the composites (which are one in form but many in number (1074a32–33)) is instructive. In other words, the above contrast can be seen clearly when we are not speaking universally. And this contrast[32] is employed by Aristotle in the argument of Λ8, 1074a31–38.

The accuracy of my examination notwithstanding, we now have a problem. Although we can appeal to the different contexts to explain away the discrepancy between Z8 and Λ5, are we now compelled to accept that, when we are not speaking universally, that is, when we are discussing the actual ontological status of the forms, forms are individuals rather than universals? But if the form of a composite is individual, for example, as in the case of the form of Callias or of Socrates, how can it be eternal? When Callias or Socrates dies, his individual form ceases to exist; the individual form of a destructible being is also destructible. But then does it mean that it is universal?

Aside from the evidence I have given, the fact that Aristotle is speaking universally in Z8 can also be confirmed from the reason he gives for the fact that "that which begets" and "what is begotten" have the same form, for he claims that "the form is indivisible" (1034a8). But the indivisibility of form suggests a unity, not of the individual, but of the universal. In I1, where the "one" is identified as indivisible in many senses, the text reads:

> The individual is indivisible in number, and what is in knowing and in knowledge is indivisible in form.[33] (1052a31–33)

And Aristotle understands the prior distinction as the distinction between individual and universal (1052a35–36).

But if "one in form (ἓν εἴδει)"[34] is a mark of universality, then in the *De Anima*, where Aristotle states that certain living things partake of the eternal and the divine, he is speaking universally:

> So since each [living thing] is unable to share continuously in the eternal and the divine, because it is not possible for [each] of the destructible things to preserve itself one and the same in number, insofar as each is able to partake of them, some share in these more and others less, but each [thing] does not preserve itself but [something] like it, one not in number, but one in form.[35] (415b3–7)

Note that what is one in number is destructible. If what is one in form suggests universality (and if universals are closely associated with potentiality),[36] we have the following dilemma: if the form of a composite is individual, then it cannot be eternal, because it will be destroyed when the composite perishes; but if it is universal, then it cannot be an actuality because it is a potentiality. Therefore, the form cannot be an eternal actuality. But I have been arguing that the form, understood as a substance of a natural being, is somehow an eternal actuality.

4.3.1. The Controversy

So in order to explain how the form can be an eternal actuality, I need to solve the old Aristotelian controversy of whether the substance is individual or universal. Before we turn to my solution,[37] let me canvass the views of others.[38]

Albritton (1957) points out that in ∧ there is evidence that particular forms[39] can be expressed in a single universal definition (700). But according to him, Aristotle holds both inanimate and animate substances to have particular forms (704). Such particular forms cannot help us explain the distinction between the forms of substances and those of artifacts. Albritton, then, compares the evidence in other books of the *Metaphysics* and concludes that, except in the case of souls, no other particular forms are mentioned, though he adds that he can find only "the very *nearly explicit* attributions of particular forms to animate substances in Z, H" (707; emphasis added) and he laments[40] that he cannot find evidence for his view in other texts.

This is noteworthy, because although we cannot assume that all living things are substances, Aristotle does identify the form, that is the soul, of things that are generated by nature as the primary substance (Z11, 1037a5, 28–29). And, according to Albritton, Aristotle does not explicitly identify the soul as individual.

On the other hand, in Λ3, Aristotle identifies not the form but the composite as an individual, for example, Socrates and Callias (1070a11–13). He argues that it is one individual (a composite) that is the principle of another (e.g., the principle of Achilles is Peleus (1071a22)). From this, Lesher (1971) rightly concludes that "this does not mean that the form which is the cause of your form is an individual, but only that the form which is the cause of your form exists in an individual substance." (175)

Frede,[41] who also argues that the form is individual, identifies it as a disposition, organization, function, or capacity. What sets living things apart from artifacts is what he calls the notion of "continuity of organization," which is the characteristic of living things. This capacity or organization in the living thing is called the soul. The problem with Frede's account is that this capacity or organization enables a living thing to function continually only for some time, but "when a living thing *has lost* this capacity that we say it is no longer alive or no longer exists" (67; emphasis added). This implies that Frede excludes the possibility that an individual form can be eternal. Frede's proposal therefore cannot solve the dilemma I have formulated, for I have argued that a substance is somehow eternal.

What is interesting, however, is Frede's admission that "in individuating a form, we shall need to go *beyond* a specification of a disposition or capacity, if we are to have an individual substance" (68; emphasis added). Modrak (1979), who argues that forms are substance types (a kind of universal), also identifies the form with "the functional organization" and says, "if forms are individuals, they cannot be identified with the functional organization of living things" (376). Despite their contrary views, Frede and Modrak[42] agree that *dynamis* as such cannot be identified as individual.[43] Perhaps this is so because the form is universal.

Woods (1967) introduces the distinction between τὸ καθόλου λεγόμενον (being predicated universally) and τὸ καθόλου (being a universal).[44] The former, which is applicable to genera only, is not a substance, but the latter, which signifies a species form, is a substance. This view has been criticized by a number of scholars,[45] however, regardless of the accuracy of Woods's interpretation of Z13, his insight that Aristotle has indeed made something like the prior distinction should be noted. So the dichotomy of individual and universal will be split into the following trichotomy: individual, universal, and universal predicate. But the question we need to ask ourselves is this: what is the precise ontological status of this third alternative—universal?[46]

Prior to Woods's article, a number of other scholars argued that Aristotle's species should be understood as a nonconceptual sense of universal.[47] The problem with all of these views is that they do not clearly explain the ontological status of the nonconceptual sense of universal. It is not enough to posit and simply claim that it is immanent in the natural substance, or that it exists as an actuality. How is that possible, especially when Aristotle associates potentiality with the universal?[48] In other words, one must explain *how* the nonconceptual sense of universal (if indeed there is such a thing) exists immanently as an actuality.

Similarly, it is not enough to identify different senses of universals to resolve the problem as if it is merely a logical puzzle. For example, Lewis[49] argues that forms are both universals and "thises," that is, some universals "are not suches but thises" (329). Forms are universal when they are predicated of the composite individuals (which are "thises"), but when a form is predicated of matter, that is, when it is universal to matter, form is a "this," but matter is not a "this." This solution does not help because, like words such as "embodiment," "instantiation," and "participation,"[50] "predication" has no explanatory force. Even if the form can be understood as a predicate of matter,[51] it cannot account for its being the principle of coming-to-be insofar as it is a predicate.

In contrast, Hughes (1978), who is sympathetic to Woods's proposal, also attempts to understand the distinction between universal and universal predicate. He does so not in terms of language or logic, but in terms of Aristotle's theory of potentiality and actuality. He understands matter as "potentially an indefinite number of substances" but it is not "something which indefinitely many substances share in common" (122). Similarly in the case of genera he suggests that genera, understood as universals, are potentially an indefinite number of species rather than "something in which an indefinite number of species share" (122–123). The advantage of this interpretation is that it accords with Aristotle's own solution to the epistemological problem of individual and universal that is found in M10 (which I shall examine later), in the sense that Hughes appeals to the distinction between actuality and potentiality to solve the problem.

Rist,[52] however, has an interesting objection to Hughes: "whereas the 'potential house' *is* bricks and mortar, the potential Achilles is not 'man,' but (perhaps) the seed of Peleus" (332). What the earlier observation shows is that, despite his downplaying of logic and language, Hughes is still thinking in terms of epistemological concepts, such as genera and species, and Rist thinks in terms of the problem of generation. Since I have established that the pertinent context of our discussion is that of coming-to-be, Rist's approach is more useful. If *dynamis* holds the key to our problem, then we need to clarify the specific sense of *dynamis* that is associated with the principle of coming-to-be. That may indicate that the simple distinction between actuality and potentiality may not be a sufficient one, if indeed *dynamis* (as well as actuality) is said in many senses.

Let me now turn to M10, where Aristotle solves the epistemological aspect of the dilemma. Although the epistemological problem *per se* is not directly relevant to our topic, it would be useful to examine how Aristotle solves it. In M10, Aristotle appeals to the distinction between actuality and potentiality to solve the problem (1087a15–25). The passage is very cryptic, and it is controversial as to exactly how successful Aristotle is.[53] However, a number of scholars believe that Aristotle's solution is that the substance is neither individual nor universal.[54] But there are two main objections: there is no textual evidence for it;[55] and it is unintelligible.[56] Let me examine each in turn.

4.3.2. Textual Evidence

As far as textual evidence is concerned, we should ask ourselves this question: what is evidence? Do we need to find a passage where Aristotle states his position unequivocally one way or another? It is instructive to note that Lesher (1971) believes that Aristotle is committed to the view that the form is universal, yet he says that "Aristotle does *not explicitly* say this to my knowledge" (169 (footnote 2); emphasis added).[57] But if that is so, by default, all scholars should accept that it is individual (on the assumption that there is such a passage).[58] But is there? Albritton (1957), who thinks that the soul is an individual form, cannot find the passage, for he laments:

> It is curious and exasperating that none of these passages ([Z10 and Z11] nor any in *De Anima*) quite unambiguously says that its particular soul is the particular form of a particular living thing (703).

Scholars have been presenting positions that they themselves admit there is no explicit textual support, but this has not deterred them from defending these views.

Why is there such a controversy? If there are other explicit statements of Aristotle that would either contradict or confirm one's interpretation, surely they should be considered. In other words, we should not, despite Heinaman, disregard the view that a substance is neither individual nor universal out of hand, for it seems this option is just as plausible as the others from the standpoint of textual evidence. Let us, however, point out what evidence we have gathered that would make the view—that the form is neither individual nor universal—plausible.

In chapters 2.3.4 and 2.3.6, I discovered a third sense of separation that has eluded a number of scholars. The traditional dichotomy states: in one sense, separation is applicable to the composite individual, and in the other sense, separation in form is applicable to the form of the composite and is understood in terms of separation in formula. If formulae are of universals, then the correlate of this dichotomy is the dilemma of individual and universal. If there is a third sense of separation that is applicable to the form of a composite, then it is reasonable to expect a corresponding way in which the form exists, being neither individual, in the sense of a composite, nor universal, in the sense of a formula in a mind.[59]

Since the question of separation is closely connected with this dilemma, the discovery of the third sense of separation is good evidence for the view that the substance is neither individual nor universal. Furthermore, there is an indication that the simple distinction between actuality and potentiality may not be sufficient. Thus, the dilemma we need to solve can be stated analogically in the following way: individual or universal; separation without qualification or separation in account; and actuality or potentiality, respectively. I have argued for the third sense of separation and defend the view that the form is neither[60] individual nor universal. What corresponds with the just mentioned analogy is that the form is neither actual nor potential *per se*.

4.3.3. Intelligibility

As far as intelligibility is concerned, Halper (1989) suggests an interesting reason why he believes that most scholars have a tendency to accept only an either-or proposition:

> A reason may be that they have tended to approach the *Metaphysics* from the perspective of contemporary *logic*, which recognizes only two sorts of entities, predicates and the individuals that receive them (respectively, F's or P's, and x's or a's). These correspond to Aristotle's universals and individuals. (241; emphasis added)

If Halper's conjecture is accurate, it is consistent with what I have been insisting—that the solution to our problem lies not within the context of a logical enquiry,[61] but within the context of Aristotle's analysis of coming-to-be.

I shall show that in the context of coming-to-be, it is intelligible to argue that the form is neither individual nor universal. I shall defend its intelligibility by appealing to the distinction of two senses of actuality/potentiality; there is a sense in which a form is neither actual nor potential because it can somehow be *both* actual and potential at the same time. It is most revealing that Aristotle makes this distinction when he defines the soul.

Chapter Five

Principle

In Λ3 Aristotle draws an important distinction between nature and art: "Art is a principle 'in another,' nature is a principle 'in itself'" (1070a7–8). To understand this, we need to clarify two points: Aristotle's concept of principle, and his distinction between "in another" and "in itself." In this chapter, I show that Aristotle's concept of principle is closely connected with eternity, actuality, and separation; and that "in another" and "in itself" imply Aristotle's principles of potentiality and actuality, respectively.

5.1. *Arché*

Throughout the *Metaphysics*, although Aristotle describes the science he is seeking in many different ways, it is consistently identified as the search for certain principles and causes.[1] Whether the science is called wisdom, divine, or being *qua* being (or whether the passage in question is taken from the central books, the theological book Λ, or any other book), Aristotle always insists that he is seeking the principles and causes. Thus, in order to appreciate Aristotle's enterprise, it is crucial to understand his concept of principle, especially when he always identifies it as a substance.[2]

The crucial characteristics of principle,[3] insofar as it is the principle of coming-to-be,[4] are eternal, actual, and separate[5]—the very same criteria that Aristotle ascribes to substances. Let me now turn to each of these criteria.

5.1.1. Eternity

This concept of principle is also found in a dialogue of Plato.[6] In the *Phaedrus*, to establish that every soul, understood as self-moving, is immortal, Plato argues that a principle is ungenerable (245d1) and that everything that comes-to-be comes to be from the principle, though the principle in its turn does not come to be from anything, otherwise, it would no longer be a

principle. And similarly, because it does not come into being, but everything else must come to be from it, the principle is also indestructible
(245a5–246a2). Given Plato's belief that the soul neither comes to be nor
dies,[7] Plato's concept of ungenerable corresponds with what I called the
eternal[8] sense of ungenerable in chapter 2.3.4.

In *Phys* 3.4, where Aristotle argues that the infinite cannot be a principle,
he himself makes the connection between a principle and its ungenerability.[9]
He does so when he is discussing the topic of coming-to-be. And of course,
this is the same context that we found in all of the four passages (B4,[10] K2,
H3, and ∧3) where Aristotle questions the substantial status of artifacts.[11]

Furthermore, one of his criticisms of Plato's theory of Forms is that
Forms do not account for the coming-to-be of things.[12] Aristotle replaces
Plato's theory with his own, which accounts for all comings-to-be;[13] that is,
Aristotelian forms are causes. He states that "all causes are principles" (Δ1,
1013a17), and in E1, we find the following statement: "But it is necessary
that *all causes are eternal*, and these most of all" (1026a16–17).

The phrase, "these most of all," refers to the unmoved movers, for
Aristotle makes this statement in the context in which he identifies the first
science as theology. But what is most important is that *all* causes must be
eternal. Some scholars[14] believe that Aristotle is referring only to first or
highest causes, thus, for example, Ross believes that the "thought is not
quite exact, for it is only *first* causes that need be eternal, and ταῦτα are not
some first causes among others, but the only first causes" (356). In contrast,
if the thought is exact, that is, if we take Aristotle's qualification "most of
all" seriously, then the passage suggests that there is a kind of eternity that
is not most of all. This reading is consistent with my analysis of other
passages of the *Metaphysics*, where I argue that there are at least two kinds
of eternal principles: one for destructible and another for indestructible
beings.[15] This qualified sense of eternity[16] is the key to solving our problem.

So, if we take his qualification seriously, we can now understand why
the form, understood as a principle of coming-to-be, is ungenerable in the
eternal sense; it is a principle in the sense of a cause.

5.1.2. Actuality

In ∧5, with respect to actuality and potentiality, principles are said to be the
same by analogy. Now, although in some sense principles cannot be stated
universally, in all cases, "the first 'this' which [exists] in actuality and the
other which [exists] in potentiality are the first principles of all" (1071a18–19);
that is, actuality and potentiality are terms in which we can understand the
first principles. But in Θ8, Aristotle argues that in all cases, actuality is prior
(πρότερον) to potentiality. If Aristotle employs τὸ πρῶτον and τὸ πρότερον

interchangeably,[17] and if principles can be understood in terms of actuality and potentiality, and if the former is prior to the latter, then the first principle as such must exist in actuality.

In chapter 3.2.2 (see note 57) I discussed why a mover must be in actuality by referring to Θ8, 1049b24–27. At this point I would like to focus on both the context in which this passage is found and the familiar themes connected with it. Aristotle distinguishes different kinds of potentiality. The primary sense is "the principle of change in another or *qua* another" (1049b6–7), and nature, which is a principle of the movable "in itself *qua* itself" (1049b10). In both[18] cases, what is actual is prior. Aristotle discusses the priority of coming-to-be when he argues for the temporal priority of actuality; that is, he closely associates them.[19] He concludes that actuality is prior to potentiality "according to coming-to-be and time" (1050a3). Aristotle's argument is based on the distinction between what is the same in form and what is the same in number.[20] For, although potentiality is prior to actuality in what is numerically the same (e.g., the semen is prior to an individual man), actuality is prior to potentiality in the sense that there always exists another thing (that has the same form in actuality) and that is the ultimate cause of realizing what is potential (e.g., the semen that turns into a man is produced by another man). And Aristotle appeals to the "man generates man" formula.[21]

In light of these points, I conclude that the *primary* principle of coming-to-be as such must be in actuality.

5.1.3. Separation

Let me begin with a remark of Morrison (1985c):

> Separation is a crucial metaphysical concept of Aristotle. Why does he never tell us what he means by it? . . . Perhaps there is some deep philosophical ground, one to which neither Fine nor I have yet penetrated. . . .(173)

I shall not pretend to have penetrated some deep philosophical ground, but perhaps I can suggest the reason why Aristotle has not defined the crucial concept of separation. The questions we should ask ourselves are these: Can we define everything? If Aristotle had defined separation, would separation still be a crucial metaphysical concept? If there were terms that would define separation, would they not be more crucial? Among other crucial metaphysical concepts Aristotle does not define actuality and potentiality, but he reminds us that "we should not seek a definition of everything, but should also perceive [something] by analogy" (1048a36–37). Perhaps it is not surprising[22] that Aristotle does not define separation, but we should rather expect this if indeed it is the crucial concept, for everything else is understood in terms of it. But this does not prevent our understanding *why* separation is a criterion of substantiality.

The reason lies in Aristotle's concept of principle. In *Phys* 1.2, criticizing Parmenides, Aristotle says this:

> Furthermore, there is no principle, if there is only one and in this way one, for a principle is of a some thing or things. (185a3–5)

Here, Aristotle makes a distinction between a principle and that of which it is a principle. So, in some sense of the word, a principle and that of which it is a principle are separate and not one.[23]

In *GA* 2.1, having identified the male and the female as the principles of generation (731b18–19; 732a1–3), Aristotle says this:

> But since the first mover, in which the formula and the form exist, being a cause is better and more divine with respect to nature than the matter, it is also better for what is superior to be separate (κεχωρίσθαι) from what is inferior. That is why in as many things as possible and to the extent that it is possible the male is separate (κεχώρισται) from the female, for the principle of motion, which exists in the male for what comes-to-be, is better and more divine—but the female is matter. (732a3–9)

Here, Aristotle gives the reason why one principle is separate from the other—it is better and more divine. So if a principle is, in principle, better (and more divine)[24] than that of which it is a principle (and of course if the principle is somehow eternal and the composite is destructible, then the principle is better and more divine), then we can see why Aristotle believes that a principle should be separate from the composite.

This relationship between a principle and separation is expressed in the *Metaphysics*:

> For it is necessary that the principle or the cause exists apart from the things of which it is the principle, and/or is capable of being separate from them. (B3, 999a17–19)

So, as we indicated, if substance is the principle and the cause, then we can understand why separation is a criterion of substantiality, for substance, as a principle, must be separate from that of which it is a principle.

But before I make a hasty conclusion based on the passage B3, 999a17–19, taken out of context, let me examine the context itself. The most important factor is that the passage is found in one of the *aporiai*, which means that we cannot take for granted that it represents Aristotle's actual view.[25] On the other hand, that it occurs in a dialectical passage does not automatically exclude the possibility that Aristotle is stating his own view.[26] Let me therefore examine whether there is reason for believing that the view stated in the passage is what Aristotle himself ascribes to.

The passage occurs in the seventh *aporia*, where Aristotle questions whether the highest or the lowest genus (that is, the species) should be considered as a principle. But if the highest genus is a principle because of its universality, then being and one will be principles. These cannot be genera, for otherwise differentia will neither exist nor be one. But if a principle is a unity to a higher degree, given that the higher genus is divisible into the lower ones (and given that genus cannot exist apart from species), then species will be the principle. However, Aristotle says:

> But again it is not easy to say in what way we should understand these things to be principles. For it is necessary that the principle or the cause exists apart from the things of which it is the principle, and/or is capable of being separate from them. But why should we understand that this sort of thing exists apart from the individual things except as what is universally predicated and according to all. (999a16–21)

So Aristotle defines principle in the context in which he questions how forms (that is, species) can be considered as principles. The problem is understood in terms of separation—how it is possible for form as a universal to be separate or separable. In chapter 3.2, we saw that Aristotle endorses separation as a criterion of substantiality. The problem he sees with the Platonists' position is that they separate universals as if universals were substances. Thus, what we now find is the familiar context in which we would expect Aristotle to appeal to the criterion of separation to undermine the possibility of universals being separate in the way in which substances are said to be separate.

There is a close connection between the seventh *aporia* (where B3, 999a17–19 occurs) and the eighth *aporia*. And this connection is stated by Aristotle—"that which is connected with it (ἐχομένη)"[27] (B4, 999a24). So if there is a close connection between the two *aporiai*, then there is good reason for believing that there is also a close connection between Aristotle's concept of principle and the separation that he constantly refers to in the eighth *aporia*: the separation between the form and the composite, especially in regard to the substantial status of artifacts.

The problem of separation is not unique to those who posit the Ideas, for Aristotle begins M10, where he takes up an epistemological problem:

> But let us now discuss a point which presents a certain difficulty both to those who speak of Ideas and those who do not. . . . (1086b14–15)

According to Annas,[28] "those who do not posit the Ideas" include Aristotle himself, and Ross[29] believes that the phrase refers to both Speusippus and non-Platonists (presumably this includes Aristotle). Given that Aristotle responds to this problem, the assessment of Annas and Ross seems reasonable. Then the problem of separation is a universal one and not restricted to the context of Platonic philosophy.

And what is more, in M10, Aristotle is concerned with the manner in which *principles* can be separate! He sets up the problem in the following way:

> For if someone will not posit substances to be separate, and in the way in which the individual things are said to be [separate], one will eliminate substance as we wish to mean; but if one were to posit substances as separate, how will one [posit] their elements or principles? For if they are individuals and not universals, there will be as many things as elements, and the elements [will] not be knowable. (1086b16–20).

Aristotle is focusing his attention on the problem not of individual things but of their elements or principles. And he describes the other horn of the dilemma as follows:

> But if indeed the principles are universal, . . . non-substance will be prior to substance, for the universal is not a substance, but the element or the principle [will] be universal, but the element or the principle is prior to that of which it is the principle or the element. (1086b37–1087a4)

This implies that the principle is a substance, for it is prior to that of which it is the principle. Accordingly, Aristotle is concerned with the problem of the separation of the principle of individual things, given that a substance must be separate in the way in which individual things are said to be separate.

So let us note the following points. Aristotle defines the relevant concept of principle in the context in which we would expect him to appeal to the criterion of separation in rejecting universals as substances (principles). Aristotle always endorses the view that separation is a criterion of substantiality, hence, if substance is a principle, we would expect Aristotle's concept of principle to be closely tied to that of separation. The view that the principle is somehow separate from that of which it is the principle is attested by other texts. There is a close connection between the seventh *aporia*, where Aristotle defines principle as separate, and the eighth *aporia*, where he constantly refers to separation; and it is in this context that we found the third sense of separation.[30] Separation is a universal problem that Platonists and non-Platonists alike must solve, hence, it is reasonable to believe that the prior concept of principle is not used merely as an aporetic (pace Chen) nor as a polemical device against the Academy (pace Reale).[31]

Dialectical context notwithstanding, we have good reason to believe that B3, 999a17–19, represents Aristotle's view that a principle must be separate.

But what is the exact meaning of Aristotle's statement in B3, 999a17–19? Let me examine the passage more carefully. The crucial word is καί in a18. Some scholars translate it as "or,"[32] while others "and."[33] Is καί disjunctive, conjunctive, or epexegetic? And what does "capable of being separate (δύνασθαι εἶναι χωριζομένην)" mean? Does it mean separate in thought or in some other way? Or does our answer depend on which principle we are referring to? The context is of no help, but since the Greek adjective χωριστός can be translated as both separate and separable, we would expect that a principle can be understood as at least both separate and separable, depending on the context.

But this goes counter to Morrison's (1985a) position that χωριστός means separate and never separable. He argues that given that it is reasonable to suppose that the term was coined by Aristotle, since it first appears in Aristotle's corpus and not in his earlier works (such as *Categories* and *Topics*), it is most certain that it was coined to serve as a technical or semitechnical term. Given this purpose, "he would have had no reason to make the word ambiguous from the start, and strong reason to keep it univocal once in use" (93). Hence, he concludes that the term means either separate or separable. Although he admits that his conclusion "is based on a chain of probabilities, and so is intrinsically weak," Morrison believes that "its total probability strongly outweighs any alternative" (93). He then proceeds to show how, in all the passages where χωριστός occurs in Aristotle's corpus, χωριστός can be understood as separate.

Morrison's most precarious assumption is that it is reasonable to believe that Aristotle's technical or semitechnical term is *univocal*, if he has coined it. This belief is not reasonable, given Aristotle's practices. One of the most conspicuous phrases that Aristotle employs in philosophical discussion is "said in many ways (πολλαχῶς λέγεται)." He is very sensitive to the fact that words have many meanings. His technical terms especially are said in many ways.[34] It is very difficult, if not impossible, to give an example where Aristotle always uses his technical term univocally.

Furthermore, there is a specific example of a coined technical term used equivocally. The word is ἐντελέχεια. It is agreed by most scholars that the term was coined by Aristotle.[35] It first appears in Aristotle's corpus and not in his earlier works (according to Blair,[36] it does not occur in the surviving fragments of his dialogues nor in his *Organon*). It is certainly a technical term, but it is not a univocal one, for when Aristotle defines the soul in the *De Anima*, he begins by identifying two senses of ἐντελέχεια.[37]

Note the parallel:

1.   neither χωριστός nor ἐντελέχεια appears in Aristotle's earlier works;
2.   both are technical or semitechnical terms; and
3.   both are said to have been coined by Aristotle.

Yet the term ἐντελέχεια is not univocal, hence, Morrison has not established the reasonableness of his conclusion that χωριστός is univocal. And even if he could somehow show that χωριστός can be translated as "separate" in all occurrences found in Aristotle's corpus, it does not mean that that is the right translation.

I show in this chapter and the next that χωριστός, understood as "separable," is the sense of separation that I am seeking. Hence, this is another reason why the third sense of separation has eluded Morrison and those who are persuaded by him.

Let me now return to Z1, 1028a31–34, where Aristotle argues that a substance is prior to other categories in time because it, and no other category, is separate. In chapter 2.2,[38] we saw that this passage has caused a lot of trouble for most, if not all, scholars. My interpretation is as follows.

If a substance is a principle of coming-to-be in the sense of a mover, then (1) as a principle, it is separate from that which comes to be and (2) as a mover, it exists in actuality (that is, it is prior in time to what comes to be). This is especially so if the principle is eternal, for what is eternal is prior in time to what is destructible.[39] Thus, by appealing to Aristotle's concept of a principle of coming-to-be, we can establish a connection between temporal priority and separation. If the coming-to-be of all other categories depends on a substance, then none of them can be separate or prior in time. The two criteria of substantiality—eternity and actuality—are closely connected with Aristotle's conception of separation. Despite Fine, Irwin, Frede and Patzig,[40] who eliminate the crucial connection between temporal priority and separation, I insist on its importance.

Of course, exactly *how* a substance can be separate is the task of this book—the task to which I now turn.

5.2. In Another and In Itself

Let me go back to the distinction of nature and art: "Art is a principle 'in another,' nature is a principle 'in itself'" (1070a7–8). Aristotle identifies two kinds of principle: "in another" and "in itself." Let me first examine the context for their meaning. In Λ2, Aristotle discusses all four changes (1069b9ff) to identify the principles of change. It is in this context[41] that he draws the distinction between the principle of art and the principle of nature.

Since the scope of his discussion in Λ3 is the same as in Z7–9,[42] it is reasonable to believe that the formulation of the principle of art and nature in Λ3 includes the principle of all four changes and is not restricted to the principle of generation. This can be seen from the description of nature in Δ4, 1015a13–17.[43] Here, Aristotle includes both coming-to-be and growth as instances of "a principle of motion in themselves *qua* themselves." If that is so, the distinction between art and nature made in Λ3 may not be helpful after all, especially since we cannot appeal to the principle of internal-change as a criterion of substantiality. In *Phys* 2.1, Aristotle's primary distinction between nature and art is defined in terms of internal-change proper. By internal-change, he means locomotion, qualitative, and quantitative changes, but not generation—for nothing generates itself.[44]

In chapter 2.3.6, we saw that in *Phys* 2.1, the form, understood as the principle of internal-change, can be separate or separable only in formula or thought, and that there is a possibility that the form, understood as the principle of *generation*, is separable in some other way than according to formula or thought. Yet the formulation of Λ3 is applicable to both the principle of internal-change and the principle of generation.

Nevertheless, Ross[45] says that, in Λ3, Aristotle makes his usual distinction between art and nature, but the distinction "*breaks down* in the case of generation" (355; emphasis added). If so, this formulation may be applicable in a different way to the principle of generation. Identifying this difference might confirm Ross's view.

If we turn to the GA, we find the same distinction:

> For art is a principle and a form of what comes to be, but "in others;" the motion of nature on the other hand is "in itself" as coming from another natural thing which possesses the form in actuality. (735a2–4)

Aristotle draws this distinction in the context of an account of how semen fashions the parts of the embryo—not simultaneously, but successively.[46] He points out that the motion is caused by "that which first made the motion from the outside (τὸ πρῶτον κινῆσαν ἔξωθεν). For nothing generates itself, but whenever it is generated, at that time it makes itself grow" (735a12–14). Given the context in which Aristotle formulates the distinction between art and nature and given that by "in itself" he means an entity other than the one that is being generated, it is clear that the formula refers only to the principle of generation and not to the principle of internal-change.

But in *Phys* 2.1, art is distinguished from nature because the principle of change is in another thing and is external (ἐν ἄλλοις καὶ ἔξωθεν)[47] (192b29). In Z7, where Aristotle is discussing the generation of animals, he himself identifies the efficient cause of nature as "ἐν ἄλλῳ"[48] (1032a25). Yet, in Λ3, although the principle may be external and comes from others, the principle of nature is somehow understood not as "in another" but as "in itself." This is the crucial point needing explication.

5.2.1. ∧3 and *GA* 2.1

Let me now return to the distinction between art and nature made in ∧3 and *GA* 2.1 and compare them more closely to make sure that there is no crucial discrepancy that would undermine my appeal to another treatise (the *GA*) to solve a problem found in the *Metaphysics*.[49] First, let me compare the formulations of art:

> ∧3: "Art is a principle 'in another' (ἡ μὲν οὖν τέχνη ἀρχὴ ἐν ἄλλῳ)"; and
> *GA* 2.1: "Art is a principle and a form of what comes to be, but 'in other' (ἡ γὰρ τέχνη ἀρχὴ καὶ εἶδος τοῦ γιγνομένου, ἀλλ' ἐν ἑτέρῳ)."

Does Aristotle employ the phrases ἐν ἄλλῳ and ἐν ἑτέρῳ synonymously? In I3, after stating that τὸ ἕτερον is said in many ways, Aristotle proceeds to give three senses (1054b13–22). Aristotle refers to the first sense as τὸ ἄλλο, but to the other two senses as τὸ ἕτερον. Both Ross[50] and Elders[51] believe that the first sense gives the general meaning and "the other two give varieties of this" (288). If that is so, in one sense that is at the general level, τὸ ἕτερον is equivalent to τὸ ἄλλο, but in another sense that is at the lower levels, the former concept is the species of the latter. Consequently, the distinction between them must be sought in the context in which they are used.

Perhaps in ∧3, because the distinction refers to all four changes, Aristotle uses the phrase ἐν ἄλλῳ, whereas in *GA* 2.1, because it is applicable only to the principle of generation, Aristotle decides to use the different phrase ἐν ἑτέρῳ. However, what we find in Δ12 is that they are used interchangeably. Here, Aristotle introduces his concept of potentiality in this way:

> The principle of motion or of change in other or *qua* other (ἢ ἐν ἑτέρῳ ἢ ἧ ἕτερον). (1019a15–16)

And in the same chapter, referring to this sense of potentiality, he writes:

> This is the principle of change in another or *qua* another (ἐν ἄλλῳ ἢ ἧ ἄλλο). (1020a1–2)

So Aristotle does not seem to make any distinction between ἐν ἄλλῳ and ἐν ἑτέρῳ in this context. On the strength of this evidence, let me assume that whatever subtle difference of meaning there may be, it is not crucial. We shall shortly see why this is also a reasonable assumption to make in the case of art.

Let me now compare the formulations of nature in Λ3 and *GA* 2.1:

Λ3: "Nature is a principle 'in itself;' for man generates man;" and
GA 2.1: "The motion of nature is 'in itself' as coming from another
natural things which possesses the form in actuality."

"Man generates man" is Aristotle's reason why nature is the principle "in
itself" (ἐν αὐτῷ). Aristotle also emphasizes this point in *GA* 2.1, explaining
his concept of nature:

> Well then, that which has the same name generated [the other
> entity], for example, man [generated] man. (735a20–21)

In chapter 4.2, I discussed the importance of this formula. Now we need to
understand why; although one thing is generated by another, Aristotle
maintains that nature is the principle "in itself."

5.2.2. *Generation of Animals*

I have now reached a juncture where I shall be turning to the *GA* to solve a
metaphysical problem. From the analysis of the *Metaphysics*, among other
things, we learned the following:

1. Aristotle's argument against the substantial status of artifacts
   is always found in the context of a discussion of coming-to-be
   (which includes all four changes);
2. in Z7, Aristotle identifies substances most of all with things
   that are generated by nature, such as animals and plants; and
3. in Λ3 the distinction between nature and art in terms of the
   principle of coming-to-be covers all four changes.

I am seeking the answer to why artifacts, that is, physical things such
as houses and chairs as opposed to things like health, are not substances.
Thus, as far as the topic of coming-to-be is concerned, I am interested in the
production of these physical objects; that is, the crucial difference between
natural things and artifacts lies in the distinction between the generation of
natural things (animals and plants) and the production of artifacts. But in
the *Metaphysics*, Aristotle does not explain this crucial difference.

However, in *GA* 2.1, we do find the exact formulation of Λ3, where the
distinction between nature and art is restricted to the principle of generation. So if indeed there is a solution to our problem, I can reasonably expect
to find it in the *Generation of Animals*.[52] Let me, therefore, briefly review
Aristotle's account of the generation of animals found in the *GA*.

As regards animals where male and female are found, the male and
the female are principles of generation—the principle of motion and matter,

respectively[53] (1.2, 716a4–7). Although what is generated by nature is formed from the seed, the important thing is how and from where it is generated:

> But we must not forget how this [the semen][54] happens to be generated from the female and the male. For by secretion (τῷ ἀποκρίνεσθαι) this sort of part (τὸ τοιοῦτον μόριον) [is generated] from the female and the male and the secretion (τὴν ἀπόκρισιν) is in them and from them, because of this the male and the female are the principles of generation. (1.2, 716a9–13)

Note the term ἀποκρίνω (to part or to separate). But, although Aristotle refers to semen as a part, what is secreted from the parents are not really their parts. Preus,[55] for example, says that:

> the semen is "simply" a part of the male parent, but it is a very odd sort of part which functions only when separated from the entity of which it is a part.

It is "a very odd sort of part" because it is not really a part. In *GA* 1.18, Aristotle denies that semen is a part (μέρος). It is rather a residue (περίττωμα)[56] (724b23–725a11).

Now although the male's physical secretion (τὴν ἀπόκρισιν) is the semen and the female's is the menstrual fluid, what is actually provided is both the form and the principle of motion by the male, and the body, that is, the matter by the female (1.20, 729a9–11). So what "is passed on (ἀπέρχεται)" (1.21, 729b19) from the male is the form and the principle of movement.

In *GA* 1.22, using a craft analogy, Aristotle explains what the male contributes to generation:

> Just as nothing is passed on (ἀπέρχεται) from the carpenter to the matter of the timber, nor is there any of the parts of the art of carpentry in what comes to be, but the form or shape are produced from him [the carpenter] by means of the motion in the matter. (730b11–14)

If the male provides the form and the principle of movement, then he is "the first which caused the motion from outside (τὸ πρῶτον κινῆσαν ἔξωθεν)" (2.1, 735a12–13) that is responsible for the formation of the embryo, for nothing generates itself, but "whenever it is generated it is then that it makes itself grow" (2.1, 735a13–14). This occurs when the heart is formed, for it is at this point that the separation takes place:

> It is clear that we must posit that semens and fetations which are not yet separate (μήπω χωριστά)[57] possess the nutritive soul potentially, and not actually until, just like the separated (χωριζόμενα) fetations, they draw the nourishment and perform the function of this sort of soul. (736b8–12)

Describing the point at which an embryo becomes a separate entity (that is, when the heart is developed), Aristotle makes an interesting analogy in *GA* 2.4:

> For whenever what comes to be is separated (ἀποκριθῇ) from both [parents] it is necessary that it manage itself just like a son who has settled away from his father. (740a5–7)

It is interesting that in *EN* 5.10, where Aristotle discusses justice, he refers to this analogy:

> A [father's] possession or child (until it reaches the age and becomes *separate* (χωρισθῇ) is just like *a part of himself* (ὥσπερ μέρος αὐτοῦ).[58] (1134b10–11)

What is separated is like a part of the father. It is this analogy that Aristotle evokes when he describes the stage of formation in which an embryo is said to be a separate entity. Furthermore, the fact that the offspring is separated from the parent(s) is stated throughout the *GA*.[59]

So, since the part that is separated from the father is not really a part (for what is secreted is a residue), but since what is passed on is his own form, it is this form that is separated; that is, if the male provides the form and if it is this form that is transmitted or passed on to the offspring, then it is the form that is separated to generate another entity. If that is so, the form of the male is *separable* from him. Thus, the form, understood as the principle of generation, is the principle "in itself," for the same[60] form is passed on from one generation to another.[61]

But there is still a lacuna in my explanation. Aristotle uses the analogy of craft to argue that the male transmits only his form, for what the carpenter transmits to the finished product is the shape or form and not the matter. But if that is so, the form of an artifact is also separable in the very same way. The form is separated from the producer to the product. That means that I have not yet fully grasped the sense of separation that Aristotle appeals to in distinguishing substances from artifacts.

5.2.3. Actuality and Potentiality

Let me review my analysis of the formulation:

> ∧3: "Art is a principle 'in another,' nature is a principle 'in itself;'"
> and
> *GA* 2.1: "Art is a principle and a form of what comes to be, but 'in other;' the motion of nature on the other hand is 'in itself' as coming from another natural thing which possesses the form in actuality."

Concerning the distinction between ἐν ἄλλῳ and ἐν ἑτέρῳ, I began with the working hypothesis that ἐν ἄλλῳ and ἐν ἑτέρῳ mean the same, because Aristotle formulates the definition of potentiality by appealing to both phrases as though they are synonymous. I can assume that they also mean the same in the case of art because there is a close connection between the definitions of potentiality and art. This can be seen clearly in Θ2:

> Therefore, all the arts or the productive sciences are potentialities,
> for they are principles of changeable in another or *qua* another.
> (1046b2–4)

All arts are potentialities because their principles of change exist "in another" or "*qua* another."[62] In contrast, nature, whose principle as defined in *GA* 2.1 is "in itself," is a form in actuality. So the crucial difference between "in another" and "in itself" is that "in another" indicates potentiality and "in itself" indicates actuality.

In chapter 2.1.4, I noted the need to explain why it is clear to Aristotle that the form of an artifact is not separate, except with qualification. We now know that this is so because the principle of art, the form, exists potentially. That is why it exists only with qualification; that is, in the mind of an artisan.[63]

Thus, there are two kinds of principles: actual and potential. Nature is a principle in the former sense and art in the latter. Given that actuality is prior to potentiality in every sense,[64] nature is prior to art in every sense. If priority is a mark of substantiality,[65] it threatens the substantiality of artifacts, for the realization of what is potential is always brought about by what is actual. Hence, art as a principle "in another" indicates its dependence on the existence of another principle that exists in actuality.

Why, then, does Aristotle hesitate to conclude that artifacts are not substances?[66] I suggest in the next chapter that the answer involves a final unresolved issue. Just as the form of a house exists potentially in the mind of an artisan, does not the form of the son also exist potentially in his father? Although the form of the father exists in actuality, in what sense does the form of his son exist in him that is different from the way in which the form of an artifact exists in its maker's mind?

Perhaps the simple distinction between actuality and potentiality is an inadequate tool for distinguishing the ontological status of the form of an artifact and the form of a son, both of which exist potentially in the father and in the artisan, respectively. What we may need is a different sense of potentiality.

Chapter Six

Power

To distinguish the ontological status of the form of an offspring in a male parent from that of the form of an artifact in the mind of an artisan, we need to identify a very specific sense of *dynamis*. I shall argue now that there are two kinds of active *dynamis*: potency (the *dynamis* of the complete form) and power (the *dynamis* of the incomplete form). Nature is a principle "in itself"—that is, it is an active *dynamis* that always exists in actuality, either in the form of potency in the male parent (and its offspring) or in the form of power in semen. Art, in contrast, is a principle "in another"—that is, it is not itself an active *dynamis*, but it is a potentiality that exists in the mind of an artisan. The form, understood as the substance of a natural composite, is this very active *dynamis*, which is neither individual (in the sense of a composite) nor universal (in the sense that it is that which is predicated of the many), but somehow it is both individual and universal (both in a different sense).

6.1. The Problem

Let me first elaborate on the problem by returning to the passage *GA* 2.1, 735a2–4, where Aristotle draws the distinction between nature and art. The passage itself was analyzed in the previous chapter. Now I examine its context.

The relevant distinction between art and nature is made when Aristotle presents a solution to what he considers to be "a rather great problem" (733b23): in what way does that which comes from the seed come to be? First, he identifies the three factors necessary for the analysis of coming to be (733b24–26): "from something (ἔκ τινος)," "by something (ὑπό τινος)," and "something (τι)."[1] By "from something (ἔκ τινος)" he means matter, for example, the menstrual fluid of the female.

Aristotle's problem is with the second factor, "by something"[2] (733b30–31). Either something external to the semen or something that is present in it makes (ποιεῖ) the embryo (τὸ κύημα).[3] What makes something cannot be external to what is made because, in order to make something, what makes something must be in contact with what is made. That something must exist in the semen, and is either a part of the semen or separate (κεχωρισμένον) from it, that is, that which is not a part of it. It cannot be separate from it, because we do not detect any such thing; therefore, it is a part of the semen. Now the parts of an embryo are made either simultaneously or successively. But a simultaneous formation of the parts of an embryo is impossible, because there is no evidence for it; rather, observations confirm that an embryo is made successively. Thus A must make B and B in turn must make C. But since that which makes another must possess the form in actuality, A must contain the form of B, for example, in the heart there will be the form of liver, if the heart is made first. But this is absurd. The alternative—that all parts must preexist as actualities in the semen from the outset—is also absurd. Hence, no part can exist in the semen. Therefore, it seems that what makes the embryo cannot be either external or internal to the embryo. But it has to be one or the other (733b32–734b4).

To resolve the dilemma, Aristotle makes a qualification. In one sense it is impossible for the parts to be made externally but in another sense it is possible. In his argument, he begins with the assumption that as far as the causal analysis of the formation of an embryo is concerned, there is no difference between the male and the semen. What is important is the actual motion itself (734b7–9). A moves B and B in turn moves C and so on. He compares the process with miraculous automatons.[4] Once the external mover sets the automaton going, the automaton moves itself. The external mover need not always be in contact for motion to continue; what is needed is only that "at one time it has been in contact with it (ἀψάμενον)." So what is transmitted from the original mover is a motion that in its turn can be transmitted to another motion until it reaches the final form. Aristotle thus concludes:

> So it is clear that there is something which makes [the successive parts of the embryo], but not in the way in which it is a "this" (τόδε τι), nor in the way in which it is present [in the semen] as that which has been completed at the beginning. (734b17–19)

How does Aristotle justify this move? How is it possible for what is not a "this" or the thing that does not possess the complete form in actuality to be able to act as an agent? How is it possible to claim that there is no difference between the male and the sperm, as far as an agent is concerned?

The answers to these questions can be found in the next part of Aristotle's explanation where he appeals to the distinction between actuality and potentiality to explain how each part is made. In nature or in art, a thing is always made *by* something that is in actuality *from* something that exists potentially. In the case of nature, the motion is originated by the male parent, who exists in actuality, and it is this motion that is responsible for the generation of an offspring by acting on the material (that exists as potentiality). Each of the parts is completed when the respective motion that makes them ceases, for example, the motion that makes the heart ceases when the heart is completely formed, while the motion that is responsible for the formation of liver keeps going until it makes the liver, and so on until all the parts are made. And when the respective motion ceases, each part becomes actually ensouled (ἔμψυχον), for that which is potentially a face or flesh is only so equivocally; that is, the semen possesses each part of the soul potentially. And it is possible for the motion of the semen to make the successive parts of the embryo, that is, to possess the soul of each part, because a thing can be a *dynamis* in different degrees:

> And it is possible for one thing to exist potentially by being nearer to that which it is capable of being or further from it (just as a sleeping geometer is further away from [the one who is exercising that knowledge] than the one who is awake, and the latter is further away from [it] than the one who is [actually] exercising that knowledge). (735a9–11)

The key to the problem comes down to the understanding of the relevant sense of *dynamis*.[5] It is puzzling that Aristotle believes he has really solved the problem. How can the fact that "a thing which exists potentially can be nearer to that which it is capable of being or farther removed from it" explain the successive formations of each part? Aristotle does not clarify what he means; however, he appeals to the analogy of the different levels of a knower (sleeping/waking/exercising levels) as if it were self-explanatory.

The real problem is that Aristotle does not explain this concept of *dynamis*. As a result, Cherniss,[6] for example, complains that such a *dynamis* "is obviously not the actuality of the form and yet not the potentiality of form either," but it is "a *power of producing*" (his emphasis). But then "it is only by equivocation of δύναμις that Aristotle can pass from what the sperm is *potentially* to its supposed *power* to produce that thing" (his emphasis). And "Aristotle does not attempt to say, of course, what this power or action may be which is intermediate between the actualized form which produces it and the matter which it actualizes" (473 (footnote 423)).

To appreciate Cherniss's criticism and why Aristotle finds this problem rather great, let me examine Aristotle's account in more detail. A problem with Aristotle's embryology is that he needs to explain the development of an embryo within the framework of his analysis of efficient causality. The two crucial assumptions that he himself identifies in the *GA* are: in order to move an object, the mover must be in contact with it (734a3–4); and only that which exists in actuality can realize that which exists potentially (734a30–31). These assumptions represent the fundamental principles of Aristotle's efficient causality, based on his definition of motion/change. Let me, therefore, briefly review Aristotle's concept of motion/change; it is found in *Phys* 3.1–3.

Aristotle defines motion[7] as "the actuality of the potentially existing *qua* such [that is, *qua* existing potentially]" (201a10–11). Motion is thus understood in terms of what is actual and what is potential. But it is not possible for the same thing to be actual and potential with respect to the same thing at the same time. For example, it is impossible for what is actually hot to be potentially hot or vice versa. What is actually hot is always different from what is potentially hot. Hence, in order for a thing that is potentially hot to become actually hot, given that the moved is moved by the mover, this qualitative change requires another thing—the mover—which is actually hot to act upon the moved. Even in the case where qualitative change occurs only within a single thing, one part, which is actually hot, acts upon the other part, which is potentially hot.[8]

Aristotle insists that motion "is the actuality of that which exists potentially when being in actuality it is actual not *qua* itself but *qua* movable" (201a27–29). Note the phrase—not *qua* itself but *qua* movable. He explains the meaning of *qua* by the following example. Although bronze is potentially a statue, it is not *qua* bronze that its actuality is a motion, because to be a bronze and to be movable are not the same thing, otherwise "the actuality of bronze *qua* bronze would be a motion" (201a33–34). But, as with bronze, it is always the case that what admits of motion and being a motion differ. No motion can be an actuality of the thing *qua* itself, but it is always *qua* movable.

Having emphasized in *Phys* 3.2 that the mover and the moved must be in *contact* (202a3–12), Aristotle explains in *Phys* 3.3 how the mover and the moved are related. Motion, which is caused by the mover, is the actuality of the moved. Motion occurs in the moved; that is, the mover and the moved are related by having one and the same actuality between them (202a13–14). This actuality is one and the same "not in the way that they are same by being (τῷ εἶναι) [what they are], but in the way that what exists potentially is related to what exists actually" (202b9–10). For example, although what it is to teach and what it is to learn differ, they are the very same process regarded from different perspectives, just as the road from Thebes to Athens and from Athens to Thebes is the same road regarded from two opposite directions. Without equating what it is to be (τῷ εἶναι) a mover and a moved, Aristotle explains how their actuality is one and the same. If the actuality of a mover is the same as the actuality of a moved, then the mover and the moved always occur together.[9] It is impossible to have one without the other;[10] such is Aristotle's analysis of efficient causality.

By being in contact, the mover and the moved (understood as the cause and the effect, respectively) exist simultaneously.

In Θ, Aristotle describes this doctrine in terms of two kinds of potencies:[11] the active potency (ἡ δύναμις τοῦ ποιεῖν) and the passive potency (ἡ δύναμις τοῦ πασχεῖν).[12] Although these potencies are distinct, they are in a way one (1046a19), for it is when the agent (τὸ ποιητικόν) and the patient (τὸ παθητικόν) are present that one acts and the other is acted upon (1048a6–7). Their potencies are realized when both are present. This is because the actuality of the active potency is also in the thing that is being acted upon. There is only one actuality for both. For example, "an art of building is the thing which is being built, and it comes to be and exists *at the same time* (ἅμα) in the house" (1050a28–29); that is, both active and passive potencies are realized in the patient simultaneously.[13]

Given his theoretical framework, we should expect Aristotle to defend the simultaneous, rather than the successive, formation of an embryo,[14] for the cause and the effect always occur at the same time; the actuality of the cause and the effect (or the active and passive potencies) is simultaneous. A successive or a temporal causal analysis undermines the theory. What is actual, which acts on what is potential, has the complete form. The active *dynamis* exists only in the complete form; if a form is incomplete, then its potentiality is realized by something other than itself that has the complete form, and they both must be in contact until what is potential is fully realized. So the father, who has the complete form, must always be acting on what is potential (that is, it must be always in contact with what is moved) until the moved has attained its end. If the father is in contact with the material only at copulation, then you would expect that the complete form should have been realized at that point. Otherwise, Aristotle needs to posit the active *dynamis* of an incomplete form (which on the surface seems to contradict his traditional account of efficient causality). I show how Aristotle makes this move and justifies his account.

Now Aristotle makes a move to defend the developmental thesis (to explain how the process from incomplete to complete is possible without there being what is complete), even at the cost of modifying his theory. His reason is this: "and [this] is obvious to sense-perception (καὶ τῇ αἰσθήσει ἐστὶ φανερόν)" (734a21). Aristotle actually made a careful study of the development of fertilized eggs by opening them at different times[15] and observing that the parts of an embryo are formed successively. He bases his theory on observations; he is unwilling to impose a theory on observations dogmatically. He is willing to modify the theory, if necessary, even to throw it away, if it does not conform to the evidence.[16]

Aristotle deserves our admiration, rather than harsh criticism, for his intellectual honesty. If in the *GA* he was in the process of modifying his old theory, we should try as much as possible to make intelligible the new concept of *dynamis* that he sought to develop.

6.1.1. A New Principle

Let us make sure that we understand the gravity of the situation. Aristotle's old theoretical framework fails to account for the phenomena. That is why Cherniss criticizes Aristotle for appealing to the new unexplained principle. That is why Aristotle finds the development of an embryo a greater problem. He *needs* to introduce a new theoretical framework to explain the phenomena. The crucial point is that this new theoretical framework has *grave* ramifications for his metaphysics.

Although this new theoretical framework is primarily for a physical science, because of Aristotle's methodology in his metaphysical enquiry (i.e., an investigation that *begins* with an examination of physical substances because they are more knowable to us),[17] once he introduces a new principle within his physical sciences, this introduction has a great impact on his metaphysics. This is especially so when this principle holds the key to determining the *substantial* status of natural beings and artifacts.

Let me now go back to the problem, raised in chapter 2.1.4, of Aristotle's hesitation to conclude that an artifact is not a substance, even though it is clear to him that the form of an artifact is not separate. In the *Metaphysics* there are hints, suggestions, and insinuations that he was troubled by the ontological status of artifacts. He seems to have not made up his mind whether to call artifacts substances or not, although he is *certain* of the fact that their forms are not separate.

"Perhaps ('ίσως)" (1043b21) I can suggest a reason for the hesitation, "if indeed (εἴπερ)" (1070a17) I have correctly identified the problem of Aristotle's embryology. In the *Metaphysics*, Aristotle does not explain *how* the form is transmitted from one generation to another. He simply uses the analogy with the production of artifacts to account for the generation of animals.[18] But Aristotle complains that Platonists do not explain *how* the generation of destructible beings is possible.[19] According to Aristotle, Platonists did not believe that the Forms of artifacts exist. If Aristotle agrees with them that artifacts are not substances in some sense of the word, then he must[20] explain precisely how the production of artifacts differs from the generation of animals and that, as a consequence, artifacts either are excluded from the status of substantiality or are at least substances with qualification. If an explanation presupposes an adequate theory of the generation of animals, he can do nothing until he has come up with such a theory.

We should also note that, even though art is a principle that is a potentiality (and hence cannot be separate),[21] Aristotle needs to explain how the potential existence of the form of an offspring is separate from the male parent. If explaining this requires a modification of his fundamental theoretical framework (especially, by introducing a principle of *dynamis* not found in the *Metaphysics*),[22] then we can see why Aristotle cannot confidently determine the ontological status of artifacts until he has established this new theory. In other words, his old theory is inadequate to determine the *ontological* status of artifacts. He needs a new principle; this is found in the *GA*.

It is instructive that a number of scholars[23] have observed that Aristotle's theory of reproduction in Θ7 is different from that of the *GA*. In Θ7, Aristotle argues that regardless of whether the principle of coming-to-be is external (ἔξωθεν) (1049a12) or internal (ἐν αὐτῷ τῷ ἔχοντι) (a13), a thing is potentially something when there is no need for addition (προσγενέσθαι) or subtraction (ἀπογενέσθαι) or change (μεταβαλεῖν) (a10–11):

> For example, the semen is not yet [potentially a man] (for it must [be placed] in another and change), but whenever at that time through its own principle it is such a thing, then it is potentially [a man]; but [before] that it needs another principle, just like the earth which is not yet a statue (for it [must] change to be bronze). (1049a14–18)

First of all, in the doctrine found in the *GA*, the comparison of the semen with the matter (1049a10) and the earth is inappropriate, for semen supplies only form and no matter; hence, the change that the semen brings about is not comparable to the kind of change that the matter and the earth undergo (but perhaps the change the menstrual fluid undergoes is).

Secondly, the distinction between the external and the internal principle of change *per se* is inadequate to account for the formation of an embryo. As a matter of fact, in *GA* 2.1 as we have seen,[24] Aristotle begins with his old embryology as a starting point for solving the greater problem.

It is not surprising that although the topic of Θ is *dynamis* itself, we cannot discover the sense of *dynamis*[25] sought, for it is closely associated with Aristotle's new concept of embryology in the *GA*. Thus, although Aristotle realizes in the *Metaphysics* that there is something fundamentally different about artifacts and that therefore they do not deserve the title of substances, he does not fully grasp what is required of him. He needs to revise his old theoretical framework to determine the fundamental difference. It is in the *GA* that we find this new sense of *dynamis*—a new principle.

6.2. Self-realization

In the first part of this section, I shall describe the new theoretical framework. In the second part, we shall see how we can understand Aristotle's embryology within this new framework.

6.2.1. The New Theoretical Framework

Cherniss, as we saw in the previous section, reproaches Aristotle for equivocation on *dynamis* in the *GA*. Let us see whether this accusation is justified.

Aristotle himself identifies two senses of *dynamis* in *GA* 1.19 when he defends the view that semen has "a great *dynamis*" (726b11–12):

Semen is potentially these sorts of things, either according to its own bulk or it has a certain *dynamis* in itself. (726b17–19)

He offers these two alternatives because he says that it is not yet clear whether it is "the body" of the semen or the fact that "it has a certain disposition and a principle of motion (ἔχει τινὰ ἕξιν καὶ ἀρχὴν κινήσεως)" that is the cause of generation.

In *GA* 1.21, Aristotle opts for the latter solution. Because the male contributes only the form and the principle of motion and not its own matter,[26] the semen is *dynamis* in the second sense. This second sense of *dynamis* is described as that which is associated neither with the body nor with "the quantity (τὸ ποσόν)" but, rather, with "the quality (τὸ ποιόν)"[27] (730a21–23). Here, Aristotle does not equivocate but determines the sense in which he is using the term *dynamis*.

It is by means of this *dynamis* present in semen, the *dynamis* provided by the male parent, that the semen can produce the parts of embryos successively (727b15–16; 739a17–18).[28] But the question remains: what kind of *dynamis* is it? Although it is not the *dynamis* that is associated with the matter, it cannot be the one that is associated with the form *per se*, because there is no such form in the semen. Such a form only exists in the male parent.

To answer this question, let me refer to the *De Anima*, for it is not only in the *GA* but also in the *De Anima* that the required sense of *dynamis* is explained. The *GA* passage is this:

And it is possible for one thing to exist potentially by being nearer (ἐγγυτέρω) to that which it is capable of being or further from (πορρωτέρω) it (just as a sleeping geometer is further away from (πορρωτέρω) [the one who is exercising that knowledge] than the one who is awake, and the latter [is further away from it than] the one who is [actually] exercising that knowledge (τοῦ θεωροῦντος). (735a9–11)

In *GA* 4.3,[29] by *dynamis* Aristotle is referring to such things as male, a kind of male, and a genus. It is in this sense that "some things are nearer to (ἐγγύτερον) or further from (πορρώτερον) that which generates (τῷ γεννῶντι), by virtue of being a generator" (767b26–28). For example, although Coriscus is both a man and an animal, man is closer to his own property (ἐγγύτερον τοῦ ἰδίου) (b31–32) than animal. If the degree of *dynamis* is understood in terms of the different levels of universals, and if the semen is nearer or further away from that which it is capable of being, then the direction in which an embryo develops is from universal to individual.[30] Aristotle himself draws an analogy to painting; nature is like painters because they "having sketched in [the figure] of an animal in outline in this way apply the colour" (743b23–25); similarly, an embryo first attains general characteristics, such as animality, and then progressively its specific properties.[31]

Another puzzle is the significance of the sleeping geometer. Does this illuminate the required sense of *dynamis*? To answer this question we may now turn to the *De Anima*, for here Aristotle uses the same analogy.[32]

In *De An* 2.1, while defining soul, Aristotle identifies two different senses of actuality:

> But this [actuality (ἐντελέχεια)] is said in two senses, as in the case of knowledge (ἐπιστήμη) and as in the case of exercising knowledge (τὸ θεωρεῖν). But it is clear that [the soul] is [an actuality] as in the case of knowledge, for sleep and wakefulness belong to the soul, and just as the latter is analogous to exercising knowledge, the former is analogous to the one who has knowledge but is not exercising it (τὸ ἔχειν καὶ μὴ ἐνεργεῖν). (412a22–27)

Analogically speaking, the two senses of actuality are these: sleep: the possessing but not exercising of knowledge (τὸ ἔχειν καὶ μὴ ἐνεργεῖν); and wakefulness: the exercising of knowledge (τὸ θεωρεῖν).

In *De An* 2.5, Aristotle uses this analogy to identify different senses of *dynamis*:

> For it is in this that way one is said to be knowledgeable (ἐπιστήμον) as we would say a man is knowledgeable, because man belongs to the class of knowledgeable being and has knowledge, but we also say this because the one already has acquired knowledge, such as grammatical [knowledge]. But it is not in the same way that each of them is δυνατός, but the former is so because he belongs to this sort of genus and the matter, and the latter because having wished he is able to exercise knowledge (δυνατὸς θεωρεῖν), if nothing external prevents him (417a22–28).

In contrast to the one who is actually exercising knowledge (ὁ ἤδη θεωρῶν) (417a28–30), the one who is able to exercise knowledge (δυνατὸς θεωρεῖν) is said to have a kind of *dynamis*. But there is an overlap. The one who has the knowledge but is not exercising it (τὸ ἔχειν καὶ μὴ ἐνεργεῖν) is equivalent to the one who is able to exercise knowledge (δυνατὸς θεωρεῖν). Therefore, the same thing is considered both as a kind of actuality and a kind of *dynamis*.[33] How should we understand this hybrid?

In *De An* 3.4, Aristotle describes it as follows:

> And whenever in this way [the intellect] becomes each thing in the sense in which the knower (ὁ ἐπιστήμων) is said to be so in actuality (ὁ κατ' ἐνέργειαν) (and this occurs when he is able to realize [the knowledge] by himself (δύναται ἐνεργεῖν δι' αὐτοῦ)), even then [such a thing] exists somehow potentially (ἔστι μὲν καὶ τότε δυνάμει πως), although not in the same way as prior to learning or discovering it. (429b5–9)

Here, Aristotle introduces a kind of actuality that exists somehow potentially (δυνάμει πως). And the mark of this kind of actuality is that an agent is able to realize [its own potentiality] by itself (δύναται ἐνεργεῖν δι' αὐτοῦ). Let me call it an ability for self-realization.

Let me clarify my terms. By "internal-change," I mean the natural change that the things that exist by nature undergo, such as qualitative and quantitative changes and locomotion. In *Phys* 2.1, Aristotle lists animals, their parts, plants, and elements as having the principle of internal-change.[34] By "self-motion," I mean the locomotion of animals.[35] The mark of self-motion is that an agent has the ability to cause both motion and standstill;[36] that is, an agent can *initiate* motion.[37]

If we turn to *Phys* 8.4, there is evidence that self-realization is not an instance of self-motion, for Aristotle denies[38] that elements[39] are self-movers. Thus, if the upward movement of fire were an instance of self-motion, fire would also be able to move downward. Hence it cannot initiate its own movement; it cannot move away from its own appropriate place, but once it has been displaced from the appropriate place by force, it is able to realize its own potentiality to move back toward its own appropriate place, if it is not impeded.

How can we account for such motion? Aristotle analyzes the natural motion of the elements by distinguishing different senses of *dynamis*,[40] using the same analogy of the different levels of a knower that we met in the *De An* and the *GA*. In other words, Aristotle seems to be appealing to the doctrine of self-realization to account for elemental motion.[41]

Aristotle's principle of self-realization does not conflict with his traditional analysis of efficient causality.[42] In his traditional analysis of efficient causality, it is always what is actual that causes the realization of the potentiality in another being. For example, it is a teacher who, actually possessing knowledge, acts on a student to realize the student's potentiality as a knower. In the case of self-realization, having once learned the knowledge, the student can now realize this potentiality on his own, although he may not always be exercising his knowledge. So if my analysis of *De Anima* and *Phys* 8[43] is correct, then Aristotle introduces the principle of self-realization by distinguishing the different senses of *dynamis*; he recognizes that there is a kind of *dynamis* that no longer needs another actuality to realize its potentiality. It can do so on its own, for it is also a kind of actuality; that is, a being, although incomplete, exists in actuality such that it can realize its own potentiality to attain its completion. Let me refer to this kind of *dynamis*[44] that can realize its own potentiality as power.[45]

6.2.2. Aristotle's Embryology

Let us now see how Aristotle applies the new theoretical framework in the *GA* to account for his embryology. First, in the *De An* Aristotle identifies soul as first actuality, which, as we saw, can also be considered as the second *dynamis*—that is, potency.[46] That means it is a potency or a set of potencies,[47] given that there is more than one potency. Second, we saw that as for the semen (τὸ σπέρμα) and that from which the semen comes (ἀφ' οὗ τὸ σπέρμα), there is no difference "insofar as [the semen] has the motion in itself which *the latter caused* (ᾗ ἔχει τὴν κίνησιν ἐν ἑαυτῷ ἣν ἐκεῖνο ἐκίνει)." (734b8–9)

The motion is originally caused by the male parent, for the semen is produced by the male parent.[48] In this way (just as in *Phys* 8) Aristotle is able to maintain his fundamental view of efficient causality; it is always the form that exists in actuality that is ultimately responsible for the motion.[49] The difference between the male parent and the semen is this: while the male parent is able to *initiate* the motion (by means of its potency), the semen can only *maintain* it (that is, to realize its own potentiality) once the semen has been "in contact (ἁψάμενον)" (734b15) with that actuality that caused that motion[50] (by means of its power). But the semen itself cannot initiate any motion, for it does not have a form in actuality.

If it is in this motion that there is the power to develop an embryo, then the potency that exists in the male parent has been transmitted to the form of the motion of the semen as power; that is, this very *dynamis* (potency) also exists in the semen itself as power. In chapter 5.2.2, I showed that the male provides the form that is transmitted or passed on to the offspring. In this way, the form of the male is separable from him. Hence, the form is the principle in itself, because the same form is passed on from one generation to another. This would mean that it is *the same dynamis* that is passed on from the male parent to the offspring.[51] The *GA* confirms this.

In *GA* 2.4, where Aristotle again draws a distinction between art and nature, he criticizes Democritus and those who believe that the external parts of an embryo are formed prior to the internal ones. Living things are not formed like the carvings of wood or stone, for the carvings do not possess any first principle. But all animals and plants have the internal principle, that is, a heart or something analogous to it, which is formed first. By means of this first principle, they form the subsequent parts. It is at this point that an animal takes nourishment on its own provided by its mother (739b33–740a24).

However, there is a problem. If blood is the nourishment that comes from outside (e.g., in the uterus from the mother), from where did the first nourishment, that is blood, enter the embryo prior to the formation of the heart, when the heart already contains blood at the time of its formation? The answer is that the residue (τὸ περίττωμα) of the female provides the nourishment from the outset (740b7–8). That means that the residue is both the matter that will be formed to generate the offspring and the matter that provides the original nourishment.

Having established this point, Aristotle again turns to the formation of the parts of the embryo. He argues that it is not because "like makes its way to like" that the parts are formed, but because the female provides the residue that "is potentially the sort of thing such that it is an animal by nature (δυνάμει τοιοῦτόν ἐστιν οἷον φύσει τὸ ζῷον)" (740b19–20) and this potentiality is realized when the active factor (the principle of motion), which is provided by the male, is present.

It is in this context that Aristotle compares and contrasts art and nature:

> Just as the things that come to be by art do so by means of instruments, or it is more true to say by means of their motion, and this motion is the activity of the art (but art is the form of the thing that comes to be in another) the power (δύναμις) of the nutritive soul behaves in the same way. And just as also in the case of these animals and plants, by using hot and cold (for in these the motion of power resides) like instruments, they *later* themselves grow from the nourishment, in the same way the thing that is generated by nature is formed from the *beginning*, for the matter by which an entity grows and from which it is *first* formed are the same. Consequently, the active power (ἡ ποιοῦσα δύναμις) is also the same. (740b25–35)

Three things are being compared: art, the power of the nutritive soul, and the matter. Why does Aristotle not simply compare the production of art and the generation of animals as before? What crucial information is provided in the analogy with the matter?

We saw that Aristotle asks where the first nourishment comes from prior to the formation of the heart. His response is that it is originally derived from the residue. This is the notion that Aristotle appeals to in the comparison between matter and power.[52]

Aristotle first compares art and the power of the nutritive soul: both employ the motion in the instrument to accomplish their task. Having established that similarity, he then points out that, in the same way the matter is provided by the female, the power of the nutritive soul forms the things that are generated from the beginning. Note the *temporal* emphasis. The power of the nutritive soul in animals nourishes them *later*, but at the *beginning* it forms them. The analogy is this: just as the matter by which an embryo grows and from which it is formed is the same, the active power by means of which it grows and from which it is formed is the same. If this same active power exists both prior to and after the formation of heart, the nutritive soul also generates the entity. What is passed on from the male to the offspring is this *dynamis*.[53]

Aristotle distinguishes art and nature by the manner in which they are formed: art lacks the first principle of formation that nature possesses. But his distinction can be made only after the formation of the first principle, the heart, or what is analogous to the heart. Prior to the formation of the heart, that is, when the first principle is absent, what is the difference between art and nature?

The answer is that since the power that makes an entity grows after its formation of the heart is the very same power that forms the heart itself, and since this *dynamis* (power) in the semen is the same *dynamis* (potency) that exists in the male parent, it is this principle, understood both as potency and power, that is always operative in the generation of animals. The same *dynamis* is always in *actuality*!

But what does the same *dynamis* mean? Let me now turn to the crux of our problem: to the notorious Aristotelian dilemma.

6.3. Individual or Universal?

In chapter 4.3, we were faced with the dilemma: is the form, understood as the substance of a composite, individual or universal? In *De An* 2.4,[54] each destructible substance partakes of the eternal and the divine not as one in number but as one in form. In I1,[55] one in number is understood as individual and one in form as universal. This distinction between individual and universal (or one in number and one in form, respectively)[56] is problematic, because a substance is somehow an eternal actuality. Hence, we were faced with the following dilemma: if the form of a composite is individual, then it cannot be eternal, because it will be destroyed when the composite perishes; but if it is universal, then it cannot be in actuality because it is potentiality. Therefore, the form cannot be an eternal actuality.

Since Aristotle denies that which partakes of the eternal is one in number, our problem stems from the other horn of the dilemma: to explain how it is possible for what is one in form to be an eternal actuality.

This dilemma can be posed analogically as follows: is the form, understood as the substance of a composite, separate without qualification (one in number) or separate in formula (one in form)? I have argued that the form of a natural substance can be separate in another sense.[57] The form is separable in the way that it *can* be transmitted from one generation to another. It is neither separate without qualification (as in the way in which an *individual* composite is) nor separate in formula in the way in which the form exists (as *universal*) in the mind of a person. Therefore, the form (which is separate in the third sense) is neither individual nor universal. Let us now retrace my argument to see how this third sense of separation can be understood as one in form.

In chapter 5.2, we saw that Aristotle distinguishes art and nature as a principle "in another" and a principle "in itself," respectively. This very distinction is somehow applicable also to the principle of generation. Although nothing generates itself, that is, although the principle is external and comes from another, the principle of natural generation, unlike the principle of artificial production, is somehow understood not as "in another" but as "in itself." My analysis of the *GA* showed[58] that the part that is separated from the father is his own form; that is, the father provides the form that is transmitted or passed on to the offspring. In this way, I explained that the form is separable. The form, understood as the principle of generation, is the principle in itself, because the same form is passed on from one generation to another. The problem, however, is to explain what is meant by the same form. Let me take three examples to illustrate my quandary.

(1) Suppose there are two amoebae, A and B. By means of fission, they reproduce their offspring: A' and B', respectively. We have now four amoebae. Each amoeba is one in number, and all four amoebae have the same form in the sense that they are one in formula. Yet, amoebae A and A' share the same form, which is different from what amoebae B and B' share. But in what sense?

(2) Suppose there are two relay teams, each consisting of four members. One team has a red baton, the other, blue. What is peculiar about this race is that instead of a baton being passed on from one runner to another, it is being replicated. When a runner touches another teammate, a new baton is created, and all the runners keep their own baton. So, although we began with two batons, at the end of the race, there are eight batons, four red and four blue. Each baton is one in number and all eight batons are one in form in the sense that they are one in formula. Yet, red batons somehow share the same form, which is different from the form of blue batons. But in what sense?

(3) Suppose there are two fathers, each with two sons. Each man is one in number and all six men have the same form in the sense that they are

one in formula. Yet, one set of brothers shares the same form not only with each other but also with its father, which is different from what the other set of brothers shares with each other and its father. But in what sense?

Forms that are duplicated, replicated, or copied are somehow closely related. In Aristotle's embryology, the crucial stage of replication of forms occurs when the semen is concocted.[59] There is no difference, Aristotle insists, between the semen and that from which the semen comes (ἀφ' οὗ τὸ σπέρμα) "insofar as [the semen] has the motion in itself which the later caused" (734b8–9). I understand this to mean that in the motion of the semen there is the power to develop an embryo. This is the *dynamis* that has been transmitted from the father to the semen. Hence I concluded that the same form that is passed on from one generation to another is *the same dynamis*. What does this mean? To answer this question we can now turn to *GA* 4.1–3.

In *GA* 4.1, Aristotle distinguishes male by a certain potency and female by a lack of potency (765b8–9). The male has the potency to concoct semen to transmit its form and the principle of motion. Given that *dynamis* and lack of *dynamis* are opposites, when the agent does not master the material toward a certain end (or form) that it is working on, then it must turn into the opposite condition (766a18–21). Successful generation occurs when the semen, or the motion of the male, makes the shape according to its own form (καθ' αὑτὴν ποιήσει τὴν μορφὴν ἡ τοῦ ἄρρενος κίνησις) (767b17–18). Any offspring that does not take after the male parent is in a way a monstrosity (767b6). The first deviation is to produce female instead of male offspring; a female is generated when the semen fails to transmit its own form to the offspring. Since male and female are distinguished in terms of potency, and since what the male transmits to the offspring is *dynamis*, then to the extent that it fails to do so, the offspring is deficient with respect to that *dynamis* (767b20–23).

In this context, such *dynamis* (that is, power) is defined by Aristotle as follows: male, a kind of male, and a genus[60] (767b24–26). They all exert influence on the formation of an embryo, but in a different degree, for what is peculiar and individual (τὸ ἴδιον καὶ τὸ καθ' ἕκαστον) always exerts (ἰσχύει) *more* (μᾶλλον) influence (767b29–30). But this means that genus also exerts some influence:

Now both the individual (τὸ καθ' ἕκαστον) and the genus (τὸ γένος) generate [what comes to be], but especially the individual, for this is the substance (ἡ οὐσία). In fact, what comes to be comes to be on the one hand as a certain quality (ποιόν τι), but on the other hand as "a this" (τόδε τι)—and this is the substance (ἡ οὐσία). (767b32–35)

It is from the powers of these (the individual and the genus) that the motions exist in the semen (767b35–36). And these powers exist as actualities:

> Some of the motions exist in actuality, while others potentially; *the motions* of the generator and *of universals* (τῶν καθόλου), such as man or animal, *exist actually*, but those of the female and of the ancestors exist potentially. (768a11–14)

Both individual and universals, such as man and animal (more than one universal), exist in the form of motions as actualities in the semen. That is why there is no difference between the father and his semen because all the essential[61] properties of the father (both individual and universal ones) exist in the semen in the form of powers, which exert influence on the menstrual fluid to produce an offspring. The father has the potency to duplicate all his essential forms (both individual and universal) as powers that exist in the movement of the semen. In this way, the same *dynamis* is transmitted from one generation (in the form of potency) to another (in the form of power that eventually becomes potency for the most part).[62]

6.3.1. Nutrition and Generation

Let us now return to the crucial passage of *De An* 2.4 and its context to confirm some of our findings:

> For the most natural function in living things, as many of those that are complete and not defective or are generated by chance, is to produce another like itself (ἕτερον οἷον αὐτό), on the one hand an animal [produces] an animal, and on the other hand a plant [produces] a plant, ... So since each [living thing] is unable to share continuously in the eternal and the divine, because it is not possible for [each] of the destructible things to preserve itself one and the same in number, insofar as each is able to partake of them, some share in these more and others less, but each [thing] does not preserve itself but [something] like it (οὐκ αὐτὸ ἀλλ' οἷον αὐτό), one not in number, but one in form (ἀριθμῷ μὲν οὐχ ἕν, εἴδει δ' ἕν). (415a26–b7)

What is one in form is the generator and something like itself (οἷον αὐτό).[63] This comparison is made in the context where Aristotle explains the two functions of the nutritive soul: "to generate and to use food" (415a26), for "the same *dynamis* of the soul is nutritive and generative (ἡ αὐτὴ δύναμις τῆς ψυχῆς θρεπτικὴ καὶ γεννητική)" (416a19).

As a nutritive *dynamis*, the function of nutritive soul is to digest nourishment. Insofar as it is undigested contrary is nourished by contrary (τὸ ἐναντίον τῷ ἐναντίῳ τρέφεται), but when it is digested like by like (τὸ ὅμοιον τῷ ὁμοίῳ) (416b6–7); that is, the nutritive soul transforms what is contrary to the thing nourish to what is like it. And this very *same* nourishment is also used in generation, for semen is a residue of the useful nourishment.[64]

In *GA*, Aristotle identifies blood (or what is analogous to it) as the ultimate nourishment (726b1–2)[65] because it is distributed to the various parts of the body.[66] What is concocted from the ultimate nourishment is the semen.[67] That is why the offspring come to resemble the generators (τὸ ὅμοια γίγνεσθαι τὰ ἔκγονα τοῖς γεννήσασιν)" (726b13–14),[68] for "what is carried to the parts resemble what is left over" (726b14–15), just as the paint left over on a pallet resembles what is used in a painting (725a25–27). Accordingly, the semen has a great *dynamis* (μεγάλην δύναμιν) (726b11–12) because all the parts exist in it, just like the blood[69] (or what is analogous to it).[70]

So, destructible entities partake of the eternal and the divine by means of the two functions of the nutritive soul: nutrition and generation. By means of nutrition, the individual animal is preserved, and by means of reproduction, its species continues to exist by the transmission of this very *dynamis* to another entity.[71] The replication of forms is possible in the form of *dynamis* because it is the same *dynamis* of the nutritive soul that is responsible for both preserving the individual animal and generating its offspring.

The eternal actuality exists as a *dynamis* in the male parent (whether as a principle of nutrition or generation) as the motion in the semen and as the first principle of growth in the offspring. In contrast, in the case of the production of artifacts, there is no such transmission of active *dynamis*. The form in the mind of an artisan exists potentially, and it is brought to actuality by an artisan only when an artifact is made.

Thus, the ontological status of the form of an artifact exists both as a potentiality (when it is in the mind of an artisan) and as an actuality (when an artifact is produced); however, the ontological status of the form of a natural entity always exists as an actuality, in the form of active *dynamis*, regardless of whether an entity is an adult male, semen, or a young male offspring.[72]

It is by means of the different senses of *dynamis*[73] that we can clearly differentiate the two principles: nature and art. While art is a principle that exists potentially in the mind of an artisan, nature is a principle, understood as an active *dynamis* (both in the sense of potency and power), that *always* exists in actuality, passing from the male parent, *via* semen, to the offspring.

We need not, therefore, assume that one in form always indicates universal. It can also mean the same *dynamis*. Thus, what partakes of the eternal, that is, the form understood as *dynamis*, is neither one in number (understood as individual) nor one in form (understood as universal).

We may, however, ask what is *dynamis* (both in the sense of potency and power), which is neither individual nor universal? Is it neither because it is both individual and universal or is it neither because it is a different kind of thing all together? And if it is a third thing, what is it? I have no definitive answer to these questions. However we may construe this third option, it is somehow a combination of individual and universal (both in a different sense). It is not an individual in the sense that it is a composite of form and matter; rather it is individual in the sense that the form, when it attains its completeness as an individual adult composite, has the *dynamis* to perpetuate its form (a monstrosity, whose form lacks such *dynamis* is called the universal most of all).[74] It is not a universal in the sense that it is predicated of many; rather it is universal in the sense that the same *dynamis* is shared by one's families and ancestors (and of course that is why family resemblances exist).[75] Perhaps Cooper (1988) is right in believing that the decision "whether Aristotelian forms are individual entities or in effect some sort of universals will have to be made on other grounds," (38) that is, other than "Aristotle's clear commitment in the *GA*" (38).

Nevertheless, as far as my topic is concerned, the discovery of power, which is somehow both potential and actual, is sufficient to solve the dilemma as *I have formulated it*, for I am interested only in explaining *how* a natural substance can be an eternal actuality such that we can distinguish it from an artifact.

The form, understood as *dynamis*, is neither individual nor universal. Thus, although an individual such as Socrates is destructible, there is a potency in him that *may*[76] partake of the eternal by transmitting itself (by duplicating or by making a copy of itself) to the next generation in the form of power. The form of a substance, therefore, is always in actuality: in the complete form of an adult, in the movement of the semen as a power, and as a principle of growth in the embryo, once the heart is formed. They are one in form in the sense that the same active *dynamis* is passed on from one generation to another.

Hence, I have explained how the form of a natural substance can be separ*able* in a way that is different from the form of an artifact and in the way in which it is *able* to be an eternal actuality—in the form of active *dynamis*.

6.3.2. Inconsistency in the *GA*

Let me conclude this chapter by defending Aristotle from a charge of inconsistency in the *GA*. I have presented his embryology as a consistent and coherent theory (at least within the *GA* itself). A number of scholars, most notable Furth,[77] argue that the theory of *GA* 4.3 is inconsistent with the prior passages of the *GA* in regard to the following points: (1) the transmission of an individual form and (2) the active motion of the menstrual fluid. I shall deal with only (1), for whether Aristotle has changed his mind in *GA* 4.3 about the menstrual fluid (from being a passive to an active agent in the process of reproduction) does not concern my thesis.[78]

As far as the transmission of an individual form is concerned, Furth argues that there is weighty evidence[79] that, prior to *GA* 4.3, Aristotle did not believe that what is transmitted is a parental form, for Aristotle always discusses the transmission in terms of a specific form. For example, Aristotle's formulation is "man begetting man, *not* Alexander begetting Alexandrovich or Alexandronova" (134).

I have already discussed a similar problem in chapter 4.3, where I dealt with the apparent inconsistency between the doctrine of Z8 (where the form is a "such") and that of Λ5 (where the form is a "this"). I have suggested that the apparent inconsistency can be resolved by noting that Aristotle's analyses often take place at different levels of generality depending on the context. And we find in Λ5 that Aristotle formulates his principle at both individual and universal levels:

> an individual is a principle of an individual, for a man is a principle
> of man universally (but no one is [a universal man]), but Peleus is
> a principle of Achilles, your father of you. (1071a20–22)

In the same way, I shall resolve the apparent inconsistency of the *GA*.[80] In *GA* 4.3, the topic is parental and ancestral resemblance; hence, in order to account for the resemblance, Aristotle must present his discussion at the level of the peculiar and individual (τὸ ἴδιον καὶ τὸ καθ' ἕκαστον) (767b31) properties of parents. As far as the *GA* in general is concerned, we should note the *scope* of his discussion. For example, in *GA* 2.1, 735a21, where Aristotle refers to his formula "man generates man," he is explaining in general how any plant or any animal is formed from the seed or semen (733b23–24).[81] Since Aristotle's theory of reproduction encompasses *all* animals,[82] we should be sensitive to the fact that his analysis often takes place at a certain level of generality.[83]

Thus, we need not charge Aristotle with inconsistency as regards the transmission of forms in the *GA*.

Chapter Seven

Artifacts

Since substances are principles of coming-to-be, they must be separate from those of which they are the principles in the sense that they are eternal and actual. How this is possible in the case of natural substances can be seen in the *GA*. Relying on my analysis of the *GA*, I am now in the position to present what would have been Aristotle's unequivocal view on the status of artifacts in the *Metaphysics* had he already completed his study of embryology. Artifacts are not substances at all in the *Metaphysics* because their existence is ontologically depended on other beings (God, heavenly spheres, and natural substances) that are eternal actualities.

7.1. *Pros Hen*

In Γ2, Aristotle argues that just as in the case of health, being is neither a univocal nor an equivocal term, but rather a πρὸς ἕν term.[1] And thereby he shows that it is possible for there to be a single science of being *qua* being; that is, there is a being (or are beings) in the primary sense such that all other beings are understood in relation to it (or them). However, there is a long-standing controversy as to exactly how we should understand what Aristotle's first philosophy is all about.[2] I argued that substances understood as metaphysical principles are causes that exist as eternal actualities. These metaphysical principles do not come to be. On the contrary, the existence of all things that come to be depends on these principles; that is, they are the focal beings (beings in the primary sense). Everything else is explained in relation to these principles, thus we can construe Aristotle's *Metaphysics* literally as the first philosophy—the science of first principles.

Although there are many principles, Aristotle identifies only three kinds of substances: unmoved mover(s),[3] heavenly spheres, and plants and animals.[4] It is easy to see how the criteria of substantiality (eternity, actuality, and separation) are applicable to the eternal substances (the first two kinds).

The Unmoved Mover is an actuality (1072b27); an eternal, immovable substance that is separate from the sensible things (1073a4–5). It is the principle of motion by being an object of desire for the heavenly bodies (1072a26–27). Heavenly bodies, in turn, are always active (1050b22) and, given that they are eternal, they are separate from the destructible entities.[5] They are principles in the sense that they are responsible for the generation and destruction of sublunary beings by their circular (ecliptic) motions.[6]

As we have seen, the problematic cases are the destructible substances. It is instructive, at this point, to turn to Λ8, 1074a31–38, where Aristotle distinguishes the Unmoved Mover from composite entities, such as men, in terms of form and number. The Unmoved Mover is both one in form and one in number; that is, it has no matter. It is an eternal actuality that has an infinite *dynamis* (1073a8), and it is eternal *most of all* (1026a17). In contrast,[7] destructible substances try to partake of the eternal[8] and the divine as much as they can. They accomplish this not as one in number but as one in form.[9]

In *Phys* 2.7, Aristotle says the three causes (formal, final, and efficient) often amount to one:

> For what it is and that for the sake of which are one, and that from which the first motion comes is the same in form (τῷ εἴδει ταὐτό) with these, for *man generates man*. (198a25–27)

Because the formal, the final, and the efficient causes are one (note the key formula that I have been emphasizing throughout the book: "man generates man"), natural substances are able to partake of the eternal and the divine.[10] In other words, they are substances because their principle, understood as an active *dynamis*, is separa*ble* from one generation to another,[11] thus, the form is an eternal actuality. An individual form of Peleus perishes when he dies, but his *dynamis* lives on in Achilles and in his offspring for the most part.[12] In this way, the form of composites is both destructible and eternal.[13] It is possible for the form to be ungenerable and indestructible in both senses: the eternal sense (form as an active *dynamis*) and the noneternal sense (an accidental form of an individual that comes into being without the process of coming-to-be and that is destroyed without the process of destruction).[14] So what makes destructible substances substances is that their substantial forms are eternal actualities; that is, the substantial status of destructible composites depends on the ontological status of their substantial forms. In the case of those composites whose substantial forms are not eternal actualities, they are not really substances (in the sense that they are not metaphysical principles).

From the description of three kinds of substances, we can easily see the πρὸς ἕν relation, even among substances. God, which is eternal most of all, is the ultimate principle. Its existence and Its activity (thinking) do not depend on anything else. Although the existence of heavenly spheres does not depend on God's existence, their activities (eternal circular motions) depend on the existence of their object of admiration (God). Animals and plants, which partake of the eternal and divine by means of procreation, need the climate provided by the motions of heavenly spheres, for in a way they also generate animals and plants. But they do so only indirectly (and of course God is also indirect, but twice removed); heavenly spheres (and in turn God) only provide the necessary, but not sufficient, condition for animals and plants to thrive. Animals and plants (or more specifically, their forms) are their own principles, that is, substances in the metaphysical sense, because they are responsible for perpetuating their own species.

7.2. *Pneuma*

Not all living things can partake of the eternal and the divine. In chapter 1.3, I showed that there is no clear evidence in the *Metaphysics* that Aristotle ever held the view that all living things are substances most of all or substances with qualification. If I have accurately identified the active *dynamis* to partake of the eternal (i.e., in the case of destructible substances the potency to procreate or to pass on its own *dynamis*) as the standard by means of which to measure substantiality, then to the degree in which a thing is deficient with respect to this potency it loses its substantiality; hence it is either a substance with qualification or not a substance at all. The question we need to ask is this: why do some things possess such a potency most of all while others possess it to some degree and still others not at all—What makes possible the presence of a degree of such potency? I suggest that the answer lies in Aristotle's doctrine of *connate pneuma* (as far as the material cause is concerned).

Since my topic is not *pneuma per se* but the substantial status of artifacts, I shall not enter into the more controversial aspects of Aristotle's doctrine.[15] I shall direct my attention only to the role of *pneuma* in the generation of animals[16] with a view to determining the substantial status of living things.

In *GA* 2.3, it seems to Aristotle that there is some kind of connection (κεκοινωνηκέναι) (736b31) between the *dynamis* of every soul and the divine body that differs from the so-called four elements. And it is characterized as something hot, although not in the way in which fire is hot (for fire does not generate any animal (737a1)). That is why, in contrast to fire, only the heat of the sun and the heat of animals can generate other animals; hence, the close analogy[17] between *aether* and *pneuma* (736b29–737a7). So whatever *pneuma* may be, it is hot and its presence as heat in the animal plays a vital role in the generation of other animals. Throughout the *GA*,

Aristotle always refers to the amount or degree of hotness to explain the ability of animals to reproduce; this heat is responsible for the concoction necessary for generation.[18] Let us take a number of concrete examples.

In the *GA*, apart from actual physical appearances, the most important way in which Aristotle distinguishes between the male and female is by means of potency (1.2, 716a17–25). While in the male there is a potency to generate, in the female there is not enough potency to concoct semen (1.20, 728a17–21), for male is by nature hotter than female.[19] Women cannot concoct semen "because of the *coldness* of their nature" (1.20, 728a21).[20]

Similarly, the semen of effeminate men (ἄνδρες θηλυκοί) is thin and cold (2.7, 747a1–3), and cold semen is not capable of generation (1.7, 718a24–25). Also because of the deficiency of heat, both the young and the old[21] have a tendency to produce female offspring,[22] or deformed[23] or infertile[24] males. Women, effeminate men, youths, and old people are all in some sense impotent because of the lack of heat.[25]

As we noted in chapter 1.2, one reason mules are infertile is that they are generated "contrary to nature" (2.8, 748b16). Another reason[26] Aristotle gives is that the animal is cold. Although other hybrids are fertile[27] (748a12–13), an ass is by nature cold and hence its semen is cold (748a31–32), so its offspring tend to be infertile. Though the male mule may occasionally generate, since the male is by nature hotter than the female (748b31–32), the female is totally infertile (747b25–26).

Because they are bloodless, insects are cold by nature (3.8, 758a5–6); hence we understand why Aristotle believes that some of them need the heat in the environment to generate them.[28]

Furthermore, it is because of its heat that an animal is said to be perfect and to produce perfect offspring (2.1, 732b31–733b16). Solmsen[29] notes that Aristotle "correlates the greater or lesser degree of internal heat in various animal classes with their capacity of producing offspring in varying degrees of perfection." We also see that Aristotle accounts for degrees of perfection, as regards the production of eggs in different animals by appealing to the varying degrees of hotness (3.1, 750b26–752a10).

The amount of internal heat enables an animal to concoct semen, which has the principle of movement (that is, the potency to transmit the form). If that is the standard measure of substantiality, then we can conclude that males (at their prime) are substances most of all. But we should note that females are also fertile to the extent that their "semen" is potentially alive in the sense of being a nutritive soul. This can be clearly seen, says Aristotle, in the case of animals whose females produce wind-eggs (2.5, 741a13–32). Therefore, I conclude that although females are not substances most of all, they are substances with qualification, that is, substances to the extent that they are able to reproduce.[30] And as far as others are concerned, such as young or old people, their degree of substantiality would correspond with their degree of ability or of heat needed to reproduce. Animals that are so cold that they are totally infertile, such as some[31] mules or spontaneously generated organisms, do not make the grade of substantiality.[32]

So, since the substantial form exists as varying degrees of active *dynamis*, a composite with a complete form, that is an adult male, is the substance most of all, for its form has the *dynamis* to procreate another being. Although semen is compared to a tool (730b21), it possess the soul potentially, in the sense of varying degree of active *dynamis* (735a9–11); that is, its ontological status differs from that of the tool of a craftsman such that semen (which is composed of *pneuma* (*GA* 2.2, 736a1–3)) has the active *dynamis*. Thus, semen, which has neither a complete or incomplete form whatsoever, is the substance in the most removed sense (but nevertheless it is a substance in some sense of the word—to the extent that it has the active *dynamis*; of course, the semen of some animals, such as mules, would not possess this *dynamis*, and therefore is not a substance at all). Each successive stage of developing embryo, as it progressively attains its form, corresponds to a varying degree of substantiality. Even a male child is a substance but not most of all, since his form is not yet complete in the sense that he cannot procreate. An organism becomes a substance in the true sense when its *dynamis* is not in the sense of power but that of potency. The substantial form is the active *dynamis* that causes both the life of an organism *and* that of its offsprings, and the composite becomes a substance most of all when it is capable of both of these functions.

7.3. Dinosaurs

Substances, as metaphysical principles, are eternal actualities. Dinosaurs are extinct, therefore they are not substances. As a matter of fact, no species is eternal. In the course of evolution, species come into, and go out of, existence. That means there are no substances in the physical world (even the heavenly spheres are not eternal); at least no living things can be considered substances. Whatever principle (or principles) that caused their comings-to-be is (or are) prior to them.

Aristotle believed that he lived in a stable world, where the universe is eternal, and so are the species. Thus, for him, the extinction of species is not real possibility. All species exist for an infinite duration of time. If there were any real possibility for such an extinction, then it would have occurred in an infinite duration of time. Since no such extinction has occurred, there is no reason to believe that it will occur in the future.

In Θ8, Aristotle argues that in one sense, actuality is prior to potentiality in time. It is prior in the sense that there always exists a thing of the same species in actuality that is responsible for generating another thing. Here, Aristotle assumes that species are eternal, for man generates man (1049b17–1050a3). In Z3, Aristotle assumes that there are substances among sensible things, thus, he can begin his ontological investigations into the nature of substances by studying the substances in the physical world, although they may not be knowable by nature (1029b3–12), unlike the substance *par excellence*—God. Aristotle's whole enterprise of first philosophy as envisioned by Aristotle is, therefore, untenable. He has no basis for assuming that there are substances in the sensible world, since species are not eternal. If so, he cannot grasp the nature of metaphysical principles that are operative in the world, for they do not exist (or at least he has misidentified them as the forms of (some) living things). In that case, his conclusions about the nature of substances are suspect (e.g., actuality is prior to potentiality in time).

A similar view has been expressed correctly by Grene (1963) over thirty-five years ago:

> We live for better or worse in an evolutionary universe, and, in the
> last analysis, evolution and Aristotelian science will not mix.[33]
> (232)

I shall go further: not only will evolution and Aristotelian science not mix, but his metaphysical enterprise itself, in an evolutionary universe, is obsolete![34] No ifs, ands, or buts. Of course, this does not mean that we cannot learn from Aristotle, who has introduced many important metaphysical concepts, such as form and matter, actuality and potentiality, to name a few, nor does it mean that we are prevented from engaging in an Aristotelian inspired metaphysics. But whatever the form this inspired investigation may take, it is NOT Aristotle's metaphysics—which is a dinosaur.

7.4. *Pragmata*

Now let me finally turn to artifacts. First of all, the substantial status of women, children, semen, mules, and other natural beings *per se* has no bearing on the ontological status of artifacts. I say *per se* because regardless of the accuracy of my understanding of *pneuma* with respect to the degree of substantiality, artifacts are not substances because their principles are not active *dynameis* (either in the sense of potency or of power), but potentialities. Consequently, artifacts are not substances, with or without qualification.

However, generally speaking, for the same reason mules and spontaneously generated organisms fail to be substances, so do artifacts. The existence of mules depends on the prior existence of horses; without horses there would be no mules. To understand what it is to be mules presupposes the understanding of what it is to be horses. The *logos* (formula or definition) of mules, therefore, includes that of horses. The existence of horses, in turn, does not depend on the existence of mules; horses could perpetuate their species without mules. The understanding of what it is to be horses does not presuppose the understanding of what it is to be any other species (except in the sense that the necessary conditions of all sublunary substances are the eternal motions of heavenly spheres, whose activities in turn depend on the Eternal Unmoved Thinker). The *logos* of horses, therefore, does not include that of any other species (except for the same qualification made with regard to the heavenly spheres and God). Thus, horses are prior to mules in time, knowledge, and *logos*. In the very same way, heavenly spheres are also prior to spontaneously generated organisms, and these are the priorities that exist between substances and nonsubstantial beings.[35]

Let me now spell out the relationship between artisans and artifacts.[36] The existence of artifacts depends on the existence of the prior existence of artisans; without artisans there would be no artifacts. To understand what it is to be artifacts presupposes the understanding of what it is to be artisans; that is, artifacts are kinds of things that come into existence by art that exists in the mind of artisans, rather than by nature. Hence the *logos* of artifacts includes that of artisans. The existence, knowledge, and *logos* of artisans (that is, human beings), in turn, does not depend on the existence of artifacts. Thus, artifacts are not ontologically prior beings; that is, they are not substances at all.

We can now understand Aristotle's argument against the substantial status of artifacts as follows: the form of an artifact is potential—a potentiality in the mind of an artisan (and not itself an active *dynamis*); hence, it cannot exist apart from the composite in the same way that substances (which are eternal and actual) do, although it is separate with qualification because it can exist (as a universal) in the mind of an artisan. Therefore, (without any hesitation we can conclude that) an artifact *is not* a substance at all (in the primary[37] sense in which substance is used in the *Metaphysics*).[38]

If artifacts are not substances, what are they? At Z17, 1041b28–31, Aristotle identifies two kinds of *pragmata* (πράγματα): substantial and nonsubstantial.[39] Substantial *pragmata* are things that are formed according to nature (1041b29–30). Obviously, only substantial *pragmata*, natural substances, can be either substances most of all or substances with qualification.

Nonsubstantial *pragmata* include *inter alia*[40] mules,[41] spontaneously generated organisms, parts of animals, elements, and artifacts. The mark of nonsubstantial *pragmata* is that they are not eternal actualities; that is, in some sense of the word they are potentialities.[42] Defective things (πηρώματα) and things that are generated by chance do not partake of the eternal and the divine (*De An* 2.4, 415a26–b7). For example, the forms of mules[43] exist potentially in horses, which are responsible for the generation of mules; similarly, the forms of spontaneously generated organisms exists potentially in the heat generated by the sun. Neither elements[44] nor parts of animals are substances (in the primary sense) because they are "potentialities" (Z16, 1040b5–10). And as we saw,[45] all the arts (πᾶσαι τέχναι) are potentialities because "they are principles of changeable 'in another' or *qua* another" (Θ2, 1046b2–4).

Unfortunately, except for elements (which are said to be like heaps),[46] Aristotle does not have names for all the subgroups of nonsubstantial *pragmata*. I can, therefore, only specify that artifacts belong to a group of nonsubstantial *pragmata*—that is, artifacts are simply *things* (πράγματα).

Appendix A

An Analysis of the Principle of Internal-Change in *Physics* 2.1

Aristotle defines "nature (φύσις)" as "a certain principle and a cause of being moved or of standstill in the thing to which it belongs primarily according to itself and not accidentally (ἐν ᾧ ὑπάρχει πρώτως καθ' αὑτὸ καὶ μὴ κατὰ συμβεβηκός)" (192b21–23).[1] The things that have this principle—animals and their parts, plants, and elements—all exist by nature, and they have this principle of change and standstill with respect to either place, quantity, or quality. In contrast to this, things that exist by "art (τέχνη)," such as beds or garments or other artifacts, have no natural tendency in themselves for changing, but they have such a tendency insofar as they are made of earth or stone; that is, the principle of change for the artifacts is in other things and/or is outside of themselves (ἐν ἄλλοις καὶ ἔξωθεν). In the case of those things existing by nature, this principle of change must belong to them by virtue of themselves and not accidentally (κατὰ συμβεβηκός). An example that Aristotle gives is medical art; it is possible for the same person to be both a doctor and a patient although this happens by accident; he is not a doctor by virtue of being a patient.

Furthermore, in his discussion of the priority of form over matter, Aristotle distinguishes between nature and art by the manner in which natural and artificial beings are generated.

For the defense of the priority of matter, Aristotle refers to an argument of Antiphon: if one were to plant a bed, and if it were to have the capacity to sprout, what should result would not be a bed but wood; thus, what is arranged by art is mere accident but what will persist is the underlying matter. However, Aristotle counters it by saying this:

> Furthermore, a man is generated from a man, but not a bed from a bed; that is why they say that the shape is not the nature but the

wood, because not a bed but wood would be generated, if it [a bed] were to sprout. But if as a consequence that this [wood] is nature, then the shape will also be nature; for a man is generated from a man. (193b8–12)

In other words, in the case of man, it is not the matter that is ultimately responsible for generation but the form that exists in him, for man generates man.

But for now, we should note that, by the principle of internal-change, Aristotle refers to locomotion, qualitative, and quantitative change; that is, he does not include generation. This is what the Greek text says:

τούτων μὲν γὰρ ἕκαστον ἐν ἑαυτῷ ἀρχὴν ἔχει κινήσεως καὶ στάσεως, τὰ μὲν κατὰ τόπον, τὰ δὲ κατ' αὔξησιν καὶ φθίσιν, τὰ δὲ κατ' ἀλλοίωσιν. (192b13–15)

In *Phys* 2.1, Aristotle nowhere identifies generation as an instance of internal-change.[2] It is important to distinguish clearly between the principle of generation and the principle of internal-change because, as I argue in this book, it is the former, not the latter, that holds the key to discovering the criteria of substantiality.

The fact that Aristotle does not identify generation as an instance of internal-change accords with the view expressed both in *GA* 2.1 and in *De An* 2.4.[3] In the *GA*, he says that "nothing generates itself (οὐθὲν γὰρ αὐτὸ ἑαυτὸ γεννᾷ), but whenever it is generated, from that point on it makes itself grow" (735a13–14); that is, "on the one hand it is the synonymous being (τὸ συνώνυμον) that generated [another], for example a man generates a man, but on the other hand it grows by means of itself (αὔξεται δὲ δι' ἑαυτοῦ)" (735a20–21).

So in *Phys* 2.1, Aristotle appeals to the difference between natural generation and artificial production to distinguish nature from art and to argue that form is prior to matter. But one should note that in his definition of "nature," in contrast to "art," the difference *per se* is not given any particular emphasis. In this chapter, the crucial distinction between nature and art is defined in terms of internal-change.[4]

Appendix B

A Summary of the Five Passages in the *Metaphysics* Examined in Chapter One

The passages are (1.) Z7, 1032a18–19, (2.) Z8, 1034a3–4, (3.) Z17, 1041b28–31, (4.) H3, 1043b22–23, and (5.) Λ3, 1070a17–19:

1. Substances most of all are things that are generated by nature (τὰ φύσει γίγνεται).
2. The most likely and safe reading is the same as in (1).
3. Naturally formed (κατὰ φύσιν συνεστήασι) substances do not include syllables and flesh.
4. Naturally formed (φύσει συνέστηκεν) substances do not include elements (including nonliving natural phenomena, such as ice and winds), parts of animals, and artifacts.
5. Substances most of all are things that are generated by nature (τὰ φύσει γίγνεται) and most likely in the same sense as (1).

Appendix C

The Common Context of the Four Passages in the *Metaphysics* Where the Argument Against the Substantial Status of Artifacts Occurs

The common immediate context is printed in italic script:

B4:

999a24–b4—the discussion of an epistemological problem*
999b4–12—the discussion of coming-to-be
999b12–16—the discussion of form and matter as ungenerable
999b17–20—the argument against the substantiality of artifacts
999b20–24—the discussion of whether the substance of all individuals is one or many

K2:

1060b19–23—the discussion of an epistemological problem*
1060b23–26—the discussion of form as indestructible
1060b26–28—the argument against the substantiality of artifacts
1060b28–30—the discussion of whether the principles are one in kind or numerically the same

H3:

1043b4–14—the discussion of substance as the cause of existence
1043b14–18—the discussion of coming-to-be and of form as ungenerable

1043b18–23—the argument against the substantiality of artifacts
1043b23–32—the discussion of definition

∧2: 1069b7–34—the discussion of the principle of change and motion
∧3:

1069b35–1070a4—the discussion of form and matter as ungenerable
1070a4–9—the discussion of coming-to-be
1070a9–13—the discussion of three [sorts] of substances
1070a13–20—the argument against the substantiality of artifacts
1070a21–30—the discussion of coming-to-be
∧4: 1070a30–b10—the discussion of principles and causes as being distinct
and yet same analogically

(* The discussion of why the epistemological problem is not directly
relevant to my topic is found in chapter 3.1.2.)

Appendix D

An Analysis of B4, 999a24–b20[1]

1. 999a24–26 (cf. chapter 5 (note 27))

> And what comes next (ἐχομένη) is to examine the hardest and the most pressing of all difficulties, which the argument has now imposed [on us].

The important word is ἐχομένη, which means "that which follows" or "that which is connected with." It shows a connection between what came before (the seventh *aporia*) and what is to follow (the eighth *aporia*). I show that the crucial concept that links Aristotle's argument in the preceding *aporia* and this one is separation.

2. 999a26–32 (cf. chapter 3 (note 31))

> If there is not anything which is apart from (παρά) individual things, and the individuals are infinite, how is it possible to obtain knowledge (πῶς ἐνδέχεται λαβεῖν ἐπιστήμην) of infinite things? For insofar as something is one and the same, and insofar as it belongs universally (καθόλου), because of this we know all things. But indeed if this must be the case and it is necessary for there to be something apart from (παρά) the individual things, it would be necessary that the genera, whether the highest or the lowest, exist apart from (παρά) individual things; but that this is impossible we have just now discussed.

In this passage Aristotle questions the possibility of knowledge (πῶς ἐνδέχεται λαβεῖν ἐπιστήμην) of individual things, given that the object of knowledge is universal (καθόλου). The crucial concept is ἐπιστήμη (knowledge), for I show that what purports to be the doublet (K2, 1060a3–27) employs a different sense of ἐπιστήμη (science).

3. 999a32–b4 (cf. chapter 3 (note 33))

Furthermore, if as much as possible there is something apart (παρά) from the composite (<and by composite I mean> whenever something is predicated of matter)—if this is so, is it necessary for something to be apart from (παρά) all things, or is it necessary for something to be apart from (παρά) some things but not from others, or apart from nothing at all? But if there is nothing apart from (παρά) the individual things, nothing would be knowable but all things would be sensible and there would not be knowledge of anything, unless one says that sensation is knowledge.

In this passage, by παρά (apart from) Aristotle refers to the separation that may be possible between that which is predicated of matter (namely, form) and the composite. The crucial concept is παρά, for I show (just as in section 2) that what purports to be the doublet (K2, 1060a7–13) employs a different sense of παρά or χωριστός (separate).

4. 999b4–12 (cf. chapter 3 (note 4) and chapter 5 (note 10))

Furthermore, nothing would be eternal (ἀΐδιον) or unmovable (for all sensible things are destroyed (τὰ γὰρ αἰσθητὰ πάντα φθείρεται) and in motion); but indeed if nothing is eternal (ἀΐδιον), no coming-to-be is possible. For it is necessary that there is something that comes-to-be, that is,[2] that from which it comes to be, and that the last of these be ungenerable (ἀγένητον), if indeed [the series] stops and it is impossible to come to be from what is not. Furthermore, if there are comings-to-be and motions it is necessary for there to be a limit (for no motion is infinite but there is an end for all [motions], nor is it possible for what is unable [to complete] its coming-to-be to come to be; but it is necessary for there to be that which has come to be when it has first come to be).

In this passage, Aristotle argues for the necessity of something eternal to account for the coming-to-be of destructible beings, because there cannot be an infinite regress of what comes to be and because nothing can come to be out of what is not. I argue that this eternal principle exists within the destructible beings.

The fact that the principle of coming-to-be must be eternal or ungenerable and indestructible (see chapter 2.3.4) is stated in *Phys* 3.4 (where Aristotle argues that the infinite cannot be a principle):

Furthermore, as a principle a thing is both ungenerable and indestructible (ἀγένητον καὶ ἄφθαρτον), for it is necessary for what comes to be to attain an end, and there is a terminus for every destruction (203b7–10).

Note that Aristotle's concept of principle must be ungenerable and indestructible.

5. 999b12–20

Furthermore, if indeed matter exists because it is ungenerable (ἀγένητος), it is even more reasonable for the substance, which at one time (ποτέ) the matter comes to be, to exist; for if neither the latter nor the former will exist, nothing at all will exist; but if this is impossible, it is necessary for something, the shape or form, to exist apart from (παρά) the composite. But if again someone will posit this, one is at a loss as to whether one will posit this for something and not for another thing. It is clear that it is not possible [to posit this] for all things; for we would not posit a house apart from (παρά) individual houses.

5.1. (cf. chapter 3 (note 4) and (note 36))

Aristotle identifies matter as ungenerable. But if that is so, he argues that there is a better reason for believing that the form exists as ungenerable (although Aristotle never explicitly claims that the form is ungenerable in the above passage, it is reasonable that this is implied in the text. See Ross I (1924), 241 and Apostle (1966), 278). The reason is this: the substance is that which at one time (ποτέ) the matter comes to be. Note the word "ποτέ." It is the *temporal* factor that is decisive for the form's being ungenerable. Because the matter takes on the form at one time or another, it is more reasonable for the form to be ungenerable. Thus, the form is more permanent in some relevant way than the matter,[3] although both are ungenerable.

Aristotle has already indicated (in section 4) that there must be something *eternal* to account for the coming-to-be of destructible beings. This passage indicates that form (as the permanent or the eternal[4] element) is a principle of coming-to-be.

5.2. (cf. chapter 2 (note 31))

Given that it is impossible for others to exist without these two ungenerable elements, not only matter, but also something else (namely, the form), must exist apart from the composites; that is, the substance which is ungenerable is the form. Aristotle assumes that if there is a form that is ungenerable, it must exist apart from the composite.

So the connection between the context and its argument against the substantial status of artifacts (see section 5.3.) is this: if the form is ungenerable, then it must exist apart from the composite.

5.3. (cf. chapter 2, (note 4))

Having identified the substance, which is ungenerable, with the form, Aristotle concludes that the form must exist apart from the composite. But the problem is that this is not always the case, for an obvious exception is an artifact; that is, the form of an artifact, such as that of a house, does not exist apart from the house. The implication is that the form of an artifact is not an ungenerable substance.

Thus, the argument is that the form of an artifact does not exist apart from the artifact; hence, it is possible that[5] the artifact is not a substance.

Notes

Introduction

1. Gerson (1984) makes the following comment on the ∧3 passage where Aristotle questions the substantial status of artifacts: "This passage has difficulties not sufficiently appreciated by the commentators and translators" (53).

2. Cf. *Republic* 4, 420c7–8.

3. *EN* 1.1, 1094b23–27.

4. Although the developmental thesis was advocated earlier, for example, by T. Case in 1910 (see his discussion in Case (1925)), it was Jaeger who made the greatest impact on Aristotelian scholarship.

5. This is so, even if we can determine the relative date of different books, for example, by reference to the celebrated thesis of Jaeger—the first person plural, "we," indicates the passages written by Aristotle when he was a Platonist and the third person plural, "they," indicates those written when he was a non-Platonist. Cf. Jaeger (1948), 171.

6. See Wians (1996), xiii.

7. Berti (1996), 128, agrees with this order, however.

8. In this respect, Peck's (1942) assessment of the treatise is telling: that the student of reality should pay special attention to Aristotle's doctrine of reproduction (v).

9. See the methodology of Furth (1988), 5–6 and 67–75.

10. Gerson (1984), 50.

11. Cf. Ross II (1924), 410 and Annas (1976), 137–139.

12. As far as other passages of B are concerned, if I believe that they represent Aristotle's view, I argue for the reasonableness of my belief. See chapter 5.1.3.

1. Substances Most of All

1. καθ' ὑποκειμένου λέγεται and ἐν ὑποκειμένῳ ἐστίν. According to Dancy (1975), "this is a distinction Aristotle has left pretty much unexplained" (343). For a standard interpretation, see Ackrill (1963), 74–76.

2. Although Anscombe, in Anscombe and Geach (1961), believes that the doctrine of *Cat* "is very straightforward" (7), there is a controversial debate on the ontological status of a "particular property." See Owen, "Inherence," reprinted in Owen (1986), 252–268; Frede, "Individuals in Aristotle," in Frede (1987), 49–63; Matthews and Cohen (1968); R. Allen (1969); Heinaman (1981); and Irwin (1988), 502–503 (endnote 21).

My thesis is not affected by this controversy, for I am interested only in showing that, in the *Cat*, the criteria that pick out primary substances are also applicable to artifacts.

3. According to Lear (1988), "Aristotle uses the expression 'this something' as a placeholder for a definite, ontological basic item" (270).

4. The translation of ἄτομος (3b12) follows Ackrill (1963) and Apostle (1980). Literally, it is "indivisible."

5. Indeed, Aristotle even flirts with the notion that a picture is a primary substance (1a1–2). In his analysis of *Cat* 1a, Anton (1968) also comes to the same conclusion: ". . . artifacts are not reducible to accidental properties" (263); and also he says: "Since portraits are not things that are said to be in a subject, they are included in the category of *ousia*" (264).

In fact, even body parts seem to qualify (3a28–32; 8a19–22; and 8b15).

6. This is the predominant interpretation of the passage. The only exception (that I know of) is found in Aquinas' Commentary (Lesson 5, 1386). According to Aquinas, Aristotle identifies composites (rather than forms) as substances most of all! Since this reading clearly goes against the rest of Aristotle's views found in the *Metaphysics*, and since my task is to undermine the view of other scholars who uses this passage as the evidence for ascribing Aristotle the belief that all living things are substances most of all, I simply follow the interpretation of the many (contra Aquinas). As a matter of fact, if Aquinas is correct, my task becomes much easier (although I believe that he got it wrong).

I am grateful to Tim Huson (the commentator of the earlier version of this chapter, presented at 1997 Central States Philosophical Association) for pointing out to me this reading of Aquinas'.

7. In *De An* 2.1, 412a11–13, both animate and inanimate natural beings are called substances most of all.

8. Furthermore, in a number of passages of the *Metaphysics*, the substantial status of artifacts is questioned: B4, 999b17–20; H3, 1043b18–23; K2, 1060b23–28; and Λ3, 1070a13–18. In chapter 2, I discuss these passages in detail.

9. See Gerson (1984), 51; Gill (1989), 62; and Kosman (1987), 360.

10. Furthermore, the scope of the discussion is not limited to the category of substance, but also includes other categories, such as quantity and quality. In the case of art, the things that come to be by art include not only artifacts like houses but also health (1032a32–b14). Thus, we should not equate artifacts with "the things that come to be by art." To indicate this scope of generality, γίγνεται is translated as "comes to be;" but where the context is clear that Aristotle is specifically talking about substantial change, it is translated as "is generated."

11. This passage makes it clear that, although in lines 1032a20–22 Aristotle mentions both nature and art in describing matter as potentiality (just before he summarizes "things that comes to be by nature"), this does not imply that the remarks to follow (22–25) are about both natural and artificial comings-to-be; that is, Aristotle's discussion in (22–25) is restricted to the things that come to be by nature.

12. They are briefly examined in Z9, 1034b4–7.

13. One might argue that the phrase "which indeed we call substances most of all" might be an *endoxon*; hence, Aristotle is not making a fine discrimination among animals, as I have suggested. On the contrary, it is Aristotle *himself* who makes the fine discrimination between "the things that come to be by nature" and "the things that come to be by chance" and it is *he* that brings up the topic and then postpones the discussion of the coming-to-be of spontaneously generated organisms.

14. I use the word "among" rather than "as" because the context is not clear whether Aristotle identifies *all* or only *some* things that come to be by nature as substances most of all.

15. τὰ μὲν φύσει γίγνεται, γίγνεται τὰ γιγνόμενα διὰ τὴν φύσιν, and ἐν τοῖς ἀπὸ φύσεως γιγνομένοις, respectively. In *De An* 2.4, 415a23–b7, where Aristotle also discusses the generation of natural things, he says they act "*according* to nature (κατὰ φύσιν)" (415b2).

16. For example, *Meta* Δ4, 1014b16–1015a19.

17. *Phys* 2.1, 192b8–34.

18. Cf. *GA* 2.7, 746b19–20.

19. I discuss the other reason in chapter 7.2.

20. *GA* 2.8, 748b16.

21. *HA* 6.23, 577b15–18.

22. Even monstrosity is not contrary to nature in all respect (*GA* 4.4, 770b9–11).

23. *GA* 2.3, 737a1–7. See also *GA* 3.11, 762a13–18. Cf. G. E. R. Lloyd (1996), 118.

24. See *HA* 5.15 and 5.19.

25. I establish in the course of this book that form, in its role as the principle of generation, is the key to identifying the criteria of substantiality.

26. I discuss the importance of this formula in chapter 4.2.

27. We should also note that "the things that come to be by art," such as health, are said to resemble the natural coming-to-be, for Aristotle says "*in a way* health comes to be from health, and a house from a house (τρόπον τινὰ τὴν ὑγίειαν ἐξ ὑγιείας γίγνεσθαι καὶ τὴν οἰκίαν ἐξ οἰκίας)" (1032b11–12).

28. Note that Aristotle thinks that the generation of a woman is an exception to the rule, "man from man" (ἐξ ἀνθρώπου ἄνθρωπος), which is more often formulated as "man generates man" (ἄνθρωπος ἄνθρωπον γεννᾷ). This *may* suggest that in this context by ἄνθρωπος Aristotle means male and NOT human!

29. Aristotle often draws an analogy of male/female to form/matter. See *Meta* A6, 988a3–7 and *Phys* 1.9, 192a20–25.

30. *GA* 1.20, 728a17–18; 5.3, 784a4–6; and 5.7, 787a28–30.

31. Note also that Aristotle often emphasizes that eunuchs and castrated animals, who have lost the male form, resemble females. See *GA* 1.2, 716b5–9; 4.1, 766a25–28; 5.3, 784a6–7; and 5.7, 788a6–13.

32. I give credence to this suggestion in chapter 7.2.

33. I determine the ontological status of both spontaneously generated organisms and mules in chapter 7.2.

34. For the purpose of my criticism of the views of other scholars, I do not distinguish between the denial of artifacts as substances with or without qualification, because I show that in either interpretation, the arguments against the substantiality of artifacts implicitly or explicitly make an unwarranted assumption that *all* living things are substances, with or without qualification.

35. The main text that supports this view is found in *Phys* 2.1. See Appendix A for the analysis of the principle of internal-change.

This view is advocated by Sellars (1967), especially 78 (footnote 11) and 119–124, and Lewis, (1994), especially 263–265.

36. This view is based on Aristotle's identification of the soul with the first substance (*Meta* Z11, 1037a5). By first substance, he means "that which is not said to be something else in another or in an underlying [subject] as matter" (1037b3–4). But this definition of first substance is applicable to both the form of artifacts and that of living things. What is decisive, however, is that the form as the shape of a statue differs in its actuality from the form as the soul of a body (for a hand or an eye severed from the body is said to be a hand or an eye equivocally, although the severed part has the same shape (*Meta* Z10, 1035b24–25 and Z11, 1036b30–32)); that is, the key to understanding the criterion of substantiality is to identify this unique actuality—the psychic activity or function of living things. But in order to understand this activity or function, we need to know the nature of the

soul, and this is defined in the *De An* 2.1, where Aristotle clarifies the two senses of actuality: having knowledge and actually exercising it (412a22–26 (I discuss the importance of this passage in chapter 6.2.1); see also *Phys* 8.4, 255a30–b5; *De An* 2.5, 417a21–b2; and *GA* 2.1, 735a8–11).

By drawing this distinction, Aristotle defines the soul as "the first sense of actuality of a natural body which has life potentially" (412a27–28). And although the object of sleep is to preserve the life of an animal, "the waking state is its goal" (*De Som* 2, 455b22–23); that is, the second sense of actuality (that which is analogous to the exercise of knowledge) is the most proper activity or function of the soul. Thus, the second sense of actuality (actuality in the full sense) is the criterion of substantiality, for the Unmoved Mover, the substance in the primary sense, is actuality without qualification. It is a thinking substance that is always realizing its activity. The other living things, on the other hand, try as much as possible to be in this state by exercising the self-preserving and self-maintaining activities of natural bodies, the activities that artifacts lack; therefore, artifacts are not substances.

Of course, even in the case of artifacts, the two senses of actuality can be analogously applied. For example, a television set that is turned off is analogous to a person who has knowledge or a person who is asleep. When the set is turned on, it is analogous to a person who is exercising knowledge or a person who is awake. So, anyone who advocates this view must clearly distinguish the different ways in which the second sense of actuality is understood in living things and in artifacts. Those who object to this example being anachronistic should note that in *GA* 2.1, where Aristotle explains how the parts of animals are formed in succession and not simultaneously, he appeals to both "the miraculous automatons" (734b10) and to the different senses of potentialities (735a11–12) (I discuss its importance in chapter 6.2). For a discussion of what these automatons could be, see Preus (1975), 291–292 (endnote 32). For the purpose of my criticism of this view, I shall simply assume that we can clearly establish the difference and that the main distinction lies in the "*self*-preserving and *self*-maintaining activities" of living things, which artifacts lack.

Gill (1989), argues for a similar view. She claims that Aristotle denies that artifacts are substances, because the former are only analogous to the latter (161). By drawing the distinction between motion and activity, she emphasizes the importance of what she calls "the second potentiality–actuality model," which she identifies with a psychic activity:

The motion proper to the second potentiality–actuality model (i.e., activity) is thus vital for self-preservation. And given the vital role of activity in self-preservation, an entity that possesses an active capacity for such activity can maintain its own unity. (221)

Hence all living organisms are primary substances (242) because their soul—the active potentiality—is "their immanent form" (213); but not so with the artifacts, because they "are not self-preserving systems but depend on external agents both for the full realization of their being and for their maintenance" (213).

Irwin (1988) also seems to hold a similar view; see 571–572 (endnote 8) and 640 (endnote 54).

37. This view is based on the fact that the form is the cause of the unity of composite substances. But unity is said in many senses. In *Meta* Δ6, Aristotle says that "things that are continuous by nature are more of a unit than those that are so by art" (1016a4; cf. *Meta* I1, 1052a19–20 and 1052a22–25).

The cause of this intrinsic unity is ascribed to the relationship that exists between the soul and the body, while the kind of unity that exists between the shape or form of artifacts and their matter is accidental or imposed. For this reason we can separate in thought the form of the circle from its matter, whether the circle is made of bronze or stone; but in the case of a man, who always exists in flesh and bone, we are unable to separate in thought the form of a man from his matter (*Meta* Z11, 1036a31–b7). Thus the substantial unity of natural substances is more of a unity than that of artifacts; that is why artifacts are not substances or at least not substances most of all.

This view is held, among others, by Gerson (1984), Halper (1989), 171–172, Kosman (1987), Ferejohn (1994), and Block (1978).

38. In *Meta* Z2, 1028b8–13 and H1, 1042a7–11, Aristotle gives the following list of the physical substances: elements, animals and plants, their parts, heavenly spheres, and their parts. In the Z2 passage, Aristotle is not committed to the list, for he simply lists them as a starting point for his investigation (1028b13–15). Nor is it clear that in the H1 passage, he endorses it. It is highly unlikely that he does so, given that in Z16, 1040b5–10, he denies the substantial status to elements and parts of animals.

39. I am not the first to question the substantial status of mules. Rorty (1973), 393–420, argues that mules are not substances but things (414).

40. The translators either literally translate the Greek phrase or understand it to mean "natural beings." For example, Frede and Patzig II (1988) translate it as "bei diesen Gegenständen" and in their commentary understand it as "bei den natürlichen Gegenständen" (146); and Ross II (1924) comments on it in this way: "τούτοις, sc. τὰ φυσικά (1033b32), living things" (189). Of course, while I agree that in this context ἐν τούτοις refers back to ἐν τοῖς φυσικοῖς, I am challenging the view that τὰ φυσικά means living things *per se*.

41. A possible meaning of this verb, in contrast to the verb γίγνεται, is discussed in chapter 1.3.3.

42. See *Phys* 2.1, 192b8–34 and *PA* 1.1, 639b16–17.

43. Cf. Ross II (1924), 354.

44. Ross II (1924), 354.

45. Alexander of Aphrodisias. *In Metaphysica Commentaria*, 673, 34. Ross II (1924), 356, also notes that the sentence in question follows the phrase μετὰ ταῦτα ὅτι. The Greek text reads: "μετὰ ταῦτα ὅτι ἑκάστη ἐκ συνωνύμου γίγνεται οὐσία (τὰ γὰρ φύσει οὐσίαι καὶ τὰ ἄλλα)" (1070a4–6).

46. In *Meta* Z9, 1034a22ff, instead of ἐκ συνωνύμου, Aristotle uses the term ἐξ ὁμωνύμου, to defend the view that in a way a house comes from a house. Strictly speaking, the proper term is ἐξ ὁμωνύμου, because a house does not generate a house (*Phys* 2.1, 193b9). Aristotle does not always clearly distinguish between ἐκ συνωνύμου and ἐξ ὁμωνύμου. For example, *Meta* α1, 993b25.

47. The root of a plant is said to be analogous to the head of an animal. See *De An* 2.4, 416a4.

2. Separate

1. ἀγένητος, which could be translated as "ungenerated," is rendered "ungenerable" throughout this book. My thesis is not affected by either translation. *Mutatis mutandis* this applies to ἄφθαρτος.

2. See chapter 2 (note 36).

3. See Appendix C.

4. See Appendix D, section 5.3.

5. See *Meta* Z3, 1029a27–28.

6. See Introduction, section 3.

7. I am indebted to Alan Code for this objection.

8. Aristotle employs παρά and χωριστός interchangeably in the passages that we have examined. χωριστός is used in H3, 1043b19, and K2, 1060b28. Thus, for the purpose of my exposition I shall simply assume that they are synonymous, for I am interested only in the sense of separation that Aristotle has in mind in these passages.

9. He also mentions the third type that he calls χωριστὸν νοήσει. But he considers it "sekundär" because it "ist kein seinsmäßiger Chorismos, sondern ein erkenntnismäßiger" (173).

10. Chen (1976).

11. Spellman (1994), 11.

12. However in Spellman (1995), Spellman emphasizes the importance of teleology as the justification for the ontological priority of substances (106). She identifies biological natural kinds that have the capacity to reproduce as the paradigm cases of substances (113). Unfortunately, as Spellman herself admits, she does not "have any novel criteria for judging

of any given kind whether it is natural" (112). In the *Metaphysics* she observes (rightly, as we saw) that "it is a bit unclear whether he wants to limit natural kinds to *biological* species" (113); that is, she does not explain how the teleological factor of the "independent being" of biological kinds can be distinguished from that of artifacts.

13. G. Fine (1984), 31–87.

14. In chapter 1.3, we saw that some scholars hold this view. See chapter 1 (note 37).

15. *Meta* Z1, 1028a32–33.

16. See her footnote 18 on page 35.

17. See, for example, *Meta* Θ8, 1049b17–1050a3. Cf. Ross II (1924) (his commentary on 1038b27–28), 210–211.

18. I henceforth accept this interchangeability. See *Phys* 8.6, 260b15–19.

19. See the emendation of Lord as γνώσει and the commentary by Ross II (1924), 210–211.

20. Cf. Ross II (1924), 160–161.

21. See also *Phys* 8.7, 260b19, where Aristotle draws a distinction between priority in time and priority according to substance.

22. Irwin (1988), 553–554 (endnote 8).

23. Frede and Patzig II (1988), 19–22.

24. See Burnyeat and others (1979) 4–5 and Bostock (1994), 57–60.

25. One of the strengths of my thesis is that I am able to provide a possible solution to the above cryptic passage, which is consistent with the criteria of substantiality that I shall be defending. See chapter 5.1.3 for my solution.

26. For example, Preiswert (1939) makes a similar distinction (192) and de Strycker (1955), referring to the above dichotomy, says this: "En un mot, la notion de séparation sert à Aristote pour distinguer l'ordre réel de l'ordre logique" (138).

27. Morrison (1985b), 155.

28. Chen (1940), 126–129.

29. Although Chen does not say so, I presume that he has something like "teaching" in his mind. Cf. Broadie (1987): "Crafts are learnt, and they are passed on by teaching" (48).

30. In this section, I focus on the very *specific* topic of coming-to-be that was discovered in all of the previous four passages: namely, the identification of the form as ungenerable or indestructible. In chapter 3, I expand the context to include the topic of coming-to-be in general. Since this specific topic occurs in all of the four passages, while the expanded context does not (notably in K2), this method enables me to focus on the essential connection that occurs in *all* the passages and helps me establish a firmer framework for my exposition.

31. See Appendix D, section 5.2.

32. See chapter 2.1.1 for the translation of the passage.

33. See chapter 2.1.2 for the translation of the passage.

34. See chapter 2.1.3 for the translation of the passage.

35. A standard interpretation of (2) is that the form comes to be without being in the process of coming to be; that is, it comes to be instantaneously (and *mutatis mutandis* this applies to indestructible). For the textual basis of this interpretation see *Meta* B5, 1002a32–b5. Cf. Shields (1990), 367; Ross II (1924), 188; and Dooley and Madigan (1992), 188 (footnote 444).

Furth (1988) finds this sense of ungenerable and indestructible non-sensical (195). But his view is based on *his* (and not Aristotle's) concept of what coming-to-be is (194). For the purpose of my thesis, I am interested only in the fact that Aristotle makes this distinction and that however one understands this sense of ungenerable and indestructible, what is important is that Aristotle believes that some forms are ungenerable and indestructible in the eternal sense.

36. Note how Aristotle closely relates ungenerable and indestructible; that is, the passages that appeal to them are dealing with the same topic. Thus, I am justified in considering K2 (where the implication is only that the form is indestructible) as dealing with the same topic as the other passages (which discuss forms as ungenerable).

Von Leyden (1964) also refers to "the inter-dependence of the terms γενητός-φθαρτός and ἀγένητος-ἄφθαρτος" (42).

37. See *Meta* E2–3, especially, 1026b22–24 and 1027a29–31.

38. See *Meta* H5, 1044b21–28.

39. See *Meta* Z15, 1039b23–26.

40. Sorabji (1983) makes a similar analysis: ". . . certain forms escape such a process [the non-eternal sense of ungenerable] merely by being *ever-lasting*. . . . This may be true of the forms of natural substances, but not . . . of forms such as white or *forms of artifacts*" (11, (footnote 5); emphasis added).

41. Among other meanings, "ungenerable" (ἀγένητον) can be understood in the following two senses:

(A) If something exists now but not before without coming-to-be and change (ἐὰν ᾖ τι νῦν πρότερον μὴ ὂν ἄνευ γενέσεως καὶ μεταβολῆς) (280b6–7).

(B) If something in general is unable to come-to-be so that at one time it exists but another time it does not exist (εἴ τι ὅλως ἀδύνατον γενέσθαι, ὥσθ ὁτὲ μὲν εἶναι ὁτὲ δὲ μή) (280b11–12).

Furthermore, "indestructible" (ἄφθαρτον) can be understood in the following two senses:

(C) That which without destruction at one time exists and at another time does not exist (τὸ ἄνευ φθορᾶς ὁτὲ μὲν ὂν ὁτὲ δὲ μὴ ὄν) (280b26–27).

(D) That which exists but is unable to be destroyed in such a way that it exists now but later does not exist or cannot exist (τὸ ὄν μέν, ἀδύνατον δὲ φθαρῆναι οὕτως ὥστε νῦν ὄν ὕστερον μὴ εἶναι ἤ ἐνδέχεσθαι μὴ εἶναι) (280b32–33).

In *DC* 1.12, 282a27–b9, Aristotle identifies (B) and (D) as the primary sense of ungenerable and indestructible, respectively. If they are said to imply each other (see chapter 2 (note 36)), that is, if what is ungenerable (in the sense of B) is indestructible (in the sense of D) and vice versa, then together they mean eternal. (A) and (C) correspond with the non-eternal sense of ungenerable and indestructible that we have already identified.

Note that in the *DC*, Aristotle identifies more than two senses of ungenerable and indestructible (for they could also mean that which cannot be easily generated or destroyed (280b16–20; 24–25)).

42. Ross II (1924), 356.

43. Elders (1972), 107.

44. Alexander of Aphrodisias. *In Metaphysica Commentaria*, 677, 2–12.

45. Elders (1972), 107.

46. I show in chapter 4.2 that Aristotle appeals to the eternal sense also.

47. See chapter 2.2.

48. For example, Owens (1978), 381 (footnote 19) refers to it to justify the equivalency of separate in notion (λόγῳ) with separate in form.

49. See Appendix A.

50. See *Meta* Z7, 1032a25. I discuss the importance of "in another" in chapter 5.2.

51. See Apostle (1966), 348 and Ross II (1924), 227.

52. In Λ3, 1070a24–26, Aristotle indicates that nothing prevents intelligence (*nous*) from surviving and suggests that, with the possible exception of *nous*, no form of any destructible composite can exist apart from the composite. Again this reading is consistent with the possible alternative interpretation of the passages discussed in chapter 2.1.5. However, if *my* reading is accurate, then this is not the kind of separation Aristotle had in mind, for beings without *nous* (plants and animals) are also substances.

53. See *Meta* A1, 981a5–7.

54. Cf. *Meta* Λ6, 1071b14–16. Matter is also ungenerable and indestructible (*Phys* 1.9, 192a25–29).

3. Eternal and Actual

1. In the previous chapter, in order to establish a firmer framework for my account of the status of artifacts in the *Metaphysics*, I focused my attention on the specific topic of coming-to-be (namely, the identification of form as ungenerable and indestructible) because it occurs in *all* of the

pertinent passages (that is, in B4, K2, H3, and Λ3). But this immediate context (that is, the context in which the specific topic is found) provides us with insufficient information. Thus, we need to go beyond this context. The wider context, common to all the passages (except K2), is the topic of coming-to-be. So, it is reasonable now to turn to this wider context and see if we can establish the essential connection between it and the more immediate context. Two types of passages provide a wider context: (1) where Aristotle discusses difficulties or *aporiai* and (2) where Aristotle criticizes Plato's theory of Forms.

Type (1) is appropriate because Aristotle himself emphasizes the importance of the prior discussion of the *aporiai*, for "it is not possible to untie a knot if one is ignorant of it" (995a29–30) and those who attempt to investigate without knowing the *aporiai* are "like those who are ignorant of where they should go" (995a34–36). Therefore, it is an appropriate starting point, since the text itself provides the justification for it. This is especially so, since there is a passage that relates to the question of the substantiality of artifacts.

Type (2) is appropriate because Aristotle is said to have been a student of Plato for twenty years, beginning at the age of seventeen or so. Therefore, regardless of whether he ever accepted Plato's theory of Forms, we cannot deny the influence that the theory had on him. Thus, it is appropriate first to understand Aristotle's objections to the theory of Forms.

2. For the purpose of my discussion, I shall simply accept the prevailing view that Aristotle does not clearly distinguish between the terms αἴδιον and ἀεί (which may indicate the distinction between eternal and everlasting); see Kneale (1961), von Leyden (1964), Whittaker (1968), and Lennox (1985), 68. See also chapter 7 (note 8). I also simply take the terms ἐνέργεια and ἐντελέχεια synonymously; that is, I do not concern myself with a subtle difference of nuance that may exist between them; see W. Ritter (1932; 1934), Blair (1967), Graham (1987), 183–206, and Rist (1989), 105–119.

3. I deal with Aristotle's discussion of *aporiai* first and then his criticism of Plato's theory of Forms and not vice versa, although historical considerations would demand an enquiry in the reverse order. The justification for this procedure derives from the texts themselves. It is in the former, and not in the latter, that Aristotle connects the immediate context to the wider one; hence, we can demonstrate at once their relevance. Having done so, it is easier for us to see how the wider context can help us show the connection between the immediate one and the argument.

4. See Appendix D, sections 4 and 5.1.

5. At this point, those who read the *aporiai* as merely dialectical may take this conclusion as a working hypothesis. See Introduction, section 7.

6. The advantage of this interpretation is that we can read the text of the B4 passage without doing harm to the structure of Aristotle's argument (i.e., without abruptly changing the topic of the discussion from the Unmoved Mover to the form of a composite). Furthermore, by contrasting the passage in B4 with that in K2 (which purports to be the doublet of B4), I show later that in B4 Aristotle is not concerned with the Unmoved Mover.

7. Note the term *principles*. I shall discuss its importance in chapter 5.1.

8. My task is to provide this lengthy discussion.

9. I draw this distinction in chapter 7.1.

10. See Appendix C.

11. This is one of the important motifs that I emphasize throughout the book.

12. The relevant passages of the *Metaphysics* are as follows:

(1) So [Plato], unlike Pythagoreans, made the one and the number apart from the things and his introduction of Forms was due to his enquiry in [the area of] *logical* [matters] (διὰ τὴν ἐν τοῖς λόγοις ἐγένετο σκέψιν) (A6, 987b31–32);

(2) . . . but philosophy has become *mathematics* (τὰ μαθήματα) for the present day [thinkers] (A9, 992a32–33);

(3) For the genera are universal, which [the present day thinkers] say are rather principles and substances because they seek *logically** (διὰ τὸ λογικῶς ζητεῖν) (Λ1, 1069a27–28);

(4) The cause of the error they fell into is that they sought after at the same time from [the standpoint] of *mathematics* (ἐκ τῶν μαθημάτων) and *universal expressions* (ἐκ τῶν λόγων τῶν καθόλου) (M8, 1084b23–25); and

(5) . . . but with respect to only *logical difficulties* (πρὸς τὰς λογικὰς μόνον δυσχερείας), which they avoid because of the fact that they themselves employ *logical demonstrations* (διὰ τὸ καὶ αὐτοὶ λογικὰς φέρειν τὰς ἀποδείξεις) (N1, 1087b19–21).

*λογικῶς could be translated as *verbally*. More often than not Aristotle means logically. See *Meta* Z4, 1029b13.

13. *Meta* M2, 1077b12–14.

14. Cherniss (1936) defends the "epistemological necessity for the existence of the Ideas" (449). See also Cherniss (1944), 213–214 (footnote 127).

15. Alexander of Aphrodisias. *In Metaphysica Commentaria*, 79, 3–80, 6.

16. For the full discussion, see for example G. Fine (1993), 66–102 and D. Frank (1984).

17. See *Meta* A1, 981a5–7.

18. Alexander of Aphrodisias also states that both ἐπιστήμη and τέχνη "περὶ τὸ καθόλου συνίσταται" (*In Metaphysica Commentaria*, 199, 35–36).

19. Ross I (1924), xxviii.

20. Chapter 2.2.

21. It is interesting to note that both Chen (1976) and Spellman (1994) consider that this kind of separation is closely related to definition. Chen says this: "For Aristotle definition corresponds to essence; the former is the latter put into words. What is one is *eo ipso* true of the other" (226); and Spellman calls it "correlate of separation in definition" (11). See also Spellman (1995) 3 and 86.

22. Of course, we could try to distinguish artifacts and substances by appealing to the distinction between the accidental and the essential unity of form and matter, respectively. But it is hard to see how such a distinction could be made without making the unwarranted assumption that all living things are substances. See chapter 1.4.

23. Cf. also *De An* 2.1, 412b10–17.

24. See chapter 3 (note 73).

25. See Appendix B.

26. Although it is not so clear-cut in Z17, it seems to be the case in that chapter also, for Aristotle mentions the cause of coming-to-be and destruction (1041a31–32). Ross says:

And, though his language in Z17 carelessly suggests that some things are to be explained teleologically and others mechanically, his real view is that the same thing which is due to *a final cause* is also due to *an efficient cause* (cxii; emphasis added).

27. See Introduction, section 4.

28. See Ross II (1924), 311; and Owens (1978), 238 (footnote 96).

29. See Ross II (1924), 311; and Owens (1978), 247 (footnote 122).

30. The *aporia* of K2 begins thus: "Furthermore, ought we to posit something apart from (παρά) the individual things or not, or are they rather the object of the science that is being sought (ἡ ζητουμένη ἐπιστήμη)? But these things are infinite (ἄπειρα). And indeed the genera and the species are apart from (παρά) the individual things, but the science that is being sought now (ἡ ζητουμένη νῦν ἐπιστήμη) is none of these things. For why it is impossible has been stated." (1060a3–7)

31. For the analysis of B4, 999a26–32, see Appendix D, section 2.

32. K2 continues: "In fact generally there is a problem as to whether or not one must assume a certain substance which is separate from the sensible substances, that is, those that are here (χωριστὴν παρὰ τὰς αἰσθητὰς οὐσίας καὶ τὰς δεῦρο); but these are the things that exist and wisdom is concerned with these things. For we seem to be seeking something else, and the matter before us is this—I mean to see if there is something that is separate according to itself and does not exist in any of the sensible things (χωριστὸν καθ' αὑτὸ καὶ μηδενὶ τῶν αἰσθητῶν ὑπάρχον)." (1060a7–13)

33. For the analysis of B4, 999a32–999b4, see Appendix D, section 3.

34. K2 concludes: "Furthermore, if there is another substance apart from (παρά) the sensible substance, apart from (παρά) what sorts of sensible thing must one posit this to be? For why will one posit this to be apart from men or horses or the rest of animals rather than the inanimate things generally? Indeed to establish (κατασκευάζειν) other eternal [substances] equal to sensible and destructible substances would seem to fall outside [the realm] of reasonableness. But if the principle that is being sought right now is not separate from (χωριστή) the bodies, what other things would one posit than the matter? Indeed this does not exist in actuality, but exists in potentiality. But the form and the shape would rather seem to be a principle and more so than this [the matter]. But this [the form] is destructible (φθαρτόν) so that there is no eternal substance separate and according to itself (χωριστὴ καὶ καθ' αὑτήν). But this is strange; for it seems also that this is being sought by nearly [all of] the most educated men as being a principle or a substance of this sort; for how will there be an order (τάξις) unless there is something eternal and separate and permanent?" (1060a13–27)

35. Of course I have been arguing that the form of a composite substance is somehow eternal. In chapter 7.1, I discuss how the form of a composite substance can be *both* eternal and destructible.

36. For the analysis of B4, 999b12–20, see Appendix D, section 5.1.

37. K2, 1060a27–36, runs as follows: "Furthermore, if indeed there is a substance and a principle of the sort of nature which we are seeking, and if this is one for all and the same for eternal and destructible things, there is a difficulty as to why indeed being the same principle some are eternal that fall *under* the principle (ὑπὸ τὴν ἀρχήν) while others are not eternal (for this is strange). But if there is one principle for destructible things and another one for eternal things, and if that of destructible things is also eternal, then similarly we will be at a loss as to why, although the principle is eternal, those that fall *under* the principle (ὑπὸ τὴν ἀρχήν) are not eternal; but if it is destructible, some other principle comes to be and another that is different from the latter and this proceeds *ad infinitum*."

38. B4, 1000b20–31, runs thus: "But the difficulty that is now being discussed is why some are while others are not [destructible], if indeed they are *of* the same things (ἐκ τῶν αὐτῶν). Let so much be said, that they could not be the same principles. If principles are different, then there is a problem as to whether these things will be indestructible or destructible, for if on the one hand they are destructible, it is clear that it is necessary also that these things are *of* something (ἔκ τινων) (for all things are destroyed into these things *of* which they are (εἰς ταῦτ' ἐξ ὧν), and as a consequence other principles will be prior to these, but this is impossible,

even if [the process] stops or advances *ad infinitum*. Furthermore, how will there be destructible things, if principles will be annihilated? But if on the other hand they are indestructible, why will these things that are *of* indestructible substances (ἐκ μὲν τούτων ἀφθάρτων οὐσῶν) be destructible, while those that are *of* others (ἐκ δὲ τῶν ἑτέρων) be indestructible?"

39. We can see this, for example, in the context in which Aristotle is discussing the Unmoved Mover in *Meta* Λ10, where he presents the following dilemma: ". . . how does the nature of the whole as the good or the best exists, whether as something *separate* and *according to itself* (κεχωρισμένον τι καὶ αὐτὸ καθ' αὐτό) or with respect to *order* (τὴν τάξιν)" (1075a11–13).

40. Of course, it is not enough simply to show that there are two notions of separation (one for the Unmoved Mover and the other for the form of a composite) because there are also two ways in which separation between the form and its composite is possible. See chapter 2.3.6. But for the purpose of distinguishing B4 and K2, this difference is sufficient.

41. One might argue that my reading of K2 and B4 opens up the developmental problem of the *Metaphysics* (See Introduction, section 5), if they cannot be taken as presenting the same *aporiai*. I have shown that in *some cases* the *aporiai* of K should not be taken as simple doublets of B. This neither affirms nor denies either developmental or unitary interpretations of the *Metaphysics*. Therefore, the controversy of K notwithstanding, it will not directly affect my position.

For a brief historical survey on the controversy of book K and the relevant literature as well as his unitary interpretation, see Reale (1980), chapter 6, 247–294. From the analyses of B4 and K2, suffice it to say that I disagree with Reale's assessment of the eighth *aporia* of B and K as identical in "spirit" (257) and of the tenth aporia of B and K—he believes that aside from the historical part "the rest corresponds well" (259).

42. For a brief historical summary of the controversy see G. Fine (1984), 31–34. See also footnotes 1–15 for some of the relevant literature that deals with this question. For a further reference, see Morrison (1985b), 126 (footnote 3).

43. See Cherniss (1944), 376–478, especially 379–380 and 450–451; Merlan (1960), 201–202 and 201 (footnote **), on some of the relevant literature; and Gallop (1975), 185, for the discussion and other relevant literature.

44. For the discussion and the summary of the relevant literature, see G. Fine (1993), 81–88 and 101–102, and Leszl (1975), 119–140.

45. *Phaedo* 100D. Cf. Ross I (1924), 199.

46. Note that Aristotle's basic criticism of the theory of Forms lies in the identification of the Forms as universals. Cf. Cherniss (1944), who says: ". . . Aristotle grants that if the ideas were substances they would be

separate but objects that it is wrong to make the universal an εἶδος" (188 (footnote 111)). This accords with his criticism of the *method* of Platonic philosophy, which he finds to be based solely on logical or epistemological considerations (see chapter 3 (note 12)).

47. In *Meta* M9, the same point is emphasized; that is, the cause of the difficulty concerning the Forms lies in the separation of the universal from the individual (1086a32–b7). Cf. Cherniss (1944), who says that according to Aristotle "the fundamental source of all the difficulties in the theory" is that "χωρίζειν means the separation of universals as οὐσίαι παρὰ τὰς αἰσθητάς" (205).

48. See also D. Frank (1984): "Aristotle's objection is that no universal exists apart from the individuals *as a substantial entity*" (136 (footnote 69)). See also chapter 3 (note 46).

49. Although Alexander of Aphrodisias mentions that Forms are not final causes (*In Metaphysica Commentaria*, 121, 14–15), he emphasizes that they are not movers in the sense of efficient causes (121, 29–30). See also 96, 12–16 and 38.

50. Mabbott (1926), 73.

51. "But this [the mover] acts by touching (θίξει), as a result at the same time it is also acted upon; therefore, motion is an actuality of movable, insofar as it is movable. And this happens by touching (θίξει) of that which moves, as a result at the same time it is also acted upon."

I discuss the importance of touch or contact with respect to Aristotle's analysis of efficient causality in chapter 6.1.

52. "The first mover, not in the sense of that which is for the sake of, but that from which the beginning of motion [originates], is together with (ἅμα) that which is being moved. And by together (ἅμα) I mean that there is nothing intermediate between them; for this is common (κοινόν) in every case between the things being moved and the mover."

53. Note the parallel. We see in *Phys* 2.1 that Aristotle does not include generation as an instance of an internal change (see Appendix A); and in chapter 2.3.6, we saw that form is separate in formula or in thought insofar as it is a principle of internal change.

54. *Meta* Λ7, 1073a3–5: "It is clear from what has been said that there is a substance which is eternal and immovable and *separate* (κεχωρισμένη) from the sensible things."

55. "But indeed if there is that which can move or affect [others], but is not actually [doing so], there will be no motion, for it is possible for that which has potentiality not to act. Consequently, it is not useful even if we make substances eternal, just as those who [posit] the Forms do, unless in them there is a principle which can [cause] changes; but even this is not

sufficient, nor any other substances apart from the Forms, for if it will not be in actuality, there will be no motion."

56. See also *Meta* Θ8, 1050b34–1051a2. Cf. Cherniss (1944): "The ideas are at best potentialities . . ." (380).

57. *Meta* Θ8, 1049b24–27: "For always that which is in actuality comes to be from what is potential by what is actual, for example, man from man, the musical by the musical, since always there is a first that which moves [others]; but the mover is already in actuality."

58. Cf. Cherniss (1944): "This neglect of efficient and final causality is for Aristotle an indication that these thinkers have substituted mathematics for philosophy" (223). Also note that when criticising Pythagoreans, Aristotle says that the mathematical objects are without motion and therefore cannot be the principle of motion and change (*Meta* A8, 989b29–990a12).

59. In order to account for eternal motion, according to Aristotle, both Leucippus and Plato posited "eternal actuality (ἀεὶ ἐνέργειαν)" (*Meta* Λ6, 1071b32). Note that in that passage Aristotle does not reproach them for having posited such an entity, but for not having explained *how* such an entity exists and is able to cause motion and change.

60. I confirm this finding from other contexts in chapters 4.2 and 5.1.

61. In chapter 4, I discuss Z7–9 in detail.

62. Ross II (1924), 188.

63. I discuss the importance of this formula in chapter 4.2.

64. Shields (1990), 369–371.

65. This term is equivalent to what I mean by the eternal sense of ungenerable.

66. It is interesting to note that Ross does not identify form with universal in the passage cited.

67. See chapter 7.2.

68. I determine the substantial status of spontaneously generated organisms and mules in chapter 7.2.

69. See chapter 3 (note 7).

70. See chapter 6.3.1.

71. And if I am successful, I shall be immune to the criticism of Shields, who understands sempiternality in terms of instantiation.

72. See also *De Gen et Corr* 2.9, 335b19–23.

73. This methodology is consistent with Aristotle's general approach to solving problems—to begin with what is knowable to us (although it may have little or no being) to what is knowable by nature. Cf. *Meta* Z3, 1029b3–32. See also Jacobs (1978), 24–27 and Broadie (1987), who says that the craft as the model of nature is not surprising "since we have a better pre–reflexive grasp of the idea of craft than we have of the idea of a thing's nature" (36).

4. Individual or Universal

1. We need not worry about taking the chapters Z7–9 out of context in book Z. Most scholars agree that, although these passages may be shown to be related to the rest of *Meta* Z, they were written separately (see Ross II (1924), 181; Owens (1978), 358 (footnote 45); Reale (1980), 204; and Burnyeat and others (1979), 54). And regardless of whether they were inserted later by Aristotle, they can stand on their own. As a matter of fact, several scholars believe that we need to show how they are found in the appropriate context (see Mansion (1975) and Halper (1989), 89–97). That means that there are well-defined boundaries to the context of which I take full advantage.

2. In this chapter, I only introduce this dilemma; in the next two chapters, I show how its solution is connected to the ontological status of artifacts.

3. The fact that Aristotle also discusses nonsubstantial categories in *Meta* Z7 is noted by Burnyeat and others (1978), 53 and 55. See also Furth (1988), 233.

4. Aristotle says that it is common to all primary [categories] (περὶ πάντων ὁμοίως τῶν πρώτων) (1034b9). But what are primary [categories]? He identifies only whatness, quality, and quantity (1034b13–14). See chapter 4 (note 12).

5. Contra Elders (1972), 107. See chapter 2.3.5.

6. Contra Elders (1972), 107; and Ross II (1924), 356. See chapter 2.3.5.

7. *Meta* Z15, 1039b23–26 and Λ3, 1070a13–20.

8. *Meta* Z7, 1032a19.

9. I show in chapter 7.1 how it is possible for the form of a natural substance to be ungenerable in both senses.

10. Scaltsas (1994a) distinguishes two ways in which the substantial form can be actual: *as* an actuality and *in* actuality (167). The distinction is described thus: "The abstract universal form is *an* actuality that has the potential of being actualized into the particular substance, which is the form *in* actuality" (169 (footnote 6)).

11. Note that by "τί" (1032a14) Aristotle also means "πού" (1032a15). This point seems to have escaped a number of scholars who have offered interpretations of *Meta* Z7–9. For example, Owen, "Particular and General" reprinted in Owen (1986), 279–294, does not seem to be aware of the scope of Aristotle's discussion. He emphasizes that "whatever becomes, becomes or is becoming *something* (*ti*)" (293), and he explicitly refers to the previous passage. His view is based on the previous translation. But how can we translate *ti* as "some*thing*," when it also refers to "some*where*?"

Ross II (1924), 182, says that the expression καθ' ἑκάστην κατηγορίαν is not exact and does not discuss the question of scope.

12. Aristotle makes no qualification by adding "and other categories" as he usually does in other passages. For example, in *Meta* Z9, where he refers to primary [categories], we find the following: ". . . for example quantity, quality, and the other categories" (1034b9–10); and ". . . in the case of whatness, quality, quantity, and the other categories" (1034b13–14).

Note that we can consistently hold that by primary [categories], Aristotle has in mind the four categories that correspond with the four changes. Perhaps, this is what Aristotle means by primary [categories] (1034b9). See chapter 4 (note 4).

13. I confirm this in chapter 6.1.

14. I discuss the importance of this expression, "in another," in chapter 5.2.

15. This is noted by Ross II (1924), 188. His example is "white does not generate white." See chapter 3.2.2.

16. However, Aristotle may not be always that careful. For example, in *Meta* Θ2 the text reads: "Health produces (ποιεῖ) health" (1046b18). Of course, we should also note that health is not necessarily produced artificially.

17. See chapter 1.2.

18. According to Dancy (1981), 85–86, Aristotle hopes "to save himself from Platonism" by means of his version of "the Principle of Eponymy"— ἐξ ὁμωνύμου; Brentano (1978), 50–53, 59–60, speaks of "the Law of Synonymy."

19. Cf. *Phys* 2.1, 193b8–9.

20. Leszl (1975) emphasises the importance of the ontological difference between the form that exists in the mind of an artisan in contrast to the immanent form of natural substances:

> Evidentemente per lui la forma nella mente dell'artigiano non ha una realtà ontologica sua propria (in tal caso si dovrebbe parlare di una sua esistenza separata rispetto ai prodotti delle arti) ma va trattata piuttosto come uno schema mentale a cui non corrisponde un universale vero e proprio (123).

But in the case of natural things, there is such a correspondence between the form and "l'universale" because species are eternal and this is accomplished by means of reproduction (122–123; see also 111 (footnote 15)). My task is to explicate clearly the above insight of Leszl. See also Irwin (1988), 588 (endnote 13).

21. According to Alexander of Aphrodisias, a natural generation occurs "according to the cause (1) 'in itself (ἐν αὐτῷ)' and (2) 'principle (ἀρχήν)' and (3) 'power (δύναμιν)' to move in some way" (103, 16–17). Topic (1) is discussed in chapter 5.2; (2) in 5.1; and (3) in 6.2.1. and 6.2.2.

22. *Meta* Z7, 1032a25 and Λ3, 1070a8.

23. I discuss the importance of the two functions of the nutritive soul (nutrition and generation) in chapter 6.3.1.

24. See *GA* 1.20, 728b10–12; 2.7, 746b14–16; and 2.8, 747a24–25.

25. The importance of this formula is explored by Oehler (1962) reprinted in Oehler (1969). He sees the formula as the paradigm in which artificial and spontaneous generation, as well as that of mules, are explained; that is, they are all instances of the ἄνθρωπος ἄνθρωπον γεννᾷ rule and that their differences are only "diese Unterscheidung der verschiedenen Modi," which "bleibt äußerlich"(130). Therefore, he emphasizes the "bio-logischen Ursprünge der Aristotelischen εἶδος-Lehre" (134). Although that may all be true, what I have emphasized is that as a pedagogical or heuristic procedure, Aristotle rather appeals to the production of artifacts as a paradigm to explain the coming-to-be of all things, including natural substances.

Oehler was inspired by the earlier work of E. Frank (1927). Frank sees the origin of the ἄνθρωπος ἄνθρωπον γεννᾷ formula in Diotima's speech in *Symposium* 207D, where Plato explains the reproduction of living things as the means in which mortal beings partake of the eternal and the divine (625).

26. Pellegrin (1986) notes a similar point: "Aristotle does not list reproduction among the fundamental functions that define the animal" (199 (endnote 14)), because there is a class of animals that does not reproduce, the class of spontaneously generated beings.

However, we should note that Aristotle is ambivalent in some cases. See *GA* 3.11, 761b25ff and 763a26ff for his discussion on the Testacea.

27. See chapter 4 (note 18).

28. See chapter 3 (note 2).

29. See also *Meta* H1, 1042a28–29 and Λ3, 1070a11–12.

30. See Chen (1976), 272–275; and Loux (1991), 133–134.

31. In chapter 6.3.2, I also appeal to the previous explanation to solve the similar controversy in the *GA*.

32. See chapter 7.1.

33. Cf. *Meta* Δ6, 1016b31–1017a3.

34. Lennox (1987b), 353–354, especially his footnote 36, emphasizes the importance of the formula "one in form." Because according to Lennox the formula is dependent on "one in account," he argues that composites (matter/form unities), and not the form–species, partake of the eternal by reproduction. Cf. Lennox (1985). See also chapter 4 (note 59).

35. Cf. *GA* 2.1, 731b31–732a2.

36. See *Meta* M10, 1087a16–17.

37. See chapters 6.3 and 6.3.1.

38. There is a large amount of literature and it would be counterproductive to examine all of it. The following should not be taken as a

comprehensive review of the problem. Furthermore, my topic is not the above controversy *per se*, but the substantial status of artifacts. Thus, I select those discussions that might help me solve our present problem. The key is this: any proposed solution must help us distinguish the ontological status of natural substances and artifacts; that is, it must solve the dilemma *as I have formulated* it.

In my formulation of the dilemma, the epistemological aspect is missing. Lesher (1971) says that "a centrally important Aristotelian view" (175) of a form being a universal is based on Aristotle's concept of the object of science or knowledge being universal and not individual. I have argued that epistemological problems have no bearing on my topic (chapter 3.1.2), thus, I deal with the dilemma to the extent that the discussion is relevant in determining the ontological status of artifacts.

39. What I mean by individual forms.

40. Albritton (1957), 703.

41. "Individuals in Aristotle," reprinted in English in Frede (1987), 49–71.See also Frede and Patzig I (1988), 48–57.

42. Modrak also identifies the form "with the soul as the complex of vital *capacities*" (374; emphasis added).

43. This is an important point, because I argue that a specific sense of *dynamis* holds the solution to our dilemma in chapters 6.3 and 6.3.1.

44. Contra, for example, A. C. Lloyd (1981), who argues that "[u]niversals are concepts and therefore belong to propositions" (2); and Scaltsas (1994a), who argues that "the path from the substantial form in actuality (= the concrete substance) to the abstracted form (= universal) is separation by abstraction. . . ." (5).

45. Most notably by Lesher (1971), 170–174.

46. Unfortunately, Woods (1991) makes a concession to those who criticized his earlier article by admitting that "it is clear that the distinction between being *katholou* and being *katholou legomenon* is not to be found in Aristotle" (45).

47. For example, Moreau (1955) identifies the primary substance with the species. The important point to note is that he does not identify the species with a universal, at least not in a rigorous sense, but it exists as an act. Otherwise, we cannot explain the specific role that the form plays in generation of animals. Thus:

L'*eidos* ou espèce n'est pas un universel ou une abstraction, mais une réalité (*ousia*), parce qu'il se traduit dans la réalité biologique, s'exprime concrètement dans le fait de la génération; et étant une réalité (*ousia*), il peut faire l'object d'une définition véritable, ayant un contenu réellement unifié (189–190).

E. Frank (1940) had already expressed the previous notion of species fifteen years before Moreau. The species is not merely conceptual (53), but "for Aristotle the sentence 'a man begets a man' becomes the formula for the real essence of the idea within the cycle of becoming" (53).

Oehler (1962), reprinted in Oehler (1969), like Frank and Moreau, sees that "Wesensbegriff," which is identical to "Artbegriff" (122), is not a purely logical concept, but "[d]iese Aussage trifft in vollem Umfang auf den Bereich der Lebewesen zu, wo sich Gattungen und Arten am deutlichsten realisiert finden" (122). He shows that "diese biologische Art," which "ist das Prinzip der immanenten Zwecktätigkeit der Natur" (124–5), characterizes its "zeitlose Allgemeinheit" (127).

48. See *Meta* M10, 1087a16–17.

49. Lewis (1991), 327–329.

50. See chapter 3.2.2.

51. See *Meta* Z3, 1029a23; Z13, 1038b6; and H2, 1043a5–6.

52. Rist (1989), 332 (endnote 49).

53. For the discussion of the problem of this passage, see Annas (1976), 188–192. She believes that "this passage is not a final and considered treatment of the difficulties facing Aristotle's theory of form" (190).

54. See Owens (1978), 379–399 and 426–434; Lear (1987), 149–174; and Lear (1988), 273–293. What is especially instructive for my purpose in Lear's (1987) article is his discussion of the varying levels of potentiality and actuality (152–160) to elucidate Aristotle's argument, for I show in chapter 6.2.1 that this distinction is crucial in solving our problem.

In contrast, see Annas (1976), 190 and Frede and Patzig I (1988), 56, who argue that, in *Meta* M10, Aristotle commits himself to individual forms. Their view is criticized by Scaltsas (1994), 252–258.

55. See Heinaman (1979): "I will ignore the claim that Aristotle's substantial forms are neither universals nor particulars. There is no evidence in Aristotle's writings to support such an interpretation" (250 (footnote 2)).

56. See Albritton (1957): "I doubt that Aristotle would have understood any better than I do the suggestion that a thing may be neither universal or particular" (699).

57. Lewis (1991), however, says this:

> Direct evidence for the view of forms as universals is not abundant in Aristotle's text. I know of only two passages in the *Metaphysics* in which Aristotle explicitly calls forms universals. At M8, 1084b5, the reference is only in passing. In Z11, however, Aristotle declares flatly that "definition is of the universal, *that is, of form*" (155; his emphasis).

Note his translation. Contra Lewis's claim, we can infer from his translation that universals are forms, but not that forms are universals.

58. Scaltsas (1994a), 166 (footnote 1), cites 1040b17.

59. The same dichotomy can be also expressed analogically by the distinction of one in number and one in form. Although in *Meta* I1, the distinction is stated in terms of individual and universal (1052a35–36), Aristotle also makes the following distinction in *Meta* I1:

> Therefore, what is one is also to be what is indivisible, just as being a this and distinct, [it is] separate either in place or in form or in thought, or even to be a whole and indivisible (1052b15–18).

If I can successfully demonstrate the existence of the third sense of separation that corresponds with the form being neither individual nor universal, then contra Lennox (see chapter 4 (note 34)), one in form is not always dependent on one in formula (in chapter 6.3 and 6.3.1, I argue for this view). Woods (1967), argues that there are three distinctions: one in number, one in form, and one in genus (222–224).

The previous dichotomy can also be expressed analogically by the distinction of a "this" and a "such." See Owen, "Particular and General," reprinted in Owen (1986), 279–294. The most revealing admission made by him from my standpoint is this:

> But the apparatus of *tode* and *toionde*, particular and general, that he [Aristotle] brings to the business [his account of change] is too primitive to illuminate them (294).

And in his "Prolegomenon to Z7–9," in Burnyeat and others (1979), he says:

> To the oversimple dichotomies of individual/sort and particular/ general we have to add a *third* with which Aristotle does not come fully to grips (52; emphasis added).

This statement is made in his qualm 2. I take his qualms about the interpretation of Z7–9 seriously.

60. Note that the word "neither" can mean either (1) that a thing is *neither* A or B because it is C or (2) that a thing is neither A or B because it is somehow *both* (A and B). I have left the option open as to which is the right sense, for now. See chapter 6.3.1 for the discussion.

61. Halper (1989), by appealing to the extended use of universal and individual, argues that form is *both* individual and universal:

> In their extended usages, universal and individual refer not to kinds but to characteristics. Accordingly, these extended usages open the possibility that something might be both universal and individual (243).

See chapter 6.3.1 for the discussion of this option.

5. Principle

1. Here is a sample of the key passages:

A1: "It is, therefore, clear that wisdom is a science of certain *principles* and *causes*" (982a1–3);

A2: "For the most divine [science] is most honorable. . . . And this alone happens to be [divine] in both of these ways: for it seems to all that god is [one] of the *causes* and a certain *principle*, and the god would possesses this sort [of science] alone or most of all" (983a5–10);

Γ1: "But since we are seeking the *principles* and the highest *causes*, it is clear that it is necessary that these things are according to itself as a certain nature. . . . Thus, we must also grasp the first *causes* of being *qua* being" (1003a26–32);

Γ2: ". . . it would be necessary for the philosopher to possess the *principles* and *causes* of substances" (1003b18–19);

E1: "*Principles* and *causes* of beings are sought, but clearly *qua* being" (1025b3–4);

E4: ". . . we must examine the *causes* and *principles* of being itself *qua* being" (1028a3–4);

Z17: "So since substance is a *principle* and a certain *cause*, we must proceed from here" (1041a9–10);

H1: "Indeed it has been said that the *causes* and the *principles* and the elements of substances are being sought" (1042a4–6);

K1: "It is clear that wisdom is a science of *principles* . . ." (1059a18);

K7: "But every science seeks certain *principles* and *causes* for each of the things that come under it" (1063b36–37);

Λ1: "The investigation is of substance, for the *principles* and the *causes* of substances are being sought" (1069a18–19); and

M1: ". . . whether the substances and *principles* of beings are Numbers and Ideas" (1076a30–31).

2. In *De An* 2.1, the reason why Aristotle calls a certain group of beings substances most of all is that they are "principles of the rest" (412a12–13). See chapter 1 (note 7). Cf. Irwin (1988): "The puzzle about principles imply puzzles about substances, since substance is intended to be some sort of principle" (164). See also Lear (1988), 248.

3. Since my task is not to examine Aristotle's concept of principle *per se*, I shall not exhaustively examine all the senses. See *Meta* Δ1, 1012b34–1013a23.

4. The text of *Meta* Δ1 reads: "So what is common to all principles is that it is first from which either [a thing] exists or *comes to be* or is known" (1013a17–19).

5. These are the very characteristics that Aristotle ascribes to the Unmoved Mover—the principle of all—in *Meta* Λ7, 1072b26–30 and 1073a3–5. See chapter 7.1.

Gerson (1990), in his discussion of Greek theology, identifies the *arché* as "divine because it is immortal and indestructible" (17) and as "a cause" (9) and as that which is "separate from or different from that which it is the *arché*" (15).

6. It is said to be what Greek philosophers in general believed. See Jaeger (1947), 203–206 (note 44). Cf. Gerson (1990), 246 (note 43).

7. To discuss whether or not this view is consistent with the creational account of souls in the *Timaeus* is outside the scope of this book. See Cherniss (1944), 423–450.

8. Plato's concept of immortal as eternal differs from the traditional understanding of the word by the Greeks. According to Reiche (1960), it was Xenophanes who challenged "the Homeric concept of deity as immortal yet born" (118). See also Jaeger (1947), 32, 206 (footnote 48), and 213 (footnote 40) for his discussion on the old concept of gods employed by Homer and Hesiod.

9. "Furthermore, as a principle, a thing is both ungenerable and indestructible (ἀγένητον καὶ ἄφθαρτον), for it is necessary for what comes to be to attain an end, and there is a terminus for every destruction" (203b7–10).

10. See especially B4, 999b8–12. Cf. Appendix D, section 4.

11. See chapter 2.1.

12. See chapter 3.2.2.

13. See chapter 4.1.

14. See Apostle (1966), 319; and Ross I (1924), 356.

15. See chapter 3.1.1.

16. See chapter 7.1.

17. I made this assumption in chapter 2 (note 18).

18. See chapter 5.2.

19. See chapter 5.1.3.

20. See chapters 6.3 and 7.1.

21. See chapter 4.2.

22. In *GA* 4.4, Aristotle says this: "The very thing that is surprising is the reason for one's being not surprised" (771a26–27). If this is so, my explanation may be on the right track. See also *Meta* A2, 983a11–21.

23. Cf. *Phys* 3.4: "For every thing is either a principle or [comes] from a principle" (203b6).

24. Cf. *Meta* Θ9, 1051a17–21:

Consequently, it is clear that *what is bad does not exist apart from the things*, for what is bad is posterior in nature to that of potentiality. As a consequence, neither in the things [that come] from the beginning (ἐν τοῖς ἐξ ἀρχῆς) or in eternal things is there bad or defective or destruction (for destruction is of bad things).

Thus, we can understand why eternity is a criterion of substantiality and why there is a connection between ungenerability and separation, for what is apart is not destructible. See chapter 2.3.4.

25. For example, Reale (1980) believes that it is a polemical argument directed at the Academy (88); Chen (1940) also interprets it as aporetic (117 (footnote 363)). Cf. Alexander of Aphrodisias who also believes that Aristotle's argument is ἔνδοξον and λογικῶς (In *Metaphysica Commentaria*, 210, 21). Madigan translates λογικῶς as "verbal;" according to Madigan, λογικῶς in Alexander is associated with dialectical argument. See Dooley and Madigan (1992), 96 (footnote 34).

26. See Introduction, section 7. See also Introduction (note 12).

27. See Appendix D, section 1.

28. Annas (1976), 188.

29. Ross II (1924), 463.

30. See chapters 2.3.4 and 2.3.6.

31. See chapter 5 (note 25).

32. For example, Apostle (1966).

33. For example, Ross (1908) and Chen (1940), 117.

34. See *Meta* Δ.

35. See W. Ritter (1932; 1934) and Graham (1987), 187 (footnote 5).

36. Blair (1967), 103.

37. *De An* 2.1, 412a22–23.

38. See also chapter 2 (note 24).

39. Cf. *Phys* 8.7, 260b29–30. See Cleary (1988), who discusses this passage, 82–83 and 119 (footnotes 57 and 60). See also chapter 2.3.4.

40. See chapter 2.2 and chapter 2 (note 25).

41. As a matter of fact, the scope of *Meta* H3 is the same, for in H1, 1042a32–b8 all four changes are mentioned. The scope of B4 also seems to be the same, for both motion and coming-to-be are mentioned (999b9).

42. See chapter 4.1.

43. "Indeed from what has been said, nature is said to be in the primary and strict sense the substance of the things which have a principle of motion in themselves *qua* themselves (ἡ οὐσία ἡ τῶν ἐχόντων ἀρχὴν κινήσεως ἐν αὐτοῖς ᾗ αὐτά), for the matter is said to be a nature by being able to receive this, and coming-to-be and growth are so by being the motions [that are derived] from them."

44. See Appendix A.

45. Ross II (1924).

46. See chapter 6.1.

47. See Appendix A.

48. See chapter 4 (note 14).

49. See Introduction, section 5.

50. Ross II (1924), 288.

51. Elders (1969), 104–105.

52. See Introduction, section 5.

53. Where male and female are not found, the seed of such living things contains the mixture (μίγμα) of both principles (724b12–19), and a thing is alive "according to its having a share of the male and of the female" (732a11–13). This includes plants.

54. Aristotle's concept of semen also includes the menstrual fluid (τὰ καταμήνια), which is "semen that is unconcocted" (4.5, 774a2). Sometimes, it is referred to as that which is analogous to the seminal fluid (γονή) in males (1.19, 727a2–4).

55. Preus (1975), 71.

56. However, in *PA* 2.2, 647b14, parts include semen (γονή). Perhaps, parts are said in many ways. Cf. *Meta* Δ25, 1023b12–25.

57. Drossaart Lulofs's emendation. Peck's emendation is this: <ἀ>χώριστα.

58. See also *EN* 8.11, 1161b18. Cf. Ross II (1924), 355.

59. *GA* 2.6, 742a2 (χωρισθέντα); 2.7, 746a28 (χωρισθέντα); and 3.3, 754b12 (χωρίζεται).

60. I clarify what this means in chapter 6.2.2.

61. Lacey (1965), 65, interprets the separation in a very similar way.

62. Cf. Alexander of Aphrodisias. *In Metaphysica Commentaria*, 389, 9–11.

63. See chapter 2.3.6.

64. Cf. *Meta* Θ8, 1049b4–1051a3.

65. See *Meta* Z1, 1028a31–33.

66. See chapter 2.1.4.

6. Power

1. As we saw in chapter 4.1, Aristotle identifies the very same three factors in *Meta* Z7, 1032a13–14, and Z8, 1033a24–27. The only difference is the accent. In *Meta* Z7 and Z8, it is "what (τί)" but in *GA* 733b26 it is "something (τι)." I wonder whether we should also emend the *GA* 733b26 to "what (τί)" in light of the *Meta* Z7 and Z8 passages.

2. In chapter 4.1, I have also focused on the importance of the efficient cause. See chapter 4 (note 13).

3. According to Peck (1942), this term "covers all stages of the living creature's development from the time when the 'matter' is first 'informed' . . . to the time when the creature is born or hatched" (lxii–lxiii). It refers also to "the fetation of plants." As a matter of fact, in the previous context, Aristotle's embryology is applicable to both animals and plants (see 733b23–24, 734a8–9, and 735a16–17). For the sake of simplicity, I focus on the development of

animals; but the importance of the *scope* of Aristotle's analysis is exploited in chapter 6.3.2.

4. See chapter 1 (note 36).

5. My topic is not *dynamis per se*; hence, I do not examine all the senses of *dynamis* in Aristotle's corpus. My target is the very specific sense of *dynamis* that helps us solve our problem.

For different senses of *dynamis*, see *Meta* Δ12, 1019a15–1020a6, and Θ1–9, 1045b27–1051a33. We see that although there appears to be some evidence, the *dynamis* sought cannot clearly be discovered or extracted from the whole of the *Metaphysics*, even from Book Θ, where the topic is *dynamis* itself! I exploit this point later.

6. Cherniss (1944), 470–474 (especially footnote 423).

7. Although Aristotle employs the word "motion (κίνησις)" in the above passage in the *Physics*, his definition and his analysis of motion applies to all four changes (201a3–9). In other words, he is using the term "motion" generically to cover all changes. Cf. Aquinas' Commentary Book 3, Lecture 2.

8. Cf. *Phys* 8.5, 257a33–b13.

9. In *Cat* 7, Aristotle points out that, for the most cases, relatives exist simultaneously by their nature (7b15). And in *An Po* 2.12, he argues that the cause and the effect occur at the same time.

10. Waterlow (1982) also says: ". . . the change *has* two sides and involves two objects, without implying that there are two *changes*" (200); and "one concrete event of which the agency of one individual and the patiency of another are distinguishable but inseparable aspects" (200–201).

11. To distinguish the *dynamis* of an incomplete form (see chapter 6.2.1), I refer to the *dynamis* of a complete form as potency.

12. Burnyeat and others (1982) also refer to the doctrine of *Phys* 3.3 to explain this distinction (51).

13. In the *De Gen et Corr* 2.9, Aristotle ascribes the active and the passive potency to the form and the matter, respectively (335b30–336a1).

14. We should expect Aristotle to be defending preformation (an embryo contains all of its parts from the beginning) rather than epigenesis (a successive development of parts). See Peck (1942), 144–145 (footnote a) and Preus (1975), 285 (endnote 6).

15. See his careful observation in *HA* 6.3, 561a3–562b2. Cf. Preus (1975), 41.

16. Having presented his theory of the reproduction of bees, Aristotle ends the enquiry with the following statement:

But the facts (τὰ συμβαίνοντα) (after Peck) have not been sufficiently gathered; and if ever they are [sufficiently] gathered, then

at that time we must trust our senses rather than our theories, and [we must trust] our theories, if they are shown to agree with the observation (τοῖς φαινομένοις). (*GA* 3.10, 760b30–33)

17. See, for example, *Meta* Z3, 1029b3–12; Z11, 1037a13–16; and Z17, 1041a6–9.
18. See chapter 4.1.
19. See chapter 3.2.
20. Peck (1953), makes a similar point:

[Aristotle] did not consider it sufficient to say that an individual is the result of a particular "form" having become embodied in a particular quantity of "matter;" he accepted the obligation to explain precisely how he thought this embodiment was effected. (112)

21. See chapter 5.2.3.
22. *Meta* Θ8 may be an exception. There, Aristotle identifies nature as a principle of motion *qua* itself (1049b8–11) and argues for a temporal causal analysis (1050b4–6). It is interesting to note that Dancy (1981) does not consider the latter as an Aristotelian doctrine because he believes the first mover is not temporally first (94–95).
23. For example, Rist (1989), 226.
24. See chapter 6.1.
25. Hence, we are not concerned with what Kosman (1984) identifies as the two senses of *dynamis* in *Meta* Θ. According to Kosman, they correspond to the two kinds of actuality—motion (an incomplete actuality) and actuality without qualification (a complete actuality). The former is "a process or activity (in the broad sense) whose end and completion lies outside itself" (e.g., walking, building), and the latter is "a process or activity whose end is nothing other than itself" (127) (e.g., seeing, thinking). We are not concerned with the first sense because it is based on the definition of motion found in *Phys* 3.1–3; that is, it is the *dynamis* that is associated with the traditional account of efficient causality. Nor are we dealing with the second sense, because the development of an embryo is not an actuality without qualification; that is, it is not the kind of process "whose end is nothing other than itself." It is a kind of motion that proceeds from an incomplete to a complete state (e.g., from a fetus to a man). See also Whiting (1992), 88–89. The earlier distinction of *dynamis* is criticized by Heinaman (1994). See also his footnote 1 for the relevant literature.
26. See chapter 5.2.2.
27. The importance of the identification of this kind of *dynamis* with the quality (τὸ ποιόν) is discussed in chapter 6.3.
28. See also *GA* 1.21, 730a2.

29. *GA* 4.3, 767b23ff. This important passage is discussed in 6.3.

30. In chapter 1.1, we saw that, in the *Cat*, the levels of universals (and hence the degrees of substantiality) are based on the different levels of subject. In the *GA*, the different levels of universals are based on the degrees of *dynamis*. In chapter 7.2, I discuss how the correspondence between the degree of *dynamis* and the degree of substantiality can be determined.

31. See also *GA* 2.3:

> An animal and man are not generated at the same time nor an animal and a horse, and similarly with the rest of animals, for the end (τὸ τέλος) is generated later, and the peculiar property (τὸ ἴδιον) is the end of each generation. (736b2–5)

Cf. Furth (1988):

> the original catamenial matter is differentiated through the series of intermediate generic phases to its final (*teleion*) fully specific phase (121).

32. See also chapter 1 (note 36).

33. This is noted by Sorabji, "Body and Soul in Aristotle," reprinted in Durrant (1993): ". . . a first actuality is also describable as a second potentiality (*De An.* 417a21–b2), in other works as a capacity" (164). See Irwin (1988), who also identifies "first actuality" as "a combination of actuality and potentiality" (21); see also 285.

34. See Appendix A.

35. *Phys* 8.2, 253a14–15.

36. *Phys* 8.4, 255a5–9.

37. It is outside the scope of this book to discuss what is meant by "self-movers," for I am interested only in showing *what* self-realization is and that it is not an instance of self-motion (Aristotle criticizes his predecessors for identifying the substance of soul as "that which moves itself (τὸ κινοῦν ἑαυτό)" (*De An* 1.3, 405b31–407b26)). For a general discussion see Furley (1978) and a number of articles on the subject in Gill and Lennox (1994). Cf. also Graham (1996).

As far as "internal-change" is concerned, in this book I simply take it as a generic term applicable to both self-realization and self-motion (as well as applying to whatever other kinds of internal-change there may be).

38. *Phys* 8.4, 255a5–6.

39. I ignore the *De Caelo*, for the doctrine of self- realization is missing, and it is irrelevant to my discussion of whether the *DC* and the *Phys* 8 present a consistent picture of elemental motion. For a general discussion of the *DC* and its relation to the rest of the corpus, see Guthrie (1933) and (1939), xi–xxxvi.

40. Phys 8.4, 255a30–256b3.

41. Lang (1992) argues that given the context of *Phys* 8, that is, given that the crucial point of Aristotle's argument is to show that "everything moved is moved by another," the problem of *"how* this mover produces motion in the elements—as a moving cause or a final cause—is not resolved, because it never arises" (64).

If we accept Lang's analysis and apply it consistently to the *GA* (for both in *Phys* 8.4 and in *GA* 2.1, Aristotle employs the same analogy to explain the different senses of δύναμις), then we also have to accept that, in the *GA*, Aristotle does not explain *how* the semen is moved.

The advantage of my analysis, contra Lang, is that I can maintain both (1) that Aristotle explains the motion of the semen and (2) that the principle of self-realization can be consistently applied to the motion of both the elements and the semen.

See also Sheldon M. Cohen (1994) and (1996), 37–45, for his discussion of elemental motion. According to Cohen, we cannot ascribe a certain natural motion to an element, because there would otherwise be a problem of accounting how, for example, a rock, once it arrives at its natural place, can perform its activity if its proper activity is to go down. The principle that explains elemental motion is rather that of rest or stasis in the sense that what is natural to earth is rest such that, if it is not in the appropriate place, its potentiality to be in that place is realized.

Since the doctrine of self-realization accounts how a being realizes its potentiality to attain its end without ascribing to it any natural motion as its proper activity, the doctrine not only avoids the problem (and my account seems to be consistent with Cohen's analysis), but also underpins the common principle that explains the motion of both the elements and the semen.

42. Bechler (1995), however, sees Aristotle's concept of natural motion (i.e. the motion of elements) and his general theory of motion to be inconsistent with each other (31).

43. If the *De An* and the *GA* are the framework from which to judge the chronology of Aristotle's corpus, then *Phys* 8 will turn out to be a rather late work.

44. A similar concept of *dynamis* is noted by Sorabji, reprinted in Durrant (1993):

> In many cases, *hexeis* and *dunameis* (capacities) are described not as mere tendencies to act, but as efficient causes of action, and as things "from which" and "through which" we act. (179–180)

45. Although we find *dynamis* in a number of passages in Platonic dialogues, this specific sense seems to be missing. Even though in some

cases, for example in *Republic* 6, 509b9, *dynamis*, for the lack of better word, can be translated as power, this is not what I mean by power. I am using the word power in a very specific sense: an active ability that can proceed from what is incomplete to what is complete. In Plato, the main sense of the *dynamis* is that which can act and be acted on (see especially *Sophist* 247d8–e8). Cf. Souilhé (1919), especially 149 and 153. Souilhé also identifies the other senses as "sens" and "facultés," which are less developed in Plato (164). See also Cornford (1957b), 234–239 and (1957a), 52–54.

This active *dynamis* (in the sense of power) is neither what Bechler (1995) calls genuine nor nongenuine (or consistency) potentiality (11–12). It is not a nongenuine potentiality, because nongenuine potentiality is not an principle of motion and can never actualize by itself (24), nor is it a genuine potentiality, because genuine potentiality contains "*all* the conditions that are necessary for the end" (16) such that it exists only in a complete form, as in the case of a man (14). I seem to be defending what he calls the traditional reading whereby "the end is the form and so, by a kind of magic, the not yet actualized form becomes the indwelling form of the object and so the force that propels the object towards its end" (2). So, I guess what I called power is "a kind of magic" according to Bechler. I hope my account will make it less "magical."

46. Recall that by "potency" I mean the *dynamis* of the complete form and by "power" I mean the *dynamis* of the incomplete form. See chapter 6 (note 11).

47. See also Sorabji, reprinted in Durrant (1993): "*the soul as capacities*" (163); "soul just *is* these capacities" (164); and "the soul as a set of capacities" (164).

48. *GA* 1.2, 716a9–13.

49. *GA* 2.1, 734b21–22.

50. *GA* 2.1, 734b13–17.

51. See chapter 5 (note 60).

52. See also Preus (1975), 93–94, for a similar analysis.

53. Preus (1975) comes to the same conclusion:

Thus it is the same power which makes the heart (or its analogue) as constructs the rest of the body once the heart (or analogue) is established (95);

nd also he says:

it *must* be the same power, movement and activity in both cases, that the nutritive and generative power of the soul has a continued existence between parent and offspring. . . . (94)

ee also Moraux (1955):

le mouvement que le sperme communique aux menstrues pour constituer les parties est le même que celui qui provoque la croissance (293).

54. *De An* 2.4, 415b3–7. Cf. *GA* 2.1, 731b31–732a2.

55. *Meta* I1, 1052a31–36.

56. In *Meta* Θ8, however, the contrast is the same in form (τῷ εἴδει τὸ αὐτό) and the same in number (ἀριθμῷ) (1049b1–19). I use the phrases "one in form" and "the same in form" (or "the same form") interchangeably, for "same" is a kind of "one." See *Meta* Δ9, 1018a4–9.

57. See chapters 2.3.4 and 2.3.6.

58. See chapter 5.2.2.

59. See G. E. R. Lloyd (1996), chapter 4, especially 91–95 for his discussion of Aristotle's concept of "concoction."

60. In *GA* 1.21, Aristotle has already stated that what the male contributes to the generation of offspring is not the quantity (τὸ ποσόν) but the quality (τὸ ποιόν) (730a21–22). See chapter 6 (note 27).

61. Insofar as the peculiar and individual (τὸ ἴδιον καὶ τὸ καθ' ἕκαστον) as well as the generic properties, such as man and animal, belong to the generator *qua* generator (καθὸ γεννητικόν) and not accidentally (ἀλλ' οὐ κατὰ συμβεβηκός) (767b27), they exert influence on the formation of an embryo. Aristotle does not explain what he means by accidental properties of a generator, but perhaps he has in mind something like a mutilated (κολοβός) part, for mutilated parents do not produce mutilated offspring (724a3–7).

62. See chapter 6 (note 76).

63. Cf. *De An* 2.4, 416b15–25.

64. See *GA* 1.18, 724b27–28; 1.18, 725a11–12; 2.3, 736b26–27; and 4.1, 766b7–9.

65. Cf. *GA* 2.4, 740a21–22; 4.1, 765b28–35; and *PA* 4.4, 678a6–10.

66. See *GA* 1.19, 726b9–11; and *PA* 3.5, 668a4–13.

67. See *GA* 1.18, 726a26–28; 1.20, 728a18–20; and 4.1, 766a30–36.

68. Cf. *GA* 4.1, 766b9–10.

69. That is why the loss of semen from the body is exhausting, because it is like the loss of fresh blood (726b12–13).

70. See *PA* 3.5, 668a26–27.

71. Furth (1988) recognizes the importance of the twofold capacity of the nutritive soul "threptic and gennetic" as a means by which destructible entities maintain their "temporal persistence," that is, partake of the eternal: "The threptic, in the individual, is the basic faculty of self-*maintenance* across time, . . . The gennetic, in the individual, is the faculty of self-*duplication*" (160–161).

72. The substantial status of female is discussed in 7.2.

73. Although Alexander of Aphrodisias distinguishes art and nature by means of rational (λογική) and nonrational (ἄλογος) *dynamis*, respectively (104,3), the distinction *per se* does not seem to help us solve our problem.

74. *GA* 4.3, 769b13.

75. I wonder if there are some "family resemblances" between this notion of universal that I am ascribing to Aristotle and Wittgenstein's discussion of family resemblances (*Philosophical Investigation*, I, 67)?

76. I say "may" because it is possible for Socrates or anyone else not to have children. We are dealing with sensible destructible substances, thus, his theory is applicable for the most part. In this regard, Aristotle's statement about the claws of crabs is instructive:

> For the most part (ὡς ἐπὶ τὸ πολύ) they all (πάντες) have the right claws bigger and stronger then the left. (*HA* 4.3, 527b6–7)

Mignucci (1981) interprets this passage as follows: πάντες "se réfère à la totalité des espèces des crabes" and (ὡς ἐπὶ τὸ πολύ) "dénote la plupart des individus dans chacune de ces espèces" (186–187).

Similarly, as a species, all men generate men, but this happens for the most part, because there are exceptions.

77. Furth (1988), 133–136.

78. See Cooper (1988) for his discussion of (2).

79. Furth (1988), 134–135.

80. See chapter 4 (note 31).

81. Cf. *GA* 2.1, 734a8–9 and 735a16–17. See also chapter 6 (note 3).

82. Cf. Morsink (1982), 147.

83. See, for example, *GA* 1.20, 729a24 (τὸν λόγον καθόλου) and 1.21, 729b9 (καθόλου).

7. Artifacts

1. For the discussion of "πρὸς ἕν," see, for example, Owens (1978), 107–135; and Owen (1960), "Logic and Metaphysics in some Earlier Works of Aristotle," reprinted in Owen (1986), 180–199.

2. Aristotle's *Metaphysics* has been understood by various commentators as theology, ontology, or something else. See Owens (1978), for the first view; Leszl (1970), for the second; and Reale (1980), for the third (he believes that it is a combination of aiteology, ousiology, ontology, and theology).

3. I do not enter into the controversial debate on how many unmoved movers Aristotle believed are required to account for the movements of heavenly spheres in Λ8. For the sake of simplicity, I refer to them (or it) as

God. See Rist (1989) 239–240 for the view that Aristotle posited only one unmoved mover.

4. *Meta* Λ1, 1069a30–35 and Λ6, 1071b3–5.

5. See *De An* 2.2, 413b27.

6. See *De Gen et Corr* 2.10, 366a15–377a34. And see also *Phys* 2.2: "Both man and the *Sun* generate man" (194b13).

7. See chapter 4 (note 32).

8. One might argue that I have been equivocating on the word "eternal." For example, von Leyden (1964) believes that 'Aion a divine nature' "must practically come to mean the same as timelessness" (47). Sorabji (1983), on the other hand, maintains that "the eternity (aiōn) of Aristotle's God is not timelessness," but "everlasting duration" (127).

Since Aristotle himself employs the same word "eternal (ἀΐδιον)" for the principles of both indestructible and destructible entities (as we saw in chapter 2.3.4 and chapter 3.1.1), I am inclined to agree with Sorabji. But even if von Leyden is correct, we need not assume that eternal is an equivocal term, for it is most likely a πρὸς ἕν term.

9. *De An* 2.4, 415b3–7 and *GA* 2.1, 731b31–732a2. See also chapter 5 (note 16).

10. Perhaps this is why, in PA 1.1, Aristotle says "the for the sake of which (τὸ οὗ ἕνεκα) and beauty (τὸ καλόν) exist rather (μᾶλλον) in the works of nature than in the works of art" (639b19–21).

11. Note that a form of a composite is always enmattered. By "separate" it does not mean that it can exist on its own apart from some particular composite or other, but rather it is separable in the sense that it can exist apart from any particular composite.

Again I need not be equivocating on the word "separate" (in the sense that it is used for the Unmoved Mover). It is most likely a πρὸς ἕν term. See also chapter 7 (note 8).

12. See chapter 6 (note 76).

13. See chapter 3 (note 35).

14. See chapter 4 (note 9).

15. For a general discussion of Aristotle's doctrine of *pneuma*, see Jaeger (1913); Solmsen (1957); Peck (1942), 576–593 (Appendix B); Peck (1953); and Freudenthal (1995). See also Freudenthal (1995), 106 (footnote 3) for other relevant literature.

16. For a similar discussion of what follows, see Rist (1989), 246–249. For the discussion of other roles that *pneuma* plays in Aristotle's philosophy, see Nussbaum (1978), 143–165; and Freudenthal (1995), especially for an account of *pneuma* in Aristotle's physiological theory.

17. I have argued that the criteria of substantiality are eternity and actuality. And if *pneuma* plays an important role in the generation of animals,

that is, if it is an instrument by means of which animals can transmit their *dynamis* and thereby partake of the divine and the eternal, then it is indeed a body more divine than the four elements. Therefore, although some scholars are reluctant to make a close analogy between *aether* and *pneuma* on the strength of this passage of *GA* (e.g., Balme (1972), 163), in light of our discussion, perhaps we may have good reason for believing that there is a close analogy, for in the *De Caelo* Aristotle argues that *aether* is ungenerable, indestructible, and divine (1.2, 269a31 and 1.3, 270a14). Cf. Peck (1942), 170–171 (footnote e). See also the discussion of this analogy in Freudenthal (1995), 115–119.

18. Cf. *GA* 3.2, 753a18–19; 4.1, 765b15–16; 4.6, 775a17–18; and 5.4, 786a17.

19. Cf. *GA* 2.8, 748b31–32; 4.1, 765b16–17; and 4.6, 775a5–7.

20. See also *GA* 1.19, 726b33–34; 2.4, 738a13; and 4.6, 775a14–15.

21. Cf. *GA* 5.4, 784a33–34.

22. *GA* 4.2, 766b29–34.

23. *GA* 2.4, 737a28.

24. *GA* 1.20, 728a18.

25. See chapter 1 (note 32).

26. See chapter 1 (note 19).

27. But we should note that eventually all hybrids end up producing females (2.4, 738b27–35).

28. *GA* 2.3, 737a3–5; 2.6, 743a35–36; and 3.11, 762b12–18.

29. Solmsen (1957), 119–120. Cf. Freudenthal (1995), 65–70.

30. See chapter 6 (note 72).

31. I say some because male mules may occasionally generate (748b31–32). For the sake of simplicity, henceforth I shall not make this qualification in the text (although the reader should keep in mind that this is implied).

32. See chapters 1 (note 33) and 3 (note 68).

33. See also Grene (1963), especially 227–233.

34. Burnyeat (1992) argues that Aristotle's philosophy of mind is no longer credible. See a number of papers in Nussbaum and Rorty (1992) for their reactions. Cf. G. E. R. Lloyd (1996), 63–65.

35. See *Meta* Z1, 1028a31–33 and Z13, 1038b27–29. Cf. also *Meta* Θ8.

36. Although I have not examined what Sheldon M. Cohen (1996) calls natural artifacts (29–31), such as spider webs, bird nests, and beaver dams, an analogous relationship exists between animals and their artifacts.

37. I say "in primary sense" because matter is also a substance (Z3, 1028b33–1029a33), that is, a metaphysical principle in the sense that it is potentiality. They are six material principles (or elements): earth, water, air, fire, *aether*, and *pneuma*. In conjunction with three kinds of substances (God, heavenly spheres, and animals and plants that are capable of reproducing), Aristotle can explain every phenomena (both supra- and sub-lunary).

38. *Nota Bene*: my topic is the substantial status of artifacts *in the Metaphysics*.

39. In other works of Aristotle (e.g., in the *Categories*), all *pragmata* may turn out to be substances.

Hence, I do not deny artifacts (or any other nonsubstantial *pragmata*) of what Husain (1996) calls "the categorical status;" that is, these *pragmata* are substances according to the categorical schema. By nonsubstantial *pragmata*, I mean those beings that are not metaphysical principles.

40. Fictitious things such as goat-stags, may also be included in the list. In this book, I am not interested in the status of nonexistent things. For a discussion of the ontological status of fictitious things, see Rist (1989), 271–272.

41. Cf. Rorty (1973), 414 (footnote 30).

42. Thus, we can understand why we could not distinguish between natural substances and artifacts by merely appealing to the categorical schema, for it is the principle of actuality and potentiality that is crucial in determining the substantial status of *pragmata*. Cf. *De An* 2.1, 412b8–9, where Aristotle identifies, among the many senses of one and being, the authoritative (κυρίως) sense as that of actuality.

43. Rorty (1973) speaks of a mule as "a potentiality" (413).

44. Cf. *PA* 2.1, 646a14–15.

45. Chapter 5.2.3.

46. *Meta* Z16, 1040b9.

Appendix A

1. Cf. *De An* 2.1, 412b15–17: "The soul is not the essence (τὸ τί ἦν εἶναι) and the formula of this sort of body [such as that of an axe], but that of natural [body] of the sort that has the principle of motion and standstill in itself."

2. Witt (1989), 65–79, seems to be unaware of this when she identifies generation as an instance of what she calls "self-change."

3. Cf. 416b16–17. See also *De Motu* 5, 700a34–b3.

4. In the course of our discussion, the importance of the difference between the form understood as the principle of internal–change and that of generation in connection with the ontological status of artifacts is fully exposed (see especially chapters 2.3.6 and 5.2).

Appendix D

1. For "Notes on Appendix D," see Introduction, section 7.

2. Following Ross, I understand καί as epexegetic. See Ross I (1924), 241.

3. In *Phys* 1.9, 192a25–29, matter is said to be ungenerable and indestructible according to potentiality (κατὰ δύναμιν).

4. Alexander of Aphrodisias also understands that Aristotle argues that the form must be eternal (εἶναι δεῖ ἀίδιον) (214, 27–28) and that this form is an active agent (τὸ ποιητικόν) (215, 17). See also Dooley and Madigan (1992), 160 (footnote 318).

5. For the phrase "it is possible that" (to indicate Aristotle's ambivalence about the ontological status of artifacts in the *Metaphysics*), see chapter 2.1.4.

Bibliography

I. Primary Sources

Plato

Burnet, J. (1900–1907). *Platonis Opera*, 5 vols. Oxford: Clarendon Press.

Aristotle

(i) *Organon*

Ackrill, J. L. (1963). *Aristotle's Categories and De Interpretatione*. Oxford: Clarendon Press.

Apostle, Hippocrates G. (1980). *Aristotle's Categories and Propositions*. Grinnell, Iowa: The Peripatetic Press.

———. (1981). *Aristotle's Posterior Analytics*. Grinnell, Iowa: The Peripatetic Press.

Forster, E. S. (1955). *On Sophistical Refutations* (Loeb Classical Library III). Cambridge, Mass.: Harvard University Press.

———. (1960). *Topica* (Loeb Classical Library II). Cambridge, Mass.: Harvard University Press.

Minio–Paluello, L. (1949). *Aristotelis Categoriae et Liber de Interpretatione*. Oxford: Clarendon Press.

———. (1964). *Aristotelis Analytica Priora et Posteriora*. Oxford: Clarendon Press.

(ii) Physical Treatises

Allan, D. J. (1955). *Aristotelis De Caelo*. Oxford: Clarendon Press.

Apostle, Hippocrates G. (1969). *Aristotle's Physics*. Grinnell, Iowa: The Peripatetic Press.

———. (1981). *Aristotle's On the Soul*. Grinnell, Iowa: The Peripatetic Press.

Balme, D. M. (1972). *Aristotle's De Partibus Animalium I and De Generatione Animalium I*. Oxford: Clarendon Press.

———. (1991). *History of Animals Books VII–X* (Loeb Classical Library XI). Cambridge, Mass.: Harvard University Press.

Charlton, W. (1970). *Aristotle's Physics Books I and II*. Oxford: Clarendon Press.

Drossaart Lulofs, H. J. (1965). *Aristotelis De Generatione Animalium*. Oxford: Clarendon Press.

Forster, E. S. (1955). *On Coming-to-be and Passing Away* (Loeb Classical Library III). Cambridge, Mass.: Harvard University Press.

Guthrie, W. K. C. (1939). *On the Heavens* (Loeb Classical Library VI). Cambridge, Mass.: Harvard University Press.

Hamlyn, D. W. (1968). *Aristotle's De Anima Books II and III*. Oxford: Clarendon Press.

Hett, W. S. (1957). *Parva Naturalia* (Loeb Classical Library VIII). Cambridge, Mass.: Harvard University Press.

Hicks, Robert Drew (1907). *Aristotle De Anima*. Salem, N.H.: Ayer Company.

Louis, Pierre. (1961). *Aristote De la Génération des Animaux*. Paris: Société d' édition.

Nussbaum, Martha Craven. (1978). *Aristotle's De Motu Animalium*. Princeton, N.J.: Princeton University Press.

Peck, A. L. (1942). *Generation of Animals* (Loeb Classical Library XIII). Cambridge, Mass.: Harvard University Press.

———. (1961). *Parts of Animals* (Loeb Classical Library XII). Cambridge, Mass.: Harvard University Press.

———. (1965). *History of Animals Books I–III* (Loeb Classical Library IX). Cambridge, Mass.: Harvard University Press.

———. (1970). *History of Animals Books IV–VI* (Loeb Classical Library X). Cambridge, Mass.: Harvard University Press.

Ross, W. D. (1936). *Aristotle's Physics*. Oxford: Clarendon Press.

———. (1955). *Aristotle Parva Naturalia*. Oxford: Clarendon Press.

———. (1956). *Aristotelis Physica*. Oxford: Clarendon Press.

———. (1956). *Aristotelis De Anima*. Oxford: Clarendon Press.

(iii) Metaphysics

Annas, Julia. (1976). *Aristotle's Metaphysics Books M and N*. Oxford: Clarendon Press.

Apostle, Hippocrates G. (1966). *Aristotle's Metaphysics*. Grinnell, Iowa: The Peripatetic Press.

Bostock, David. (1994). *Aristotle Metaphysics Books Z and H.* Oxford: Clarendon Press.
Frede, Michael and Patzig, Günther (1988). *Aristoteles, Metaphysik Z'*, 2 vols. München: C. H. Beck.
Furth, Montgomery. (1985). *Aristotle Metaphysics Books VII–X.* Indianapolis: Hackett.
Jaeger, W. (1957). *Aristotelis Metaphysica.* Oxford: Clarendon Press.
Ross, W. D. (1908). *Metaphysica* (The Works of Aristotle VIII). Oxford: Clarendon Press.
————. (1924). *Aristotle's Metaphysics*, 2 vols. Oxford: Clarendon Press.

(iv) Others

Apostle, Hippocrates G. (1975). *Aristotle's Nicomachean Ethics.* Grinnell, Iowa: The Peripatetic Press.
Bywater, I. (1894). *Aristotelis Ethica Nicomachea.* Oxford: Clarendon Press.
Fine, Gail. (1993). *On Ideas.* Oxford: Clarendon Press.
Leszl, Walter. (1975). *Il "De Ideis" di Aristotele e la Teoria Platonica delle Idee.* Florence: Olschki.
Ross, W. D. (1955). *Aristotelis Fragmenta Selecta.* Oxford: Clarendon Press.

Alexander of Aphrodisias

Dooley, William E. (1989). *Alexander of Aphrodisias: On Aristotle Metaphysics 1.* London: Duckworth.
————. (1993). *Alexander of Aphrodisias: On Aristotle Metaphysics 5.* London: Duckworth.
Dooley, William E. and Madigan, Arthur. (1992). *Alexander of Aphrodisias: On Aristotle's Metaphysics 2 & 3.* Ithaca: Cornell University Press.
Hayduck, M. (1891). *In Aristotelis Metaphysica Commentaria.* Berlin: Reimer.
Madigan, Arthur. (1993). *Alexander of Aphrodisias: On Aristotle Metaphysics 4.* London: Duckworth.

Thomas Aquinas

Rowan, John P. (1995). *Commentary on Aristotle's Metaphysics.* Notre Dame, Ind.: Dumb Ox Books.

II. Secondary Sources

Ackrill, J. L. (1973). "Aristotle's Definitions of *PSUCHE*," *Proceedings of the Aristotelian Society* 73, 119–133.

————. (1991). "Change and Aristotle's Theological Argument," *Oxford Studies in Ancient Philosophy*, Supplementary Volume, 57–66.

Albritton, Rogers. (1957). "Forms of Particular Substances in Aristotle's *Metaphysics*," *Journal of Philosophy* 54, 699–708.

Allen, D. J. (1960). "Aristotle and the *Parmenides*" in Düring and Owen (1960), 133–144.

Allen, R. E. (1969). "Individual Properties in Aristotle's Categories," *Phronesis* 14, 31–39.

————. (1970). *Plato's 'Euthyphro' and the Earlier Theory of Forms*. London: Routledge & Kegan Paul.

————. (1973). "Substance and Predication in Aristotle's *Categories*," *Phronesis*, Supplementary Volume 1, 362–373.

Annas, Julia. (1974). "Individual in Aristotle's 'Categories': Two Queries," *Phronesis* 19, 146–152.

————. (1982). "Aristotle on Inefficient Causes," *Philosophical Quarterly* 32, 311–326.

Anscombe, G. E. M., and Geach, P. T. (1961). *Three Philosophers*. Ithaca: Cornell University Press.

Anton, John P. (1968). "The Meaning of Ὁ λόγος τῆς οὐσίας in Aristotle's *Categories* 1a," *Monist* 52, 252–267.

Ayers, Michael R. (1981). "Locke verses Aristotle on Natural Kinds," *Journal of Philosophy* 78, 247–272.

Balme, D. M. (1962a). "ΓΕΝΟΣ and ΕΙΔΟΣ in Aristotle's Biology," *Classical Quarterly* N.S. 12, 81–98.

————. (1962b). "Development of Biology in Aristotle and Theophrastus: Theory of Spontaneous Generation," *Phronesis* 7, 91–104.

————. (1984). "The Snub" reprinted in Gotthelf and Lennox (1987), 306–312.

————. (1987a). "Aristotle's Biology was not Essentialist" revised in Gotthelf and Lennox (1987), 291–302.

————. (1987b). "Aristotle's use of division and differentiae" in Gotthelf and Lennox (1987), 69–89.

————. (1987c). "Note on the *aporia* in *Metaphysics* Z" in Gotthelf and Lennox (1987), 302–306.

Barnes, J., Schofield, M., and Sorabji, R., eds. (1975–79). *Articles on Aristotle*, 4 vols. London: Duckworth.

Beach, J. D. (1958). "Aristotle's Notion of Being," *The Thomist* 21, 29–43.

Bechler, Zev. (1995). *Aristotle's Theory of Actuality*. Albany: State University of New York Press.

Benn, Alfred. (1896). "The Idea of Nature in Plato," *Archiv für Geschichte Der Philosophie* 9, 24–49.

Berti, Enrico. (1975). "Logical and Ontological Priority Among the Genera of Substance in Aristotle" in *Kephalaion: Studies in Greek*

Philosophy, eds. J. Mansfeld and L. M. de Rijk. Assen: Van Gorcum, 55–69.

———. (1996). "Does Aristotle's Dialectic Develop?" in Wians (1996), 105–130.

Blackwell, Richard J. (1957). "The Methodological Function of the Categories in Aristotle," *The New Scholasticism* 31, 526–537.

Blair, George A. (1967). "The Meaning of 'Energeia' and 'Entelecheia' in Aristotle," *International Philosophical Quarterly* 7, 101–117.

Block, Irving. (1961). "The Order of Aristotle's Psychological Writings," *American Journal of Philology* 82, 50–77.

———. (1978). "Substance in Aristotle," *Paideia, Special Aristotle Issue*, 59–64.

Bluck, R. S. (1947). "Aristotle, Plato, and Ideas of *Artefacta*," *The Classical Review* 61, 75–76.

Boas, George. (1943). "A Basic Conflict in Aristotle's Philosophy," *American Journal of Philology* 64, 172–193.

Bonitz, Hermannus. (1870). *Index Aristotelicus*. Darmstadt: Wissenschaftliche Buchgesellschaft.

Boylan, Michael. (1983). *Method and Practice in Aristotle's Biology*. Washington, D.C.: University Press of America.

Brentano, Franz. (1975). *On the Several Senses of Being in Aristotle*. ed. and trans. Rolf George. Berkeley: University of California Press.

———. (1977). *The Psychology of Aristotle*. ed. and trans. Rolf George. Berkeley: University of California Press.

———. (1978). *Aristotle and his World View*. eds. and trans. R. George and R. M. Chisholm. Berkeley: University of California.

Broadie, Sarah. (1987). "Nature, Craft and Phronesis in Aristotle," *Philosophical Topics* 15 (no. 2), 35–50.

Brody, Baruch A. (1973). "Why Settle for Anything Less than Good Old-Fashioned Aristotelian Essentialism," *Nous* 7, 351–65.

———. (1980). *Identity and Essence*. Princeton, N.J.: Princeton University Press.

Brumbaugh, Robert S. (1954). "Aristotle's Outline of the Problems of First Philosophy," *Review of Metaphysics* 7, 511–521.

Buchanan, Emerson. (1962). *Aristotle's Theory of Being*. University, Miss.: <s.n.>.

Burge, Evan L. (1971). "The Ideas as Aitiai in the *Phaedo*," *Phronesis* 16, 1–13.

Burnyeat, M. F. (1982). "Gods and Heaps" in Schofield and Nussbaum (1982), 315–338.

———. (1992). "Is an Aristotelian Philosophy of Mind Still Credible? A Draft" in Nussbaum and Rorty (1992), 15–26.

Burnyeat and others. (1979). *Notes on Book Zeta of Aristotle's Metaphysics*. Oxford: Sub-faculty of Philosophy.

———. (1982). *Notes on Books Eta and Theta of Aristotle's Metaphysics*. Oxford: Sub-faculty of Philosophy.

Bury, R. G. (1894). "Δύναμις and Φύσις in Plato," *Classical Review* 8, 297–300.

———. (1895). "The Later Platonism," *Journal of Philology* 23, 161–201.

Bynum, Terrell Ward (1987). "A New Look at Aristotle's Theory of Perception" reprinted in Durrant (1993), 90–109.

Cartwright, Helen. (1990). "Commentary on Whiting," *Proceedings of the Boston Area Colloquium in Ancient Philosophy* 6, 64–75.

Case, T. (1925). "The Development of Aristotle," *Mind* 34(NS), 80–86.

Charles, David. (1994). "Matter and Form: Unity, Persistence, and Identity" in Scaltsas, Charles and Gill (1994), 75–105.

Charlton, William. (1980). "Aristotle's Definition of Soul" reprinted in Durrant (1993), 197–216.

———. (1994). "Aristotle on Identity" in Scaltsas, Charles and Gill (1994), 41–53.

Chen, Chung-Hwan. (1940). *Das Chorismos-Problem bei Aristoteles*. PhD. thesis. Berlin: Friedrich-Wilhelms-Universität.

———. (1957a). "Aristotle's Concept of Primary Substance in Books Z and H of the *Metaphysics*," *Phronesis* 2, 46–59.

———. (1957b). "On Aristotle's Two Expressions: καθ' ὑποκειμένου λέγεσθαι and ἐν ὑποκειμένῳ εἶναι," *Phronesis* 2, 148–159.

———. (1964). "Universal Concrete, A Typical Aristotelian Duplication of Reality," *Phronesis* 9, 48–57.

———. (1976). *Sophia: The Science Aristotle Sought*. New York: Georg Olms Verlag Hildersheim.

Cherniss, Harold. (1936). "The Philosophical Economy of the Theory of Ideas," *American Journal of Philology* 57, 445–456.

———. (1944). *Aristotle's Criticism of Plato and the Academy*. Baltimore: Johns Hopkins University Press.

Chroust, Anton-Hermann. (1961). "The Origin of "Metaphysics," *Review of Metaphysics* 14, 601–616.

———. (1962). "The Miraculous Disappearance and Recovery of the Corpus Aristotelicum," *Classica et Mediaevalia* 23, 50–67.

———. (1964). "Some Observation on the origin of the Term 'Philosopher,'" *New Scholasticism* 38, 423–434.

———. (1973). *Aristotle: New Light on his Life and on Some of his Lost Works*, Vols. I, II. London: Routledge & Kegan Paul.

Clagett, Marshall. (1955). *Greek Science in Antiquity*. New York: Abelard-Schuman.

Cleary, John J. (1988). *Aristotle on the Many Senses of Priority*. Carbondale: Southern Illinois University Press.

Code, Alan. (1978a). "No Universal is a Substance—An Interpretation of *Metaphysics* Z13 1038b8–15," *Paideia, Special Aristotle Issue*, 65–74.

————. (1978b). "What is It to be an Individual?" *Journal of Philosophy* 75, 647–648.

————. (1984). "The Aporematic Approach to Primary Being in *Metaphysics* Z," *Canadian Journal of Philosophy*, Suppl. Vol. 10, 1–20.

————. (1986). "Aristotle: Essence and Accident" in *Philosophical Grounds of Rationality: Intensions, Categories, Ends*. eds. R. E. Grandy and R. Warner, Oxford: Clarendon Press, 411–439.

————. (1987). "Soul as Efficient Cause in Aristotle's Embryology," *Philosophical Topics* 15, 51–59.

Code, Alan, and Moravcsik, Julius. (1992). "Explaining Various Forms of Living" in Nussbaum and Rorty (1992), 129–145.

Cohen, Sheldon M. (1994). "Aristotle on Elemental Motion," *Phronesis* 39, 150–159.

————. (1996). *Aristotle on Nature and Incomplete Substance*. Cambridge: Cambridge University Press.

Cohen, S. Marc. (1978). "Individual and Essence in Aristotle's *Metaphysics*," *Paideia, Special Aristotle Issue*, 75–85.

————. (1992). "Hylomorphism and Functionalism" in Nussbaum and Rorty (1992), 57–73.

Cooper, John M. (1982). "Aristotle on Natural Teleology" in Schofield and Nussbaum (1982), 197–222.

————. (1988). "Metaphysics in Aristotle's Embryology," *Proceedings of the Cambridge Philological Society*, 214 (NS, 34), 14–41.

Cornford, F. M. (1912). "Psychology and Social Structure in the *Republic* of Plato," *Classical Quarterly* 6, 246–265.

————. (1957a). *Plato's Cosmology*. New York: The Liberal Arts Press.

————. (1957b). *Plato's Theory of Knowledge*. New York: The Liberal Arts Press.

————. (1957c). *Plato and Parmenides*. New York: The Liberal Arts Press.

Cousin, D. R. (1933). "Aristotle's Doctrine of Substance," *Mind* 42, 319–337.

Dancy, Russell. (1975). "On Some of Aristotle's First Thoughts About Substances," *Philosophical Review* 84, 338–373.

————. (1978). "On Some of Aristotle's Second Thoughts About Substances: Matter," *Philosophical Review* 87, 372–413.

————. (1981). "Aristotle and the Priority of Actuality" in Knuuttila (1981), 73–115.

Davies, J. Llewelyn. (1897). "Plato's Later Theory of Ideas," *Journal of Philology* 25, 4–25.

Demos, Raphael. (1944–45). "The Structure of Substance According to Aristotle," *Philosophy and Phenomenological Research* 5, 255–268.

Driscoll, John A. (1981). "ΕΙΔΗ in Aristotle's Earlier and Later Theories of Substance" in *Studies in Aristotle*. ed. D. J. O'Meara. Washington, D.C.: Catholic University of America Press.

Dronke, E. P. M. (1960). Review of Charlesworth's *Aristotle on Art and Nature. The Australasian Journal of Philosophy* 38, 188–192.

Drossaart Lulofs, H. J. (1957). "Aristotle's ΠΕΡΙ ΦΥΤΩΝ," *Journal of Hellenic Studies* 77, 75–80.

Düring, Ingemar. (1956). "Aristotle and Plato in the Mid–Fourth Century," *Eranos* 54, 109–120.

———. (1960). "Aristotle on Ultimate Principles from 'Nature and Reality'" in Düring and Owen (1960), 35–55.

Düring, I., and Owen, G. E. L. (eds.). (1960). *Aristotle and Plato in the Mid-Fourth Century*. Proceedings of the First Symposium Aristotelicum. Göteburg.

Durrant, Michael, ed. (1993). *Aristotle's De Anima in Focus*. London: Routledge.

Dybikowski, James C. (1972). "Professor Owen, Aristotle, and the Third Man Argument," *Mind* 81, 445–447.

East, Simon-Pierre. (1958). "De la méthode en biologie selon Aristote," *Laval Théologique et Philosophique* 14, 213–235.

Easterling, H. J. (1966). "A Note on *De Anima* 413a8–9," *Phronesis* 11, 159–162.

Elders, Leo. (1960). *Aristotle's Theory of the One*. Assen: Van Gorcum.

———. (1972). *Aristotle's Theology*. Assen: Van Gorcum.

Else, Gerald Frank (1936). "The Terminology of the Ideas," *Harvard Studies in Classical Philology* 47, 17–55.

Ferejohn, Michael. (1994). "The Definition of Generated Composites in Aristotle's *Metaphysics*" in Scaltsas, Charles and Gill (1994), 291–318.

Field, G. C. (1967). *Plato and his Contemporaries: A Study in Fourth-Century Life and Thought*. London: Methuen & Co.

Fine, Gail. (1984). "Separation," *Oxford Studies in Ancient Philosophy* 2, 31–87.

———. (1985). "Separation: A Reply to Morrison," *Oxford Studies in Ancient Philosophy* 3, 159–165.

Fine, Kit. (1994). "A Puzzle Concerning Matter and Form" in Scaltsas, Charles and Gill (1994), 13–40.

Fortenbaugh, W. W. (1977). "Aristotle on Slaves and Women" in Barnes, Schofield, and Sorabji, vol 2 (1977), 135–139.

Frank, Daniel H. (1984). *The Arguments 'From the Sciences' in Aristotle's Peri Ideon*. New York: Peter Lang.

Frank, Erich. (1927). "Das Problem des Lebens bei Hegel und Aristoteles," *Deutsche Vierteljahrsschrift Für Literaturwissenschaft und Geistesgeschichte* 5, 608–643.

———. (1940). "The Fundamental Opposition of Plato and Aristotle," *American Journal of Philology* 61, 34–53, 166–185.

Frede, Michael. (1987). *Essays in Ancient Philosophy*. Minneapolis: University of Minnesota Press.

————. (1992). "On Aristotle's Conception of the Soul" in Nussbaum and Rorty (1992), 93–107.

————. (1994). "Aristotle's Notion of Potentiality in *Metaphysics* Θ" in Scaltsas, Charles and Gill (1994), 173–193.

Freeland, Cynthia A. (1994). "Aristotle on Perception, Appetition, and Self–Motion" in Gill and Lennox (1994), 35–63.

Freundenthal, Gad. (1995). *Aristotle's Theory of Material Substances: Heat and Pneuma, Form and Soul*. Oxford: Clarendon Press.

Furley, David J. (1978). "Self Movers" in Lloyd and Owen (1978), 165–179.

Furth, Montgomery. (1978). "Transtemporal Stability in Aristotelean Substances," *Journal of Philosophy* 75, 624–646.

————. (1988). *Substance, Form and Psyche: An Aristotelean Metaphysics*. Cambridge: Cambridge University Press.

Gallop, David. (1975). *Plato: Phaedo* (trans. with notes). Oxford: Clarendon Press.

Gerson, Lloyd P. (1983). "The Aristotelianism of Joseph Owens," *Ancient Philosophy* 3, 72–81.

————. (1984). "Artifacts, Substances, and Essences," *Apeiron* 18, 50–57.

————. (1990). *God and Greek Philosophy: Studies in the Early History of Natural Theology*. London: Routledge.

Gewirth, Alan. (1953). "Aristotle's Doctrine of Being," *Philosophical Review* 62, 577–589.

Gill, Mary Louise. (1989). *Aristotle on Substance: The Paradox of Unity*. Princeton, N.J.: Princeton University Press.

————. (1991). "Aristotle on Self-Motion" reprinted in Gill and Lennox (1994), 15–34.

————. (1994). "Individuals and Individuation in Aristotle" in Scaltsas, Charles and Gill (1994), 55–71.

Gill, M., and Lennox, J., eds. (1994). *Self-Motion: From Aristotle to Newton*. Princeton, N.J.: Princeton University Press.

Gillespie, C. M. (1912). "The Use of Εἶδος and Ἰδέα in Hippocrates," *Classical Quarterly* 6, 179–203.

————. (1925). "The Aristotelian Categories," *Classical Quarterly* 19, 75–84.

Goldin, Owen. (1989). "Problems with Graham's Two-Systems Hypothesis," *Oxford Studies in Ancient Philosophy* 7, 203–213.

Gotthelf, Allan. (1976). "Aristotle's Conception of Final Causality," *Review of Metaphysics* 30, 226–254.

————, (ed.) (1985). *Aristotle on Nature and Living Things*. Pittsburg, Pa.: Mathesis Publications, Inc.; Briston, England: Bristol Classical Press.

———. (1985a). "Notes towards a Study of Substance and Essence in Aristotle's *Parts of Animals* ii–iv" in Gotthelf (1985), 27–54.

Gotthelf, A., and Lennox, J., (eds.) (1987). *Philosophical Issues in Aristotle's Biology*. Cambridge: Cambridge University Press.

Graham, Daniel W. (1987). *Aristotle's Two Systems*. Oxford: Clarendon Press.

———. (1987). "Two Systems in Aristotle," *Oxford Studies in Ancient Philosophy* 7, 215–231.

———. (1996). "The Metaphysics of Motion: Natural Motion in *Physics* II and *Physics* VIII" in Wians (1996), 171–192.

Grene, Majorie. (1963). *A Portrait of Aristotle*. Chicago: University of Chicago Press.

———. (1974). "Is Genus to Species as Matter to Form? Aristotle and Taxonomy," *Synthese* 28, 51–69.

Guthrie, W. K. C. (1933). "The Development of Aristotle's Theology—I," *Classical Quarterly* 27, 162–171.

Hackforth, R. (1955). *Plato's Phaedo*. Cambridge.

Halper, Edward C. (1984). "Aristotle on Knowledge of Nature," *Review of Metaphysics* 37, 811–835.

———. (1989). *One and Many in Aristotle's Metaphysics: The Central Books*. Columbus: Ohio State University Press.

Hants, Harold Donovan. (1939). *The Biological Motivation in Aristotle*. Doctoral dissertation, Columbia University.

Hardie, W. F. R. (1936). *A Study in Plato*. Oxford: Clarendon Press.

———. (1964). "Aristotle's Treatment of the Relation between the Soul and the Body," *Philosophical Quarterly* 14, 53–72.

Hare, J. E. (1979). "Aristotle and the Definition of Natural Things," *Phronesis* 24, 168–179.

Haring, Ellen Stone. (1956–57). "Substantial Form in Aristotle's *Metaphysics* Z," *Review of Metaphysics* 10, 308–332, 482–501, 698–713.

Harter, Edward D. (1975). "Aristotle on Primary ΟΥΣΙΑ," *Archiv für Geschichte der Philosophie* 57, 1–20.

Hartman, Edwin. (1976). "Aristotle on the Identity of Substance and Essence," *Philosophical Review* 85, 545–561.

———. (1977). *Substance, Body, and Soul: Aristotelian Investigations*. Princeton, N.J.: Princeton University Press.

Haslanger, Sally. (1994). "Parts, Compounds, and Substantial Unity," in Scaltsas, Charles and Gill (1994), 129–170.

Heidel, W. A. (1912). "On Anaximander," *Classical Philology* 7, 212–234.

Heinaman, Robert. (1979). "Aristotle's Tenth Aporia," *Archiv für Geschichte der Philosophie* 61, 249–270.

———. (1981). "Non-substantial Individuals in the *Categories*," *Phronesis* 26, 295–307.

————. (1994). "Kosman on Activity and Change," *Oxford Studies in Ancient Philosophy* 12, 207–218.

Hintikka, Jaakko. (1981). "Aristotle on the Realization of Possibilities in Time" in Knuuttila (1981), 57–72.

Hughes, Gerald J. (1978). "Universals as Potential Substances: The Interpretation of *Metaphysics* Z13" in Burnyeat and others (1979), 107–126.

Husain, Martha. (1996). "The Ontological Status of Artifacts in Aristotle's *Metaphysics*." A paper presented at SAGP, Binghamton, New York, October 26, 1996.

Irwin, T. H. (1977). "Plato's Heracleiteanism," *The Philosophical Quarterly* 27, 1–13.

————. (1988). *Aristotle's First Principles*. Oxford: Clarendon Press.

Jackson, Henry. "Plato's Later Theory of Ideas," *Journal of Philology*: I, 10 (1882), 253–298; II, 11 (1882), 287–331; III, 13 (1885), 1–40; IV, 13, (1885), 242–272; V, 14 (1885), 173–230; VI, 15 (1885), 280–305; VII, 25 (1897), 65–82.

Jacobs, William. (1978). "Art and Biology in Aristotle," *Paideia, Special Aristotle Issue*, 16–27.

Jaeger, Werner. (1913). "Das Pneuma im Lykeion," *Hermes* 48, 29–74.

————. (1947). *The Theology of the Early Greek Philosophers*. Oxford: Clarendon Press.

————. (1948). *Aristotle—Fundamentals of the History of his Development*, 2nd ed. trans. R. Robinson. Oxford: Clarendon Press.

Jones, Barrington. (1972). "Individuals in Aristotle's Categories," *Phronesis* 17, 107–123.

————. (1975). "An Introduction to the First Five Chapters of Aristotle's Categories," *Phronesis* 20, 146–172.

Jones, Roger Miller. (1926). "The Ideas as the Thoughts of God," *Classical Philology* 21, 317–326.

Judson, Lindsay. (1994). "Heavenly Motion and the Unmoved Mover" in Gill and Lennox (1994), 155–171.

Kahn, Charles H. (1981). "The Role of *Nous* in the Cognition of First Principles in *Posterior Analytics* II 19" in *Aristotle on Science: The "Posterior Analytics*." ed. Enrico Berti. Padova: Editrice Antenore, 385–414.

Kneale, W. (1961). "Time and Eternity in Theology," *Proceedings of the Aristotelian Society* 61, 87–108.

Knuuttila, Simo, ed. (1981). *Reforging the Great Chain of Being*. Dordrecht: D. Reidel.

Kosman, Aryeh. (1987). "Animals and Other Beings in Aristotle" in Gotthelf and Lennox (1987), 360–391.

————. (1984). "Substance, Being, and *Energeia*," *Oxford Studies in Ancient Philosophy* 2, 121–149.

———. (1994a). "Aristotle's Prime Mover" in Gill and Lennox (1994), 135–153.

———. (1994b). "The Activity of Being in Aristotle's *Metaphysics*" in Scaltsas, Charles and Gill (1994), 195–213.

Kung, Joan. (1977). "Aristotle on Essence and Explanation," *Philosophical Studies* 31, 361–383.

———. (1981). "Aristotle on Thises, Suches and the Third Man Argument," *Phronesis* 26, 207–247.

Lacey, A. R. (1965). "Οὐσία and Form in Aristotle," *Phronesis* 10, 54–69.

Lang, Helen S. (1992). *Aristotle's Physics and Its Medieval Varieties*. Albany: State University of New York Press.

Lear, Jonathan. (1987). "Active Episteme," in *Mathematics and Metaphysics in Aristotle*, Proceedings of the Tenth Symposium Aristotelicum, ed. by A. Graeser, 149–174.

———. (1988). *Aristotle: The Desire to Understand*. Cambridge: Cambridge University Press.

Lefèvre, Charles. (1978). "Sur le Statut de l'Ame dans le *De Anima* et les *Parva Naturalia*" in Lloyd and Owen (1978), 21–67.

Lennox, James G. (1977). *A Study of the Interaction between Aristotle's Metaphysics and his Biological Works*. Ph.D. thesis, Toronto.

———. (1982). "Teleology, Chance, and Aristotle's Theory of Spontaneous Generation," *Journal of the History of Philosophy* 20, 219–238.

———. (1984). "Aristotle on Chance," *Archiv für Geschichte der Philosophie* 66, 52–60.

———. (1985). "Are Aristotelian Species Eternal?" in Gotthelf (1985), 67–94.

———. (1987a). "Divide and Explain: the *Posterior Analytics* in Practice" in Gotthelf and Lennox (1987), 90–119.

———. (1987b). "Kinds, Forms of Kinds, and the More and the Less in Aristotle's Biology" in Gotthelf and Lennox (1987), 339–359.

———. (1996). "Aristotle's Biological Development: The Balm Hypothesis" in Wians (1996), 229–248.

Lesher, James H. (1971). "Aristotle on Form, Substance, and Universals: A Dilemma," *Phronesis* 16, 169–178.

Leszl, Walter. (1970). *Logic and Metaphysics in Aristotle*. Padua: Antenore.

———. (1972). "Knowledge of the Universal and Knowledge of the Particular in Aristotle," *Review of Metaphysics* 26, 278–313.

Lewis, Frank A. (1991). *Substance and Predication in Aristotle*. Cambridge: Cambridge University Press.

———. (1994). "Aristotle on the Relation between a Thing and its Matter" in Scaltsas, Charles and Gill (1994), 247–277.

Lloyd, A. C. (1962). "Genus, Species and Ordered Series in Aristotle," *Phronesis* 7, 67–90.

————. (1976). "The Principle that the Cause is greater than its Effect," *Phronesis* 21, 146–156.

————. (1981). *Form and Universal in Aristotle.* Liverpool: Francis Cairns.

Lloyd, G. E. R. (1961). "The Development of Aristotle's Theory of the Classification of Animals," *Phronesis* 6, 59–81.

————. (1970). *Early Greek Science: Thales to Aristotle.* London: Chatto & Windus.

————. (1992). "Aspects of the Relationship Between Aristotle's Psychology and his Zoology" in Nussbaum and Rorty (1992), 147–167.

————. (1996). *Aristotelian Explorations.* Cambridge: Cambridge University Press.

Lloyd, G. E. R., and Owen, G. E. L., eds. (1978). *Aristotle on Mind and the Senses.* Proceedings of the Seventh Symposium Aristotelicum. Cambridge.

Louis, P. (1955). "Remarques sur la Classification des Animaux chez Aristote" in *Autour d' Aristote.* Louvain: Universitaires de Louvain, 297–304.

Loux, Michael J. (1979). "Form, Species and Predication in *Metaphysics* Z, H and Θ," *Mind* 88, 1–23.

————. (1991). *Primary Ousia: An Essay on Aristotle's Metaphysics Z and H.* Ithaca: Cornell University Press.

Lowe, Malcolm F. (1983). "Aristotle on Kinds of Thinking" reprinted in Durrant (1993), 110–127.

Luce, J. V. (1965). "The Theory of Ideas in the *Cratylus*," *Phronesis* 10, 21–36.

Lumpe, Adolf. (1955). "'Der Terminus 'Prinzip' (ἀρχή). von den Vorsokratikern bis auf Aristoteles," *Archiv für Begriffsgeschichte* 1, 104–116.

Mabbott, J. D. (1926). "Aristotle and the ΧΩΡΙΣΜΟΣ of Plato," *Classical Quarterly* 20, 72–79.

Mansion, Suzanne. (1955). "Les apories de la Métaphysique aristotélicienne" in *Autour d' Aristote.* Louvain, 141–179.

————. (1979). "The Ontological Composition of Sensible Substances in Aristotle (*Metaphysics* VII 7–9)" translated in Barnes, Schofield, and Sorabji, vol. 3 (1979), 80–87.

Marck, Siegfried. (1912). *Die Platonische Ideenlehre in Ihren Motiven.* München: Oskar Beck.

Matthews, Gareth B. (1982). "Accidental Unities" in Schofield and Nussbaum (1982), 223–240.

Matthews, Gareth B., and Cohen, S. Marc. (1968). "The One and the Many," *Review of Metaphysics* 21, 630–655.

Merlan, Philip. (1960). *From Platonism to Neoplatonism.* Second ed., rev. The Hague: Martinus Nijhoff.

Meyer, Hans. (1919). *Natur und Kunst bei Aristoteles: Ableitung und Bestimmung der Ursächlichkeitsfaktoren.* Paderborn: Ferdinand Schöningh.

Meyer, Susan Sauvé. (1994). "Self-Movement and External Causation" in Gill and Lennox (1994), 65–80.

Mignucci, Mario. (1981). "'Ὡς ἐπὶ τὸ πολύ' et nécessaire dans la conception aristotélicienne de la science" in *Aristotle on Science: 'The Posterior Analytics.'* ed., Enrico Berti, 173–203.

Modrak, D. K. (1979). "Forms, Types, and Tokens in Aristotle's *Metaphysics*," *Journal of the History of Philosophy* 17, 371–381.

Moraux, Paul. (1955). "À propos du νοῦς θύραθεν chez Aristote" in *Autour d'Aristote*. Louvain: Universitaires de Louvain, 255–295.

Moravcsik, J. M. (1975). "AITIA as Generative Factor in Aristotle's Philosophy," *Dialogue* 14, 622–638.

———. (1994). "Essences, Powers, and Generic Propositions" in Scaltsas, Charles and Gill (1994), 229–244.

Moreau, Joseph. (1955). "L'être et l'essence dans la philosophie d' Aristote" in *Autour d' Aristote*. Louvain: Universitaires de Louvain, 181–204.

Morrison, Donald. (1985a). "Χωριστός in Aristotle," *Harvard Studies in Classical Philology* 89, 89–105.

———. (1985b). "Separation in Aristotle's *Metaphysics*," *Oxford Studies in Ancient Philosophy* 3, 125–157.

———. (1985c). "Separation: A Reply to Fine," *Oxford Studies in Ancient Philosophy* 3, 167–173.

Morsink, Johannes. (1982). *Aristotle's on the Generation of Animals: A Philosophical Study*. Washington, D.C.: University Press of America.

Nussbaum, Martha C., and Putnam, Hilary. (1992). "Changing Aristotle's Mind" in Nussbaum and Rorty (1992), 27–56.

Nussbaum, M. C., and Rorty, A. O., eds. (1992). *Essays on Aristotle's De Anima*. Oxford: Clarendon Press.

Oehler, Klaus. (1962). "Ein Mensch Zeugt Einen Menschen" reprinted in Oehler (1969). *Antike Philosophie Und Byzantinisches Mittelalter*. München: C. H. Beck.

Olshewsky, Thomas M. (1976). "On the Relations of Soul to Body in Plato and Aristotle," *Journal of the History of Philosophy* 14, 391–404.

Owen, G. E. L. (1960). "Logic and Metaphysics in Some Earlier Works of Aristotle" in Düring and Owen (1960), 163–190.

———. (1976). "Prolegomenon to Z7–9" in Burnyeat and others (1979), 43–53.

———. (1986). *Logic, Science, and Dialectic*. ed. M. Nussbaum. Ithaca: Cornell University Press.

Owens, Joseph. (1978). *The Doctrine of Being in the Aristotelian Metaphysics*, 3rd Ed. Toronto: PIMS.

———. (1981). *Aristotle—The Collected Papers of Joseph Owens*. ed. J. R. Catan. Albany: State University of New York Press.

————. (1984). "The Present Status of Alpha Elatton in the Aristotelian *Metaphysics,*" *Archiv für Geschichte der Philosophie* 66, 148–169.

Page, Carl. (1985). "Predicating Forms of Matter in Aristotle's *Metaphysics,*" *Review of Metaphysics* 39, 57–82.

Paton, H. J. (1922). "Plato's Theory of ΕΙΚΑΣΙΑ," *Proceedings of the Aristotelian Society* 22, 69–104.

Peck, Arthur L. (1953). "The Connate *Pneuma*: an Essential Factor in Aristotle's Solutions to the Problems of Reproduction and Sensation" in *Science, Medicine and History* vol. 1, ed. E. Ashworth Underwood, New York: Arno Press, 111–121.

Pellegrin, Pierre (1986). *Aristotle's Classification of Animals.* trans. A. Preus. Berkeley: University of California Press.

————. (1987). "Logical Difference and Biological Difference: the Unity of Aristotle's Thought" in Gotthelf and Lennox (1987), 313–338.

Philippson, Robert. (1936). "Il ΠΕΡΙ ΙΔΕΩΝ di Aristotele," *Rivista di filologia e d'istruzione classica,* NS 14, 113–125.

Plochmann, George Kimball. (1953). "Nature and the Living Thing in Aristotle's Biology," *Journal of the History of Ideas* 14, 167–190.

Polansky, Ronald. (1983). "*Energeia* in Aristotle's *Metaphysics* IX," *Ancient Philosophy* 3, 160–170.

Preiswerk, Andreas. (1939). "Das Einzelne bei Platon und Aristoteles," *Philologus, Supplementband* 32, 1–196.

Preus, Anthony. (1975). *Science and Philosophy in Aristotle's Biological Works.* New York: Georg Olms Verlag Hildesheim.

————. (1979). "*Eidos* as Norm in Aristotle's Biology," *Nature and System* 1, 79–101.

Reale, Giovanni. (1980). *The Concept of First Philosophy and the Unity of the Metaphysics of Aristotle.* trans. John R. Catan. Albany: State University of New York Press.

Reiche, Harald A. T. (1960). *Empedocles' Mixture, Eudoxan Astronomy and Aristotle's Connate Pneuma.* Amsterdam: Adolf M. Hakkert.

Rist, John M. (1974). "Aristotle: The Value of man and the Origin of Morality," *Canadian Journal of Philosophy* 4, 1–21.

————. (1989). *The Mind of Aristotle: A Study in Philosophical Growth.* Toronto: University of Toronto Press.

————. (1996). "On Taking Aristotle's Development Seriously" in Wians (1996), 359–373.

Ritter, Constantin. (1933). *Essence of Plato's Philosophy.* trans. Adam Alles. London: George Allen & Unwin Ltd.

Ritter, William. E. (1932; 1934). "Why Aristotle Invented the Word *Entelecheia,*" *Quarterly Review of Biology* 7, 377–404; 9, 1–35.

Robin, L. (1963). *La théorie platonicienne des Idées et des Nombres d' après Aristote.* Hildesheim: G. Olms.

Robinson, Richard. (1953). *Plato's Earlier Dialectic*: Second Edition. Oxford: Clarendon Press.

Rohr, Michael David. (1981). "Empty Forms in Plato" in Knuuttila (1981), 19–56.

Rorty, Richard. (1973). "Genus as Matter: A Reading of *Metaphysics* Z–H," *Phronesis*, Suppl. Vol. 1, 393–420.

———. (1974). "Matter as Goo: Comments on Grene's Paper," *Synthese* 28, 71–77.

Ross, W. D. (1951). *Plato's Theory of Ideas.* Oxford: Clarendon Press.

———. (1960). "The Development of Aristotle's Thought" in Düring and Owen (1960), 1–17.

Ryle, Gilbert. (1953). *Dilemmas.* Cambridge: Cambridge University Press.

———. (1971). "Categories," in *Collected Papers*, vol. 2. London: Hutchinson. 170–184.

Scaltsas, Theodore. (1994a). *Substances and Universal in Aristotle's Metaphysics.* Ithaca: Cornell University Press.

———. (1994b). "Substantial Holism" in Scaltsas, Charles and Gill (1994), 107–128.

Scaltsas, T., Charles, D., and Gill, M. L., eds. (1994). *Unity, Identity and Explanation in Aristotle's Metaphysics.* Oxford: Clarendon Press.

Schofield, Malcolm. (1991). "Explanatory Projects in the *Physics*," *Oxford Studies in Ancient Philosophy*, Supplementary Volume, 29–40.

Schofield, M., and Nussbaum, M. C., eds. (1982). *Language and Logos: Studies in Ancient Greek Philosophy.* Cambridge: Cambridge University Press.

Sellars, Wilfrid. (1957). "Substance and Form in Aristotle," *Journal of Philosophy* 54, 688–699.

———. (1967). "Aristotle's *Metaphysics*: An Introduction" in *Philosophical Perspectives.* Springfield, Ill.: Charles C Thomas, 73–124.

———. (1967). "The Soul as Craftsman" in *Philosophical Perspectives.* Springfield, Ill.: Charles C Thomas, 5–22.

Shields, Christopher. (1990). "The Generation of Form in Aristotle," *History of Philosophy Quarterly* 7, 367–390.

———. (1994). "Mind and Motion in Aristotle" in Gill and Lennox (1994), 117–133.

Shorey, Paul. (1903). *The Unity of Plato's Thought.* Chicago: University of Chicago Press.

———. (1910). Review on Constantin Ritter's *Neue Untersuchungen über Platon. Classical Philology* 5, 390–393.

Skemp, J. B. (1960). "Ὕλη and ὑποδοχή" in Düring and Owen (1960), 201–212.

———. (1978). "ὄρεξις in *De Anima* III 10" in Lloyd and Owen (1978), 181–189.

Slakey, Thomas J. (1961). "Aristotle on Sense-Perception" reprinted in Durrant (1993), 75–89.

Slote, Michael A. (1974). *Metaphysics and Essence.* Oxford: Basil Blackwell.

Smith, J. A. (1921). "ΤΟΔΕ ΤΙ in Aristotle," *The Classical Review* 35, 19.

Solmsen, Friedrich. (1957). "The Vital Heat, the Inborn Pneuma and the Aether," *Journal of Hellenic Studies* 77, 119–123.

———. (1960). "Platonic Influences in the Formation of Aristotle's Physical System" in Düring and Owen (1960), 213–235.

———. (1963). "Nature as Craftsman in Greek Thought," *Journal of the History of Ideas* 24, 473–496.

Sorabji, Richard. (1974). "Body and Soul in Aristotle" reprinted in Durrant (1993), 162–196.

———. (1983). *Time, Creation and the Continuum: Theories in Antiquity and the Early Middle Ages.* Ithaca: Cornell University Press.

Souilhé, Joseph. (1919). *Étude sur le Terme ΔΥΝΑΜΙΣ dans les Dialogues de Platon.* Paris: Librairie Félix Alcan.

Spellman, Lynne. (1994). "Separation in Aristotle's Metaphysics." A paper given at SAGP, APA Central Division, Kansas City, May 6, 1994.

———. (1995). *Substance and Separation in Aristotle.* Cambridge: Cambridge University Press.

Steckerl, F. (1942). "On the Problem: Artefact and Idea," *Classical Philology* 37, 288–298.

Stenzel, Julius. (1940). *Plato's Method of Dialectic.* trans. D. J. Allan. Oxford: Clarendon Press.

Steward, J. A. (1909/1964). *Plato's Doctrine of Ideas.* New York: Russel & Russel.

Stocks, J. L. (1911). "The Divided Line of Plato *Rep.* VI," *Classical Quarterly* 5, 73–88.

Stough, Charlotte L. (1972). "Language and Ontology in Aristotle's *Categories,*" *Journal of the History of Philosophy* 10, 261–272..

———. (1976). "Forms and Explanation in the *Phaedo,*" *Phronesis* 21, 1–30.

Strycker, E. de. (1955). "La notion aristotélicienne de séparation dans son application aux Idées de Platon" in *Autour d' Aristote.* Louvain: Universitaires de Louvain, 119–139.

Sykes, R. D. (1975). "Form in Aristotle: Universal or Particular?" *Philosophy* 50, 311–331.

Taylor, A. E. "On the Interpretation of Plato's *Parmenides,*" *Mind*: I, 5 (1896), 297–326; II, 5 (1896), 483–507; III, 6 (1897), 9–39.

———. (1903). "On the First Part of Plato's *Parmenides,*" *Mind* 12, 1–20.

———. (1911). *Varia Socratica.* Oxford: James Parker & Co.

Taylor, C. C. W. (1969). "Forms as Causes in the *Phaedo*," *Mind* N.S. 78, 45–59.

Teloh, Henry. (1979). "The Universal in Aristotle," *Apeiron* 13, 70–78.

Theodorakopoulos, John. (1978). "Relations between Aristotle and Plato," *Paideia, Special Aristotle Issue*, 1–7.

Torrey, Harry Beal, and Felin, Frances. (1937). "Was Aristotle an Evolutionist?" *Quarterly Review of Biology* 12, 1–18.

Turnbull, Robert G. (1958). "Aristotle's Debt to the 'Natural Philosophy' of the *Phaedo*," *Philosophical Quarterly* 8, 131–143.

Vlastos, Gregory. (1969). "Reasons and Causes in the *Phaedo*," *Philosophical Review* 78, 291–325.

Vogel, C. J. de. (1960). "The Legend of the Platonizing Aristotle" in Düring and Owen (1960), 248–256.

von Leyden, H. (1964). "Time, Number, and Eternity in Plato and Aristotle," *Philosophical Quarterly* 14, 35–52.

Waterlow, Sarah. (1982). *Nature, Change, and Agency in Aristotle's Physics*. Oxford: Clarendon Press.

Wedin, Michael V. (1986). "Tracking Aristotle's *Noûs*" reprinted in Durrant (1993), 128–161.

———. (1994). "Aristotle on the Mind's Self-Motion" in Gill and Lennox (1994), 81–116.

White, Nicholas P. (1971). "Aristotle on Sameness and Oneness," *Philosophical Review* 80, 177–197.

———. (1972). "Origins of Aristotle's Essentialism," *Review of Metaphysics* 26, 57–85.

Whiting, Jennifer E. (1986). "Form and Individuation in Aristotle," *History of Philosophy Quarterly* 3, 359–377.

———. (1990). "Aristotle on Form and Generation," *Proceedings of the Boston Area Colloquium in Ancient Philosophy* 6, 35–63.

———. (1992). "Living Bodies" in Nussbaum and Rorty (1992), 75–91.

Whittaker, John. (1968). "The 'Eternity' of the Platonic Forms," *Phronesis* 13, 131–144.

Wians, Williams, ed. (1996). *Aristotle's Philosophical Development: Problems and Prospects*. Lanham, Md.: Rowman & Littlefield.

Wildberg, Christian. (1989). "Two Systems in Aristotle?" *Oxford Studies in Ancient Philosophy* 7, 193–202.

Wilkes, K. V. (1992). "Psuché Versus the Mind" in Nussbaum and Rorty (1992), 109–127.

Wilpert, Paul. (1949). *Zwei aristotelische Frühschriften über die Ideenlehre*. Regensburg: Josef Habbel, 15–118.

Witt, Charlotte. (1985). "Form, Reproduction and Inherited Characteristics in Aristotle's Generation of Animals," *Phronesis* 30, 46–57.

———. (1989). *Substance and Essence in Aristotle*. Ithaca: Cornell University Press.

———. (1994). "The Priority of Actuality in Aristotle" in Scaltsas, Charles and Gill (1994), 215–228.

Wittgenstein, Ludwig. (1958). *Philosophical Investigations*, 2nd ed. trans. G. E. M. Anscombe. New York: Macmillan.

Woodbridge, Frederick J. E. (1965). *Aristotle's Vision of Nature*. New York: Columbia University Press.

Woods, Michael. J. (1967). "Problems in *Metaphysics* Z, Chapter 13" in *Aristotle: A Collection of Critical Essays*. ed. J. M. E. Moravcsik. New York: Anchor Books, 215–238.

———. (1975). "Substance and Essence in Aristotle," *Proceedings of the Aristotelian Society* 75, 167–180.

———. (1991). "Universals and Particular Forms in Aristotle's *Metaphysics*," *Oxford Studies in Ancient Philosophy*, Supplementary Volume, 41–56.

———. (1994). "The Essence of a Human Being and the Individual Soul in *Metaphysics* Z and H" in Scaltsas, Charles and Gill (1994), 279–290.

Wright, Larry. (1976). *Teleological Explanation: An Etiological Analysis of Goals and Functions*. Berkeley: University of California Press.

General Index

Index of Passages Cited

Index of Greek Terms

εἴ τι ὅλως ἀδύνατον γενέσθαι, ὥσθ ὁτὲ
   μὲν εἶναι ὁτὲ δὲ μή, 127n.41
ἐκ, 46
ἐκ δὲ τῶν ἑτέρων, 133n.38
ἐκ μὲν τούτων ἀφθάρτων οὐσῶν,
   133n.38
ἐκ συνωνύμου, 22, 125n.46
ἔκ τινος, 56–57, 81
ἔκ τινων, 132n.38
ἐκ τῶν αὐτῶν, 132n.38
ἐκ τῶν λόγων τῶν καθόλου, 130n.12
ἐκ τῶν μαθημάτων, 130n.12
ἔμψυχον, 83
ἐν ἄλλοις καὶ ἔξωθεν, 75, 109
ἐν ἄλλῳ, 38, 75–76, 80
ἐν ἄλλῳ ἢ ᾗ ἄλλο, 76
ἐν αὐτῷ, 77, 137n.21
ἐν αὐτῷ τῷ ἔχοντι, 87
ἔνδοξον, 144n.25
ἔν εἴδει, 62
ἐνέργεια, 129n.2
ἐν ἑτέρῳ, 76, 80
ἐντελέχεια, 73–74, 89, 129n.2
ἐν τοῖς ἀπὸ φύσεως γιγνομένοις,
   121n.15
ἐν τοῖς διαπορήμασιν, 12
ἐν τοῖς ἐξ ἀρχῆς, 143n.24
ἐν τοῖς φυσικοῖς, 19, 124n.40
ἐν τούτοις, 19, 124n.40
ἐν ὑποκειμένῳ ἐστίν, 120n.1
ἐν ᾧ ὑπάρχει πρώτως καθ' αὑτὸ καὶ μὴ
   κατὰ συμβεβηκός, 109
ἐξ ἀνθρώπου ἄνθρωπος, 122n.28
ἐξ ὁμωνύμου, 125n.46, 137n.18
ἔξωθεν, 87
ἐπιστήμη, 42, 89, 115, 130n.18
ἐπιστήμον, 89
ἔστι μὲν καὶ τότε δυνάμει πως, 90
ἕτερον οἷον αὐτό, 96
ἔχει τινὰ ἕξιν καὶ ἀρχὴν κινήσεως, 88
ἐχομένη, 71, 115

ἡ αὐτὴ δύναμις τῆς ψυχῆς θρεπτικὴ
   καὶ γεννητική, 96
ἡ γὰρ τέχνη ἀρχὴ καὶ εἶδος τοῦ
   γιγνομένου, ἀλλ' ἐν ἑτέρῳ, 76

ἡ δύναμις τοῦ ποιεῖν, 85
ἡ δύναμις τοῦ πασχεῖν, 85
ἢ ἐν ἑτέρῳ ἢ ᾗ ἕτερον, 76
ἡ ἐπιστήμη, 46–47
ᾗ ἔχει τὴν κίνησιν ἐν ἑαυτῷ ἦν ἐκεῖνο
   ἐκίνει, 91
ἡ ζητουμένη ἐπιστήμη, 45, 131n.30
ἡ ζητουμένη νῦν ἐπιστήμη, 131n.30
ἡ μὲν οὖν τέχνη ἀρχὴ ἐν ἄλλῳ, 76
ἡ οὐσία, 95
ἡ οὐσία ἡ τῶν ἐχόντων ἀρχὴν κινήσεως
   ἐν αὐτοῖς ᾗ αὐτά, 144n.43
ἡ ποιοῦσα δύναμις, 92

θίξει, 134n.51

ἰσχύει, 95
ἴσως, 28, 86

καθ' αὑτήν, 46
καθ' αὑτὴν ποιήσει τὴν μορφὴν ἡ τοῦ
   ἄρρενος κίνησις, 95
καθ' ἑκάστην κατηγορίαν, 136n.11
καθὸ γεννητικόν, 151n.61
καθόλου, 115, 152n.83
καθ' ὑποκειμένου λέγεται, 120n.1
καί, 73, 155n.2
καὶ λόγῳ καὶ γνώσει καὶ χρόνῳ, 31
καὶ τῇ αἰσθήσει ἐστὶ φανερόν, 85
καὶ χρόνῳ, 31
κατὰ δύναμιν, 156n.3
κατασκευάζειν, 132n.34
κατὰ συμβεβηκός, 109
κατὰ φύσιν, 121n.15
κατὰ φύσιν συνεστήασι, 111
κεκοινωνηκέναι, 103
κεχωρίσθαι, 70
κεχωρισμένη, 134n.54
κεχωρισμένον, 82
κεχωρισμένον τι καὶ αὐτὸ καθ' αὑτο,
   133n.39
κεχώρισται, 70
κίνησις, 146n.7
κοινόν, 134n.52
κολοβός, 151n.61
κυρίως, 155n.42